Know How

Other FuturePace Books by the Authors:

Solutions
Practical and Effective Antidotes for
Sexual and Relationship Problems
(Cameron-Bandler)

The EMPRINT Method
A Guide to Reproducing Competence

Know How

Guided Programs for Inventing Your Own Best Future

Leslie Cameron-Bandler

David Gordon

Michael Lebeau

Published by FuturePace, Inc., P.O. Box 1173, San Rafael, California 94915.

ISBN 0-932573-00-2

Library of Congress Catalog Card Number 85-80006

Design by James Stockton & Associates, San Francisco

Dedications

To Debbie, through whose love, intelligence, and (apparently boundless) patience so much has been made possible.
DG

To Saul and Reva, with deepest love and respect. I look with appreciation to my memories of being your child as the source of my knowledge in bringing my own son to manhood.
ML

To Ken Hausman, a man of gallantry, commitment and heart. For me you freed the present from the past, and brought the future within reach.
LCB

Like the creative composer, some people are more gifted at living than others. They do have an effect on those around them, but the process stops there because there is no way of describing in technical terms just what it is they do, most of which is out of awareness. Some time in the future, a long, long time from now when culture is more completely explored, there will be the equivalent of musical scores that can be learned, each for a different type of man or woman in different types of jobs and relationships, for time, space, work, and play. We see people who are successful and happy today, who have jobs which are rewarding and productive. What are the sets, isolates, and patterns that differentiate their lives from those of the less fortunate? We need to have a means for making life a little less haphazard and more enjoyable.

Edward T. Hall
The Silent Language

Table of Contents

Note to the Reader

For many years a diverse group of researchers, educators, philosophers, and scientists have argued for the existence of a "language of the brain" that would explain how seemingly gifted people are able to manifest their unique aptitudes, skills and talents. A few visionaries have suggested that this language, once discovered, could be used to reproduce and transfer those aptitudes and skills from one person to another. Apparently, these futurists and visionaries were right.

The authors have recently discovered such a language, and they have developed a new methodology that uses that language to create methods and formats that anyone can use to tap into mankind's trove of mental resources. Their name for this new methodology is Mental Aptitude Patterning^{SM}.

Mental Aptitude Patterning enables the authors to code the patterns that underlie human aptitudes. And as the visionaries predicted, it includes a set of processes that the authors use to transform that coded information into a sequence of instructional experiences that, when followed, result in the installation of the given aptitude in any person.

This book, together with a related book titled *The EM-PRINT Method: A Guide to Reproducing Competence*, contains the fruits of the author's first harvest since their development of Mental Aptitude Patterning. As you will soon discover, Mental Aptitude Patterning and the products it has engendered hold the possibility for stimulating a renaissance of individual initiative, accomplishment, and evolution. The world may never be the same.

Preface

Have you ever wondered why some people have what seems to be a natural ability to achieve success and fulfillment, while others seem to be doomed to a life of repeated failures, disappointment and frustration? Would you like to understand talented and gifted people in a way that provides you with a choice to be more like them—a choice that offers *you* the talents of those who achieve success and fulfillment naturally? If so, read on. The purpose of this book is to give you that choice.

The following pages are the result of an exciting collaboration that has led us literally out of our own minds and into the fascinating life experiences of others. Several years ago we began to identify genius and excellence in important everyday situations, and our curiosity about talented and gifted people has led us to a fascinating discovery about *how* they are able to do those things that they do so well. We have distilled those patterns of success into simple, easy-to-use formats. Our purpose in writing this book is to provide you the formats—the thinking processes, perceptions and behaviors—that naturally lead to success and fulfillment in several of life's most challenging and potentially rewarding areas. As you read through each chapter you will be participating in a presentation and exploration that is designed to involve you in an ongoing learning process. You will be learning and changing as you read and enjoy each chapter.

The thousands of people we have helped change over the years have consistently expressed to us their surprise at discovering that change need not be difficult. It used to be thought (and still is in some circles) that making pervasive life changes is very difficult. Making major personal changes was equated with an ordeal—complete with pain, struggle, and sacrifice. This gauntlet orientation was based upon the assumption that (1) deep-seated problems and primordial issues needed to be uncovered and dealt with before desired experiences could be attained, and (2) there was no existing method which made possible the transference of successful or desirable life experiences from one individual to another.

We now have that method. Years of research have taken us into a new endeavor that is an evolutionary step beyond any of our previous work.* Recently, the focus of our research has been in specifying the ways in which each of us uses the past, present and future to determine our behaviors and the kind and quality of our experiences. We found unexpected riches in our explorations, from which we have produced a new process—The EMPRINT℠ Method—which has allowed us to map the patterns of success in many significant areas of life.

The EMPRINT Method is an accelerated skill acquisition process. Through its use we have been able to recognize and describe universally useful sequences of perceptions, thinking processes and behaviors that serve as solutions to the most frequently occurring personal challenges and problems that people experience. This book is designed to make the benefits of our new method accessible to anyone.**

Our experience in assisting people (both individually and in training seminars) to get what they want has demonstrated something very profound: *The vast majority of people do not need therapy. Instead, they need an opportunity to learn HOW to organize their perceptions, thinking processes and behaviors*

---

*In our previous work as researchers and co-developers of Neuro-Linguistic Programming we assisted people in attaining their desired outcomes and changes using a variety of techniques that we had created. Those techniques are very effective for some communication and therapeutic applications, but, like any set of techniques, their effectiveness is limited.

**For those interested in a complete presentation of The EMPRINT Method, see *The EMPRINT Method: A Guide to Reproducing Competence*, by the authors and also published by FuturePace. There you will find a thorough presentation of each aspect of the method, including guidelines and examples for acquiring the talents, skills and abilities of others. You will also find more information on the author's new endeavor: Mental Aptitude Patterning℠.

in ways that naturally lead to success. Once people know how, they translate their learnings into action and fulfill their desires rather than choosing to deny themselves those desires.

The following pages are a coalescence of a portion of our accumulated knowledge concerning the solutions to commonly experienced problems. In each of the areas covered we have described both those who respond successfully and unsuccessfully. This gives you the opportunity to find yourself and to understand the basis for your own successes and stumblings. As you identify yourself among the examples of people whose behaviors have led to a lack of success in a given area, remember that *there is nothing wrong with you.* You simply have not yet had the opportunity to *know how* to respond in those problem situations in any other way. This book gives you that opportunity—the opportunity to know how.

We believe that it is possible for you to acquire talent and to manifest natural excellence in any area of life. We wrote this book to direct you toward actualizing this belief. The following pages contain a sampling of the formats we have created from our explorations into the structure of talent and natural excellence. We present them to you with the hope that you will use them to enhance your existing talents, as well as to gain control of presently frustrating areas of your life. Read on and enjoy yourself as you acquire those skills that will make your dreams and desires come true.

San Rafael, California
September 20, 1984

1 A World of Difference

. . . I flung myself into futurity. At first I scarce thought of stopping, scarce thought of anything but these new sensations. But presently a fresh series of impressions grew up in my mind—a certain curiosity and therewith a certain dread—until at last they took complete possession of me. What strange developments of humanity, what wonderful advances upon our rudimentary civilization, I thought, might not appear when I came to look nearly into the dim elusive world that raced and fluctuated before my eyes!

H.G. Wells
The Time Machine

Like the time traveler in Wells's novel, we are about to embark upon a journey of discovery. Unlike the time traveler, however, our objective is not to discover what will be in the future, but what could be. Any future of "could be's" is richer by many magnitudes in both promise and possibility than a future of "will be's." It is our intention that by the time you have read the final words on the final page in this book you will have both the ability to perceive multitudes of possible futures for yourself, and the necessary skills and abilities to eventually make any one or all of those futures your reality.

If those sound like the introductory promises of a how-to book, you are correct. That is just what this is: a book about how to make sense out of your and other's behavior, and *how to have the choice to change your experience and behavior in effective and useful ways.* As an approach, this represents a significant new development for us. In our previous writings

1

and teachings we emphasized that every individual is just that, *an individual,* and must be approached with utmost respect for his or her personal and unique view of the world. Our belief in this presumption of uniqueness has not changed in the least. However, believing that each of us functions through our own personal view of the world does not diminish the fact that there are also many patterns of experience and behavior that most of us share. No greater proof of the existence of shared patterns of human response could be cited than the effectiveness and flourishing of advertising companies, institutions which demonstrate time and again that every individual is also a member of a culture.

There are patterns in the way we think and in the way we behave which are characteristic of large segments of our culture. In fact, some are characteristic of all human beings.[1] In this book we present you with the patterns which we have found underlying common problems as well as the EMPRINT formats which will, if used, provide solutions to those problems and make it possible for you to achieve new and, hopefully, more gratifying results in many areas of your life.

What do we mean by EMPRINT format? An EMPRINT format is an arrangement of steps or procedures which, if followed, will consistently result in the same outcome. In the following pages we have laid out some of the EMPRINT formats which are the reliable fruits of our efforts at modeling human behavior and experience as influenced by a person's use and evaluation of the past, present and future. Once we have established a shared vocabulary which we can use to talk about the specific patterns of thinking that go on in each of us with respect to time and experience, you will be able to use those EMPRINT formats to create different personal experiences and behaviors for yourself, and thus get more of what you desire in the various areas of life covered in this volume (and perhaps other areas as well). Because all of the formats have been tested, they will almost certainly impact your experience and behavior in the ways described.

We want to caution you, however, that this being a how-to book does not mean that you need only read it and then follow the recipes outlined later. This is a book about *experience.* Throughout the book we will ask you to explore your attitudes, thoughts, perceptions, emotions, and behavior in different ways. It is important that you take the few moments necessary to complete each exploration. Essentially, the EMPRINT formats that are presented throughout this book are based upon your ability to alter various aspects of your own experience in specific ways. The explorations will provide you with that ability.

As a simple first example, let us suppose that one of your children has come home from school with a note from his teacher informing you that he has not been doing his homework. You now have to decide how to respond to this situation. If you are a person for whom the future is a realm of experience about which you rarely speculate, how would you respond? How would having only a past and present affect your decision? If you do not consider the future then you are not likely to connect your son's present lack of effort to the consequences he may suffer as an adult who has failed at school or has learned sloth. And so, your response will probably not be intended to do something about the future, but about what is going on now or has gone on in the past. For instance, you might take the note as a slur on your competence as a parent and be angry with your child or with the teacher. You might recall previous notes from school that never seemed to have made much difference and, so, shrug the matter off. Or you might recall previous notes that did make a difference and, as a result, punish or reason with the boy. In each case your response is either with respect to your perceptions of what is going on or what has gone on in the past (though, of course, being angry, shrugging it off, punishing, or reasoning will each have some effect on the future).

Suppose, instead, that for you the future was of overwhelming importance, but that the past was nothing more than a few dim memories of little importance. How then would you respond to the note from school? You might start by imagining where the behavior indicated in the note might lead your son. If you could foresee no particular problems then you would probably drop the matter. If instead you imagined your son's behavior leading to future problems, then you would probably intervene, and the *intention* of that intervention would be to change your son's behavior in order to make possible some better future (or to prevent some worse future). Now this intervention may involve railing at or reasoning with the child, just as in the example above in which the past or present were most compelling. The difference to appreciate at this point is, however, that the *intention* of that railing or reasoning is to address some future possibility, rather than something that has happened in the past or the concerns of the present.

Of course, no one of us is as simply identified as, "Oh, she's totally future oriented," or "Oh, he has no past." We are all very much more complex and very much more interesting than that. As should be evident to you from considering the questions asked above, each of us has access in varying degrees and in varying ways to the past, present and future. What does this mean in terms of our ongoing experiences and behaviors?

There is within our culture a great diversity of responses to apparently similar situations. A moment's consideration of your own experience and behavior and that of those around you will undoubtedly furnish you with many examples. Perhaps you procrastinate, putting off chores, work projects or assignments until the last moment or until it is too late. Certainly you know of someone who gets their assignments done promptly. (There are even those who anticipate assignments and do them before they are asked!) Maybe you are one of those individuals who takes care of your health, abstaining from unnecessary drugs, unwholesome foods and eating practices, while making sure to get enough exercise. You can easily identify acquaintances who drink to the point of getting drunk, smoke cigarettes, eat poorly, overeat, or have been promising themselves to start regular running—for the past several years. Or perhaps you have low self esteem; that is, you have little sense of personal purpose or importance. You can probably think of people who obviously think very highly of themselves (and some of them with little apparent justification). How is it that some people achieve their business, financial or career goals, while others seem to find only a recurring lack of success and frustration? Is it just luck? Is it genetics? What makes it possible for you to procrastinate, and someone else to get things done quickly; for you to take care of your health and someone else to ingest potentially harmful drugs and foods; for you to think little of yourself while others find themselves to be worthy? How is it possible that some people have regrets, are able to plan, are able to carry out plans, be jealous, be Pollyannas, be curious, be bored, be vengeful, be hopeful, be self-sacrificing, be hedonistic, remember every occasion with a greeting card, or forget their own anniversaries? Obviously, there is a tremendous diversity of experience and behavior even among con-culturals.

We believe all of the experiences and behaviors we have just listed are the direct result of the perceptual and cognitive patterns of the individuals who have those experiences and behaviors. In other words, how an individual perceives and thinks about the world determines that person's experiences of, and responses to, the world. A person who procrastinates is using a combination of perceptions, evaluations and behaviors that result in that person being able to put things off until later. Not being able to operate *without* the imposition of those perceptions, evaluations and behaviors is what makes procrastination an attribute and a problem, as opposed to being incidental and not a problem.

Although the person who procrastinates may or may not appreciate having that attribute, it is an attribute nonetheless. Moreover, whether that person realizes it or not, procrastination can be a resource. Every one of the experiences and behaviors we have just mentioned (plus the thousands we did not) can be a blessing if used in the appropriate situation, or a curse if used in an inappropriate situation. For instance, if you need to write a grant proposal or lecture presentation it is obviously better to be motivated to get it done as soon as possible rather than procrastinate. But what happens to the person who wants to get things done right away when he goes on vacation? For the person who vacations in the same way he runs his work crew, the attribute of being able to procrastinate might be very useful when vacationing. Similarly, the asceticism that makes it possible for a person to remain svelte by eating sparingly may become a tremendous burden if applied to getting emotional needs met.

It is our contention that *the best choice is to have the widest range of useful and gratifying behaviors possible within any given situation.* Having this choice allows an individual's response to be determined by that person's intended or desired outcome, rather than by the automatic triggering of an inbred and (perhaps) inappropriate reaction. Interacting with children who are baking cookies is, in many ways, a very different activity than running a corporation. Yet a corporate executive who is accomplished at running a business may come home from work and direct her children and their baking in the same way she runs the business, and then wonder why the kids are so contrary, so messy, and so quickly lose interest in the enterprise. This executive needs the ability to set aside her corporate attributes and access the attributes that are appropriate for interacting with children engaged in projects. We call this ability to choose from a number of alternatives and to respond appropriately (rather than reflexively) a *choice response.*

A *default response,* on the other hand, occurs when an individual has only one, automatic response within a particular situation. For the person who needs to write the grant proposal or lecture material but cannot seem to get to it, procrastination is a default response in that he has only one response to the context of "paper due": procrastination. Similarly, promptness is a default response for the person who would *like* to ignore writing a grant proposal but nevertheless feels compelled to work on it. For these two individuals, procrastination and promptness become choice responses when they can choose to respond in either (or neither) way.

The experiences and behaviors which we specifically address in this book are those whose qualities are partially or wholly determined by an individual's utilization of the past, present and future. This does not narrow the field of application as much as it may seem, as it is our experience that the use and subjective perception of time affects all experiences to varying degrees. The purpose of this book is to provide you with ways of influencing and altering your experience and use of the past, present and future so that you can have the know-how to transform default responses into choice responses for yourself and for others.

Almost all of the various aspects of your experience that we will be directing you to recognize and alter occur inside you.

We call these aspects *internal processes*, and they include your thoughts, attitudes, and perceptions. It may seem to you that you simply respond to food, hopes, attractive potential mates, etc., but that is not so. Your responses are the result of a great deal of internal activity. In fact, it is this range of internal processes that determines your response; and many of these internal processes typically go on without your conscious attention or intercession. In the course of reading this book you will become familiar with this realm of your experience. In the pages to come, you will first learn to recognize what you are doing in terms of your internal processes and how they influence your behavior and the quality of your experience. Then you will learn how to alter the scope and effectiveness of your internal world such that you can respond out of choice and achieve the experiential and real world results that you desire. It is likely that you will be surprised, as we were at first, by how much difference it makes whether your evaluations are concerned with the past, present, future, or some combination of these time frames.

We want to make it clear to you at the outset that to learn you must do, and we hope that you will take to heart our suggestion that you engage yourself fully in the explorations and exercises to come. This book is a tangible demonstration of an old proverb: One who knows, *but does not do,* in truth does not know.

So that your doing and learning are enhanced, we will engage you from time to time in private conversations. We want you to receive the most enrichments possible from what we are offering, so when we feel you would benefit from an encouragement or suggestion we will quietly speak to you like this: "This is an important step, so be sure to take all the time you need to make this evaluation." Or, "Before moving to the next step, use the following space to list the short-term goals you will use as evidence of your continuing success." When you see one of these personal messages, imagine one of us sitting at your side; and hear the sound of our voice helping you apply your new skills toward the achievement of your goals.

So you, the reader, and we, the authors, will explore and learn together. The payoff in terms of personal enrichment and increased effectiveness will be well worth the effort. "But," you might ask, "suppose I just sit and read this book quietly, without doing anything?" The answer may surprise you: That is almost impossible. The method we present is so simple, so reasonable, so effective, that even an effortless reading will engage you in ways that must *improve your attitude toward yourself, toward life, and toward your ability to make changes for the better.* The choice is yours, of course. Read for pleasure and subtle advancement. Or, much better, apply yourself to making the changes you would like to see in your life.

Before turning you toward the specific exploration of the realm of internal processes, we must first acquaint you with the presuppositions which are the foundation for all that we offer you. Our presuppositions are both wise and provocative, and the foundation they form includes everything you need in order to begin to acquire the know-how for personal and professional fulfillment.

2 Into the Looking Glass

*Alice laughed. "There's no use trying," she said: "one can't be-
lieve impossible things."*

*"I daresay you haven't had much practice," said the Queen.
"When I was your age I always did it for half-an-hour a day.
Why, sometimes I've believed as many as six impossible things
before breakfast."*

Lewis Carroll
Through the Looking Glass

A presupposition is an assumption or belief under which you
knowingly or unknowingly operate. For example, some people
presuppose that everyone is pretty much the same and so they
treat everyone as though they are just like themselves; or, that
"you can't change human nature" and so accept themselves
and others the way they are; or, that "people who do bad
things are bad people," that "you can't fight city hall," that
"adults are stodgy," that "kids are lazy," and so on.

There is one presupposition which we now want to bring to
your attention: *If something is possible for one person in the
world, then it is possible for you—it is only a question of how
to make it a part of your experience.* Now, the importance of
that statement is not whether it is true or false. In fact, most
people do *not* have as a presupposition that it is possible for
them to do anything that is possible for any other human
being. We are even willing to concede that, as a generalization, it is certainly not true. We know that all generaliza-
tions are at some time false. The importance of this presup-

position lies not in its veracity, but in the *effect* it has on the individual who believes it to be true.

Let us give you an example of the phenomenon we are talking about. When you finish reading this paragraph, take a moment to search through your memories to find an example of something that at one time you thought you could not do, but later actually succeeded at doing. That "something" could be, for example, learning to do algebra, being able to ask a person out on a date, or being able to feel happy again. The only requirement is that it be something that you eventually mastered or experienced. Search through your memories and find this example now, before going any further.

You now have an example of at least once in your life in which you mistakenly thought that some outcome was beyond your abilities. Now we want you to find another kind of example: At the end of this paragraph, identify for yourself an experience, behavior, or ability that exists in the world and that you do not now have but that you want to have, *but* which you are sure is not possible for you to have. For example, having a svelte body, obedient and well-mannered children, a promotion, or a fulfilling relationship. Before reading further, take a few moments to find that example.

Sitting here, right now, you really do not know whether you are capable of getting for yourself that outcome you want but do not have. There was a time, in that first experience we asked you to recall, in which you thought that some particular outcome was beyond your grasp. Despite the sincerity and conviction of that belief *at that time*, that assessment was wrong, as demonstrated by the fact that at some later time in your life intervening experiences and changes made the attainment of that outcome possible. If you were wrong about the possibility of attaining that one outcome, what other outcomes that you presently believe to be beyond your grasp might you be equally mistaken about?

Consider for a moment the difference between a person who believes that his competence is limited to certain things, and a person who believes that she is capable of gaining competence in any situation in which it is possible for humans to be competent. You would expect very different internal experiences and external behaviors from those two individuals.

Whether able to achieve her outcomes or not, you would probably find the second person (who believes in the possibility of mastering anything that humans can master) *dauntlessly* pursuing whatever goals she has set for herself or has had set for her. On the other hand, the first person would tackle only those goals which he perceives as being already within his capabilities. Again, the point is not whether she is right or wrong to attempt what she is attempting, or whether he is right or wrong to shy away from the possibilities he judges beyond his grasp. Rather, the point is that the differences in their operating presuppositions will result in profound differences in how they think, feel, and behave when faced with a possible goal or outcome.

We cannot judge for you whether you are capable of achieving some particular goal or not. Indeed, as you discovered above, if you recall an example of something that you thought that you could not do but at some subsequent time discovered you *were* able to do, you will find that even you are not necessarily able to accurately judge for yourself the *future* range of your capabilities. What we *can* say from our remote position within these pages is that if you do *not* make some attempts toward achieving a goal, it is almost certainly *not* going to be achieved. In not pursuing your outcomes you will certainly be bolstering your confidence in your assessment of your own limitations. But the price, in terms of accumulating limitations, is very steep. It therefore seems that the question, "Is it possible for me?" is not nearly as useful as the question, *"How can I go about turning that possibility into a reality?"*

The possibilities we are talking about are those contained within the incredibly vast and varied repertoire of human experience and behavior. Every human being is a resource, a wellspring of unique experiences, behaviors and skills. Somehow each person has fashioned their unique conformation of experiences, behaviors and skills using the same neurology and perceptual systems that we all share. The fundamental tenet underlying all we are describing in these pages is this: The skills, perceptions, attitudes, attributes, thought processes, and behaviors of others are resources for *anyone* who perceives them in that way and is capable of formatting them in a way that can be learned. Although it is not necessary to have this perspective in order to benefit from the EMPRINT formats presented in this book, this perspective *is* crucial to having an understanding and appreciation for the EMPRINT method—the process we used to *generate* these formulas for human fulfillment and success.[1]

What follows is a set of examples demonstrating the diversity and range of human response possible within similar situations. You may recognize yourself or people that you know in the examples. As you read through them, compare how you respond in those same situations, and consider what makes it possible for the people described to have the responses that they have.

The Job Interview   Steve and Nate are standing outside the office of that unknown quantity, the prospective employer. They are out of work, in need of work, and are now in the anteroom of an employer who can, if he chooses, offer them a job. But first they must be interviewed.

As Steve waits to be interviewed, he recalls all those times in the past in which he had interviewed for positions and had been nervous, inept, and did not get the job—in short, all those interviews he considers failures. By the time he is called into the interview itself, Steve is feeling inadequate, and not at all hopeful of success. During the interview, Steve's feelings of inadequacy are expressed in his apologetic manner, hesitant answers, and lack of enthusiasm.

Despite having his share of botched interviews and job rejections, Nate walks into each new interview with a feeling and bearing of confidence. Although he recognizes that getting the job is certainly a way of measuring the success of an interview, Nate also considers it a success if he learns something. Accordingly, for each of his past interview experiences Nate has determined just what he learned or needed to learn. Thus, even when he recalls interviews in which he was unsuccessful at being hired, he considers them as learning experiences, not as examples of his incompetence. Nate enters the interview feeling confident, an internal state which is manifested in his relaxed and open manner, resolute answers, and optimism.

The Date Daphne is in her early thirties. Although she doesn't want to, she lives alone. She is a secretary in a large corporation where she has daily contact with several men to whom she is attracted. And even though she would like to, she has never dated any of them. Daphne's efforts at securing a date with any of these men consists of waiting behind her desk, hoping to be noticed and asked, and staring a hole through the telephone at home, where she hopes to be remembered and called. While she waits, she fantasizes about how wonderful her relationship with one or another of her prospects might be, imagining their marriage, home, children, and so on. She wants these things and experiences very badly, but often these days she despairs of ever having them, because nothing romantic has been happening in her life for some time now. In fact, it has come to the point where she alternates between resenting men for not asking her out, and feeling resigned to the fact of being unattractive.

Daphne's approach contrasts sharply with that of Sue. Sue is in her mid thirties, also works in an office, and usually dates whoever she decides she wants to date. When Sue finds a man attractive, she launches a campaign to discover what he responds to favorably and unfavorably. If, for instance, her prospective beau enjoys riddles, she will then be sure to find some which she then uses to engage his interest in her. She will also take note of his patterns of movement within the office (or wherever) so as to be able to plan when and where she can arrange to make contact with him, which she *does*. Although her approach may vary as to directness or subtlety, the consistent result of Sue's efforts is that she makes contact with the man she's attracted to, and the interaction that follows is usually one which that man enjoys.

A Marriage Proposal Lotty, Lester and Carl have each just had a proposal of marriage made to them by their respective lovers. Now Lotty, Lester and Carl must each decide how to respond to the possibility of marriage.

In making her decision, Lotty recalls her previous marriage and tries to evaluate whether it was a satisfactory marriage, whether she had been right to marry that man, whether or not her present man has revealed himself to be similar or different from her first husband, and so on. The result of Lotty's deliberations is that she turns down the marriage proposal, because she has determined that marriage was not a satisfying experience for her and that her present beau has often acted much like her detested first husband. Lotty wishes all this weren't so, but she does not want a repeat of her previous marriage.

Lester is having a wonderful time being in love with his girlfriend, so his only concern is that they be able to continue their relationship. In making his decision, Lester uses his present responses to, and perceptions of, his lady to judge how ready he is for marriage, how much he loves his lady, and whether or not she is sincere. When a helpful friend (proposing to help Lester make his decision) asks him to consider the proposal in light of his previous marriage, Lester becomes confused and a little irritated. "What does that have to do with anything?" Lester snaps back, then walks off. Lester feels he is in love, that his resolve is strong, as is his girlfriend's. He realizes that they have some problems in their relationship, but he decides that none of those problems are as great or as important as is his love for this woman. Lester decides to remarry.

Carl has never been married, but he has lived with women twice. Like Lester, Carl is having a wonderful time with his present girlfriend, but that does not move him to say yes to marriage. What Carl tries to determine is just what will happen if he marries his girlfriend. Carl considers where they would live; he imagines them having children and considers whether or not he alone will be able to bring in enough money to support them. Carl imagines what it will be like living with his girlfriend not just now, but ten or twenty years from now. He wonders if they will still love one another; and if their choices of careers will be likely to get in the way of their relationship; and so on. Carl sees himself making enough money to support a family and things going well for awhile. But then he imagines their relationship becoming strained over a continuing argument with his wife about the time demands of their respective careers. Carl wonders, "Is this what we have to look forward to?" He shakes his head and decides to postpone a decision until they can work out their potential career conflicts more satisfactorily.

Dessert   Three friends—Arbuckle, Wally and Eileen—are enjoying a delicious meal at a fine restaurant. After finishing their main courses, while all three are rhapsodizing about the meal and remarking how full they are, the waiter appears at their tableside with a pastry cart loaded with cakes and pies. The waiter asks, "Now, who would like dessert, hmm?"

Arbuckle is more than a little overweight. He often talks about how he is going to go on a diet "soon," and he knows from his own experiences of wheezing up a flight of stairs and from the cautionary magazine articles that he has read that he really must lose some weight. He recognizes that if he does not lose weight he will become more and more physically incapacitated and limited, and he does not want that to happen. Despite all this, Arbuckle orders a slice of pie. When his surprised friends ask him for an explanation, all he can say is, "I can start dieting tomorrow. This is just too delicious to pass up."

Wally (who is not overweight) also thinks the pie looks delicious, and confesses to wanting a slice. Even so, Wally ruefully declines, saying, "Naw, I'll regret it later." He then offers the excuse, "I'll wake up in the middle of the night with heartburn if I eat any more."

The pie looks just as tasty to Eileen, but she too turns it down. "Pie has never agreed with me. I *always* get heartburn," she explains. Arbuckle attempts to talk her into giving it a try, since she may have finally become immune to its effects, and if not, she could become accustomed to it by eating a little at a time. Eileen just waves him off. "Listen," she says, "I've been through this movie before and I already know how it ends." No pie for Eileen.

What is striking about all of these examples is that different people in the same situation can have very different responses. You say, "Well of course they had different responses—they're different people!" But having said that, do you take the next conceptual step which is to realize that if those individuals are having different responses to the same situations, *then it is not the situation which is determining the response?* Rather, it is the way in which each is thinking (the structure and content of that particular person's internal processes) that determines what responses he or she will have within a given situation. Thus, responding with anxiety, anticipation, inadequacy, or confidence during an interview, waiting for the phone to ring or finding a way to make it ring when you want a date, or deciding to marry or remain single are all determined to a very great extent by how you process information within each of those situations. If you change the nature of those internal processes, you will alter in some way your feelings and actions.

A simple illustration of the pervasive influence of internal processes involves identifying your existing goals and priorities. At the end of this paragraph explore your existing goals and priorities by answering the following questions: What are some of the most important things you would like to accomplish (or be) in your lifetime? What are the experiences that you absolutely want to be sure to have sometime during your stay on this earth? What pursuits and activities are important enough to be worth doing now and in the future? Your responses to these questions will be used in the next step, so take the time now to discover the answers.

Having identified your existing goals and priorities, now pay attention to the degree to which you believe you can and will achieve each one of them. In other words, determine how firmly you believe you can get that which you have identified. Do this for each of your goals and priorities before moving to the next step.

Now we will make a simple change in how you are thinking about your goals and priorities. Using your imagination, temporarily step into the reality that, because of war or a rare disease perhaps, you just found out you have only one week to live. How would you spend your time if you had only one week left in your life? What is important to you now in this time-shortened reality? As you think about your goals, with only one week to accomplish them, what feelings and sensations do you experience? Explore the degree to which this change in time frame affects your belief in your ability to achieve the goals and priorities you originally identified. Take some time now for this exploration.

Now make another simple change. Instead of one week, imagine that you have one year to live. Go through the same process of determining what you would do, who you would be with, where you would go, what would be important enough to actually make happen, if you had one *year* to live. Notice any changes in sensations or feelings. Also notice any changes in how much you really believe you could accomplish the goals and priorities you originally identified. Before you go on to the next paragraph, discover the differences created by this change.

Now we will have you make one more simple change in how you are thinking about your future. Because of an unprecedented breakthrough in bio-medical research, human life-spans have been lengthened. Instead of one week or one year, use your imagination to step into the reality that you have *two hundred* more years to this lifetime. With two hundred years to look forward to, how do your goals and priorities change? What becomes important to experience and accomplish in this time-expanded reality? Regardless of how your list changes, notice any differences in the degree to which you believe you can and will accomplish each goal and priority. How does having two hundred years to achieve your outcomes affect your belief in your ability to accomplish them? Notice how the sensations and feelings that you experience change as the span of your future changes. This is the last step in this exploration, so finish now before proceeding.

Some people change their priorities when their future is expanded, and some don't. Perhaps you merely add to your original list of wants and desires. Although there may be a wide range in *type* of internal change experienced by those who participate in this demonstration, we are sure you experienced some kind of change in response to this simple alteration in how you think about the future. As you just discovered, when you make a change in what you believe or how you are thinking, you are affecting your experience of the world. Indeed, your beliefs and internal processes combine to fashion much of what you experience as real and compelling.

The sum total of your beliefs and internal processes constitutes what we refer to as your *model of the world.* As we demonstrated above, it is your individual model of the world that creates meaning and subjective experience (your emotions and perceptions). And it is that meaning and subjective experience that guides your actions. If you change your model of the world you will necessarily alter in some way your subjective experience and behavior. This, then, is the domain within which you will be operating whenever you want to change your own (or someone else's) subjective experience and behavior: the domain of personal models of the world.[2]

If you concede (even if only for the moment) that the quality and expression of human experience is greatly influenced, if not determined, by the nature of the internal processing that each of us uses to make the world sensible and understandable, then it becomes important to discover just what kinds of internal processing lead to what kinds of experiences and behaviors. If we can sift such patterns from the convoluted layers of human information processing and experience, name those patterns, and describe them in such a way that they can become the formable clay of experience and expression—rather than the granite of genetically and historically determined responses—then we will have gone a long way toward fulfilling that dream so beautifully expressed in the opening quote from Edward Hall: that each of us can attain competence and fulfillment in pursuit of our personal dreams, hopes and ambitions.

The EMPRINT formats we are about to present are a step in that direction. They are a springboard from which to generate ever more fulfilling solutions to life's puzzles and problems. Thus, we end this introductory chapter by echoing Edward Hall's eloquent plea.

Like the creative composer, some people are more gifted at living than others. They do have an effect on those around them, but the process stops there because there is no way of describing in technical terms just what it is they do, most of which is out of awareness. Some time in the future, a long, long time from now when culture is more completely explored, there will be the equivalent of musical scores that can be learned, each for a different type of man or woman in different types of jobs and relationships, for time, space, work, and play. We see people who are successful and happy today, who have jobs which are rewarding and productive. What are the sets, isolates, and patterns that differentiate their lives from those of the less fortunate? We need to have a means for making life a little less haphazard and more enjoyable.

Edward T. Hall
The Silent Language

3 The Five Fundamentals of Success

In the chapters to follow we will explore specific areas within which people often need and want to acquire new skills, make changes, or become more effective. At the end of each chapter we present an EMPRINT format, a step-by-step procedure for acquiring skills, accomplishing change, and developing the know-how to be more effective in that particular area. All of these EMPRINT formats have certain steps in common: They all utilize the know-how for five fundamentals of success.

We discovered the significance of these fundamentals of success by discerning patterns in the people who are consistently able to achieve success and fulfillment in their careers and personal lives. We contrasted these talented people with people who are just as sincere in their efforts, who are trying just as hard to succeed, but who, despite their good intentions and best efforts, continually end up frustrated, disappointed, and unfulfilled. The people we studied vary widely in age, background, profession, interests, and economic position, but *without exception* each of those talented and fulfilled people demonstrate a common pattern: Each of those talented people incorporate into their thinking and actions most, if not all, of the fundamentals of success we are about to present. The people who are plagued by continuing failures and frustrations incorporate only a few, and oftentimes none, of these fundamentals of success.

Before specifying the necessary steps to accomplish change

in the areas described in subsequent chapters, we first want to acquaint you with these elements of success. Because they will be echoed throughout each of the EMPRINT formats in this book, we will take the time now to guide you through steps designed to assist you in gaining mastery with each of these valuable tools. The steps are numbered to make them easier to locate should you decide to repeat a step (or the entire sequence). Read through the entire step before participating in that exercise or exploration; each step contains valuable examples, instructions, and hints.

It is important that you incorporate these fundamentals of success into your thinking and behavior, rather than simply read about them. So spend the small amount of time required to engage fully in the exercises and explorations that follow. You will be rewarded for the rest of your life.

Compelling Futures

Since you are reading this with at least some intention of learning a new skill, making a change in yourself, or somehow becoming more effective, you must have some notion of a future that you desire. All of our research indicates that unless you are leaving the attainment of that desired future to the efforts of others or the generosity of fate, attaining that desired future will, in large part, depend upon your being able to generate for yourself a *compelling future* —one which is capable of motivating and guiding you so that eventually you can make that desired future a present reality. You need that compelling future whether you want to lose weight, stop smoking, invest wisely, get along differently with others, change your opinion of yourself, turn a wish into a reality, or what have you. Let us now go about the various tasks involved in building a compelling future.

Though most certainly there are situations in which you do have a compelling future, how do you know it *is* a compelling future? Remember, a compelling future is one that impacts you forcefully enough to motivate and influence you in the present. So, is there a situation in which you have a compelling future? The deciding variable will be whether or not you experience some projected future as real. To get an idea of what we are talking about, take yourself through the following experiences:

> Imagine going over to your radio and, while it is turned off, turning the volume knob *all* the way up. Moving your head so that one of your ears is next to the speaker, you place your fingers such that they are poised over the "on" switch. Now imagine what your response is as you consider turning the radio on. Do you snap it on, or do you hesitate? The degree to which you hesitate is an indication of how real the projected future auditory assault is to you.

> Imagine you are sitting on the padded table in a doctor's examination room. The doctor has decided that you need an injection of some kind. You watch as the nurse produces a syringe, jams the needle through the rubber seal on a vial, and pulls back the plunger to suck up the clear fluid inside that vial. You know what is coming. Is the approaching needle of no more significance to you than the potted ivy in the corner, or are you already recoiling from, and steeling yourself for, the stab of the needle?

> Consider staying up all night tonight. How real is the reality that tomorrow you will feel weary and strung out?

These three examples of compelling futures are set in very short time frames (with the third example set in a longer time frame than the first two), and as such are more apt to be universal. Compelling futures seem to be available to everyone provided that the time frame is one of an imminent future and that the connection of events being invoked is known and accepted. To illustrate, most people avoid eating food which is suspected of being spoiled since the likelihood of becoming ill is very real; most people avoid stepping in front of an oncoming car, and so on. These, then, are examples of situations in which the experience of a future is compelling.

As these examples illustrate, compelling futures can influence your behavior in ways that serve you well. Having a compelling future of likely negative consequences protects you from the results of reckless or foolish behavior. In fact, reckless or foolish behavior is usually a result of *not* having a compelling future with regard to the situation in which that potentially dangerous behavior is manifested. Compelling futures also spur you to behave *now* in ways that are likely to lead to greater rewards and fulfillment down the road.

Acquiring the ability to generate compelling futures is a significant step in protecting yourself from unpleasant personal experiences such as ill health, loneliness, rejection, poverty, and so on. As you will also discover, a compelling future that includes a full representation of one of your goals will influence you to behave in ways that support the attainment of that goal. The following sequence will provide you competency in generating compelling futures. Be sure to acquaint yourself with the instructions by first reading through each step, then be sure to *carry out* the instructions. By doing so you will acquire one of the internal processing talents of those gifted people for whom personal excellence is consistently expressed.

1   Unlike our previous examples, the compelling futures which are needed within certain contexts (health and investments, for instance) are generally of a long time frame, spanning at least several years into the future. To generate a long-term compelling future for yourself, you must first construct a full *visual* representation (a mental picture) of yourself being in the future. If picturing yourself does not come easily, begin by looking down at your own hand and imagine it growing older. It is just like watching the special effects we have all seen in the movies (*Little Big Man, The Portrait of Dorian Gray, The Diary of Miss Jane Pittman*) in which the actor or actress is seen growing older as the movie progresses. As you age your hand in your imagination, the skin texture changes, becoming thinner, smoother, harder, the wrinkles and folds deepen, and the veins become prominent. And you can vary the way in which your hand ages. You can watch it become discolored with liver spots and knobby with arthritis, or strong and supple, aging gracefully. Having aged your hand, you can then imagine one of your feet and then a leg aging in the same way. Then sit in front of a mirror and, using your creative abilities as would a movie special effects person, age your face in a way that makes that future real to you.

Remember, the purpose of this exercise is not to frighten

or discourage yourself concerning the consequences of aging, but rather to provide you with an experience capable of influencing your present behavior such that you *will* take care of yourself now in order to live well for now and in the future. The you that you are creating is the you from *your* future, and he or she is completely dependent upon your present actions for his or her well-being. That is, whether you are failing to save for your retirement, disregarding your relationships, over-eating, drinking, smoking, being slothful or taking drugs, it is the future you that will *most* pay for it.

2 Having done the previous exercise, it will be easier for you to construct an image of yourself in some possible future of yours. To increase the reality of this future representation of yourself, specify a future time—two, five, or ten years from now—and imagine your future self from that time standing in front of you. It might help to imagine that you are looking into a mirror that magically reflects the future. When you can see yourself clearly, imagine moving over and physically becoming that you. Feel how it feels to be there. Feel what it is like to be in your future body. Take a deep breath and explore the sensations that go along with being this much older. Then step back out, see your future self again, and ask that future you what he or she wants from you *now*. Listen well to the answer, as that future you is apt to be quite encouraging concerning the development of healthy, wise, and productive habits in the present. If *you* do not listen and respond to your future self, who will? Whatever your future self wants from you, write it down:

The future me wants me to _____

_____

_____

Yet another way to develop a compelling future representation of yourself is to notice other people who are older than you: people who are both a little older and who are a lot older. Thinking of them one at a time, imagine being just like them. Which of them represent appealing futures—ones you would want to grow into? Before reading any further, use these two methods and practice developing a representation of your future self.

3 The next step in creating compelling futures for yourself is to do an assessment, both positive and negative, of yourself in the present. Ranging through the full breadth of who you are as a person, take stock of where you live, your home life, your personal relationships, your career, health, finances, appearance, and so on. This appraisal should be your *own* honest assessment of what is *real*—not what could be, but what *is*. For instance, a very general assessment could be:

- **Housing** House in great location, but in need of repair.
- **Marriage** Mutually satisfying, enriching.
- **Children** Happy, healthy, doing well in school, but I don't spend as much time with them as I'd like.
- **Health** Mediocre, I don't eat well and I don't exercise.
- **Career** Fine, but unfocused; not sure of where it will go. It lacks security.
- **Finances** Less than secure, but treading water just fine. No long-range plan.
- **Appearance** Same as health. I don't take good enough care of myself.

The following lines are provided for you to write down your general assessment of your present situation. You will use this information in the following step, so make that honest assessment now.

General Assessment of My Present Situation

Housing _____

_____

Marriage (or love relationship) _____

_____

Children _____

_____

Health _____

_____

Career _____

_____

Finances _____

_____

Appearance _____

_____

? _____ _____

_____

? _____ _____

_____

4 Now, recall how you were within those same areas of your life five years ago. How was your health five years ago? What was the state of your finances? What was the quality of your relationships? Here are the answers for the person we used as an example in the previous step:

■ **Housing** Terrible. A temporary solution to housing needs.

■ **Marriage** Bad shape. It needed all the attention that has subsequently been given to it.

■ **Children** OK, but also in need of attention. They probably were suffering from the effects of the troubled marriage relationship.

■ **Health** Fine. Youth made up for the lack of care.

■ **Career** It was just forming, just getting off the ground.

■ **Finances** Erratic. Over my head a lot of the time.

■ **Appearance** Fine. Youth made it easy.

Use the following lines for your assessment of the same areas *five years ago.* Be sure to make this review before going on to the next step.

General Assessment of My Situation Five Years Ago

Housing _____

_____

Marriage (or love relationship) _____

_____

Children _____

_____

Health _____

_____

Career _____

_____

Finances _____

_____

Appearance _____

_____

? _____   _____

_____

? _____   _____

_____

5 Having done that, assess how your behavior since that time has (for better or for worse) contributed to creating your present situation. In other words, determine how your actions during the last five years have helped shape your present self and circumstances. This is an important step, so be sure to take all the time you need to make this assessment.

6 After you have completed that assessment, imagine in what ways you would now be worse off had you behaved *very* inappropriately (badly, rashly, irresponsibly, compulsively, etc.) during the last five years. You will soon discover how to benefit from making this kind of evaluation, but first you need to realize that you could be a lot worse off today had you behaved differently in the past.

7 The next step is to determine what else you could have done (other than what you actually did) during the last five years that would have resulted in your present situation being *better than it is.* We are not talking about acts of God or fortuitous circumstances, such as winning a lottery or having Mr. or Ms. Right show up on your doorstep. Rather, we are talking about what else YOU could have *done* that would not have been a significant deprivation and would have brought you to a substantially better position today (with regard to your relationships, career, health, and so on). For example, you work as a grocery clerk and are dissatisfied with the job. Looking back on the past five years, you realize that had you gotten into some kind of computer training program during that time, you would now be making a better living, probably doing something of more interest to you. Go ahead now and imagine what you could have done during the last five years that would have made the present even better than it is.

8 Now paint for yourself two pictures of the future: the first being five years from now and containing experiences and situations that you really *do* want; and the second being five years from now and containing experiences and situations that you really do *not* want. Be sure to include in your pictures your surroundings, where you are, who you are with, what you are doing, and how you are feeling. Pay attention to interesting details. Each picture should contain a vivid representation of your future self living within that very *desirable* or *undesirable* set of circumstances. Before proceeding, use your imagination to create these two images.

9 Having created these two futures, when you finish reading this paragraph look at your desired future and say to yourself, "How can I make that happen?" Asking this question is the impetus to your identifying just what actions are likely to lead to your desired future. An extremely important standard to apply at this point is this: If any steps leading to your desired future rely upon luck or the largess of others they are unacceptable. Such steps take the attainment of your desired future out of your hands and place it in the hands of others (thus, they are default responses). In order to keep the attainment of your goal a function of choice as much as possible, any such steps must be replaced by steps/behaviors that you yourself can control or, at least, influence. For instance, suppose your goal is to be in a loving relationship with a good mate. If one of the steps toward that goal is hoping the right person will find you, then whether or not you actually attain your goal is beyond your control. That is, outside forces or fortuitous circumstances must provide the right person. By changing that step to one which involves *seeking* out a loving mate you create many opportunities and options that you would otherwise never have. If you do not have sufficient information to determine how you will make your desired future happen, use the question, "How can I learn how to make it happen?" as a way of orienting yourself toward discovering appropriate sources of information. Be sure to make a note of those behaviors that will make your desired future an upcoming reality. Look at your desired future and ask and answer those questions now, before proceeding.

Things Worth Doing

_____

_____

_____

_____

_____

_____

10 Once you have identified those behaviors that will lead to your desired future, you need to identify those behaviors that are likely to lead to the *undesired* future. In this way you will have generated for yourself both a compelling representation of a future that you *want* to have (including the necessary steps/behaviors that *you* need to take in order to attain that future), and of those behaviors which will lead you toward the future you do *not* want. To illustrate, choosing certain foods will help make you healthy, but ignoring your nutritional needs will help make you unhealthy; stretch-type exercise will make you more physically flexible, but slothfulness will make and keep you inflexible; immediately setting aside a part of your paycheck will make it possible for you to save money, but waiting until the end of the month to see what is left over will make it difficult to save money; being with your child will help foster a good relationship, but always being busy with other things will provoke alienation. Now take the time to identify the behaviors that are likely to lead to your *undesired* future. Use the space provided below to list those behaviors that will lead you away from where you want to go.

Things Worth Avoiding

_____

_____

_____

_____

_____

_____

These representations now become a resource to be used for the purpose of making ongoing evaluations of whether you are progressing toward your desired or undesired future.

11　Now that you know which behaviors will lead to which futures, obviously you will want to engage in those behaviors which will lead to your desired future and steer clear of those behaviors which will lead to the undesired future. Each time you engage in behavior that takes you toward your desired future, feel and see yourself approaching that desired future. And should you engage in behaviors which lead toward your *undesired* future, feel and see yourself approaching that undesirable future.

You now have the know-how for generating personally compelling futures. Use these personally compelling futures to guide your decision-making and behavior toward achieving your goals (and away from disappointment and regret). You can always return to this sequence of steps. We encourage you to do so anytime you feel the need to bring your life back on track and your behavior into alignment with your goals. This know-how is the means to connect today's actions with tomorrow's fulfillment. In the following chapters we will assist you in applying this know-how to your health, career, and relationships.

Flexibility of Criteria

The compelling futures you created using the previous sequence of steps result from your use of certain standards, or *criteria*. Criteria determine what it is that you are trying to fulfill in your experience. Of course, you already have criteria that you use for most of the situations in which you find yourself, including the situations in which you want to make a change. Since, to a great extent, those criteria determine what you attend to and what you overlook or avoid, it is important to consider whether or not those criteria are *appropriate* with respect to your desired future.

For example, if your desired future includes a stable, secure, long-term love relationship, and you are presently attracted to raunchy, though charming, philanderers, it is likely that your criteria for what is attractive are inappropriate for achieving your desired future. Once you have evaluated your criteria and adjusted them to assure that they contribute to the accomplishment of your desired futures (as well as your present well-being), we will teach you how to develop *criteria flexibility*. Criteria flexibility assures that you have multiple ways of meeting your standards and satisfying your desires. Like having many possible and enjoyable routes to a chosen destination, criteria flexibility provides choices in *how* your fulfillment is accomplished.

1 The first question to consider is whether or not your criteria are standards left over from some previous (and now obsolete) period of your life. For instance, are you still trying to fulfill the criterion of being nice (perhaps a criterion imposed by a parent, teacher, or member of the clergy) when it would be more appropriate to direct your efforts toward being competent? In other words, are your criteria possibly inappropriate because they are from some time in your life that is no longer relevant to who you are *now*, or are they current and, so, representative of who you are as a person now? Sort through various contexts, such as relationships, personal health, lovers, politics, life style, and career, identifying your criteria for each one. For instance, you may highly value *loyalty* in relationships, *strength* in health, *intellectual compatibility* in a lover, *socially liberal* but *fiscally conservative* politics, an *orderly* and *urban* life style, and a *challenging* career. Someone else's criteria for the same areas might focus on *fun* in relationships, *vitality* in health, *physical attractiveness* in a lover, *environmental* politics, *outdoor rural* life style, and an *individualized* career that emphasizes *independence*.

What, in *your* opinion, is important, valuable, right, wrong, and appropriate within those contexts? Before going on to the next paragraph, list what is important to you for each of the contexts you are interested in, and determine which of the listed criteria are representative of who you are now (and who you want to be), and which are standards that are no longer relevant, perhaps because they were characteristic of you at some time in the past. Listing your criteria will make it easier (and more compelling) to evaluate whether or not they are indeed representative of your own values and standards.

What Is Important Concerning:

Relationships _____

_____

Personal Health _____

_____

Lovers _____

_____

Politics _____

_____

Life Style _____

_____

Career _____

_____

? _____   _____

_____

2   Another useful way to update your criteria is to identify for yourself who you respond to as role models. Who are the athletes, media stars, business leaders, political leaders, and literary characters with whom you identify? Who are the people you know professionally and personally whom you emulate (or specifically do not emulate)? Are the standards these people/models exemplify representative of the person you are and want to be, or are they more properly representative of who you _were_ at some time in the past? For example, if you are a woman, perhaps as a teenager you thought Playboy bunnies or beauty contest winners were the ultimate role models. But now, rather than limit your striving to looking great in high heels and a bathing suit, you look to female corporate leaders, reputable women politicians, and fulfilled, nurturing mothers as women worth emulating. Whereas a sexy walk, great legs, or a flashy smile might have seemed important to you in the past, the qualities you admire now might include intelligence, wit, independence, and caring for others. Spend a minute or two using this method to update your criteria with regard to who you are and who you want to be.

Your Role Model's Qualities

The Qualities Meaningful to the Present and Future You

_____   _____

_____   _____

_____   _____

_____   _____

_____   _____

3   Having criteria that are current, however, is not necessarily the same as having the most appropriate criteria for the future that you want to attain. You should test for this appropriateness/inappropriateness by considering a *range* of criteria that includes standards of evaluation that you might not otherwise have considered. Some of those standards may prove more useful in attaining your desired futures than those you now use. Taking over-eating as an example, imagine that you are about to make your dinner selection from a menu in a familiar restaurant. Perhaps you use pleasure as the criterion by which you make your selection. Using the criterion of pleasure, what would you select for an appetizer? For your main course? For your beverage? For your dessert? Having made those selections, go through the menu again, only this time make your choices using the criterion of health. How does that change in criteria change your meal? What now do you select for an appetizer (or do you even select one)? What are healthful main courses, beverages and desserts? Taking your time, go through the following list of possible criteria (and any others that occur to you), making menu selections with regard to each one:

Pleasure

Health

Calories

New (or Different)

Familiar

Filling yourself

Lightness

How I will feel after eating

How I will feel tomorrow

4   Reviewing the choices you made under the influence of each of the above criteria, assess for yourself which of those criteria led you to make choices which *are in alignment with your desired future*. Of course, those criteria which lead you to choices which work against your attaining your outcomes are inappropriate and should be set aside in favor of those criteria which direct your attention and choices in ways which will lead you to your desired outcomes. For instance, using pleasure as a criterion for meal selection might lead you to notice and choose sausage *en brioche* and warm French bread as appetizers, lasagne for a main course, and cheesecake for dessert. What a wonderful meal . . .unless you are overweight and on a diet. It is, perhaps, mother nature's cruel prank that many of those foods and dishes that we find so pleasurable to eat wind up the next day in bulging bottoms and bellies. Nevertheless, regardless of which of the latest diet regimens you are on, losing weight means changing the kind and amounts of food you eat, and getting exercise sufficient to reduce fat reserves and increase body tone. As a criterion to use at mealtimes for selecting food, pleasure will lead most people to select dishes which do not fit with their desire to lose weight. (We say "most" because some people find either a piece of fruit for dessert, or no dessert, pleasurable, and cheesecake not at all pleasurable.) If instead of pleasure you used health as the criterion, you might instead select as your meal a salad appetizer, broiled salmon as a main course, and fresh berries for dessert. This is not necessarily a better meal than the lasagne-cheesecake one, but if your intention is to lose weight, then the salmon and berries meal is more *appropriate*. Before going on, assess for yourself which criteria led you to make choices which are in alignment with your desired future.

In the examples we have been using above, we have been presupposing that the criteria have certain meanings, or *evidence of fulfillment*. For example, among the Jewish immigrants of the first half of this century, a baby was considered healthy if he or she was fat. The criterion is *healthy*. The evidence of fulfillment is *fat*. Furthermore, since the evidence for a good mother was in part dependent upon having healthy children, women often fed their babies butter fat, and those whose babies refused to balloon kept their children inside and out of sight as much as possible (at least until the butter fat took effect). It must be remembered that criteria are simply labels for contextually significant values. We will be using the term *criterial equivalence* to mean the particular experiences used as evidence to know when a criterion has been fulfilled. For the diner, the criterial equivalence of a healthy meal might be foods that are low in fat and calories and high in vitamin content. For the Jewish mother in the 1940's, the criterial equivalence of a healthy baby often was a baby that was fat. The diners and the mothers of the above examples may both be using a criterion called health, but the experiences used as evidence of health are very different, and will cause them to experience and behave very differently.

Steve and Nate being interviewed (Chapter 2) is another example of the significance of such criterial equivalences (again, criterial equivalence being the term applied to those perceptions and experiences by which you recognize that your criteria are, or are not, being met). For Steve, the criterial equivalence for success was getting the job. Thus, when he did not get the job, he felt that he had failed. Nate certainly recognized that to get the job was to be successful, but to him learning something was also being successful. Therefore, as long as Nate could extract some kind of learning from the job interview experience he would walk away with a feeling of success, whether he got the job or not. *Flexibility in criteria and in the means by which those criteria are experienced as being fulfilled* (criterial equivalences) *creates choice.*

As another example, consider the criterion of attractiveness. For many people, the criterial equivalences which they label as attractive are accepted as those physical characteristics belonging to acknowledged beauties as portrayed in the media (models and starlets). You could, instead, evaluate people's attractiveness with respect to criterial equivalences concerning strength (attractive = powerful arms and legs), skin texture (attractive = satin-like skin), ethnic background (attractive = almond-shaped eyes), symmetry (attractive = symmetrical facial features), sincerity (attractive = sincere and gentle), and so on. It is important, then, to specify for yourself just what are the criterial equivalences (the perceptions and experiences) represented by the criteria with which you are operating.

5 Given the kinds of experiences and outcomes you want, are your criterial equivalences useful to you or not? Have you ever really sat down and thought about whether the basis upon which you evaluate both your experience and the world around you is in accord with what you want your experience to be? For instance, in an effort to be successful, you work long, hard hours, exhausting both yourself and your family in an effort to make a lot of money (success = wealth). You want to have the experience of being successful, and you also want to enjoy life and your family, as well as have the opportunity to nurture them, and so on. Is your criterial equivalence for success in accord with your outcomes?

As a further example, here is an interesting sample list of criteria and criterial equivalences: competency = being the best, success = position/title, freedom = no obligations, adventure = dangerous, life-threatening activity. These are examples of criterial equivalences that could be less than useful. Being the best is difficult to achieve and maintain in any cooperative environment. If you need to be the best in order to feel competent, you will probably spend a lot of time feeling inadequate instead. (It would be much more useful to utilize *wanting to be the best* as the fuel for the motivation and commitment necessary to constantly improve.) Using position/title as evidence of success contributes to the prosperity of those who print business cards, but it may not provide an adequate basis for the continuous experience of personal fulfillment. Take this opportunity to list several of your criteria and the evidence you presently use to signal their fulfillment. Writing them down will help you create a perspective from which you can evaluate whether or not your criterial equivalences will lead you to your chosen destinations.

Criteria		Criterial Equivalence
Success	=	_____
Intelligence	=	_____
Attractive	=	_____
Healthy	=	_____
Competence	=	_____
? _____	=	_____
? _____	=	_____

6 Once you have specified the criteria that are relevant to your desired future *and* the kinds of evidence that would exemplify their fulfillment, it is time to apply them to your desired future. Which of the experiences that you have designated as evidence of your criteria fulfillment are congruent with the outcomes that you want for yourself, and which are incongruent, hindering, or simply not helpful? Those criterial equivalences which are not supportive of your desired future should be changed. In the previous example of success = wealth, for instance, changing your criterial equivalence to success = enjoying your work would have a profound impact upon how you approached your work, family, and so on. Often, what *is* appropriate as evidence of criteria fulfillment will be obvious. For example, a criterial equivalence of healthy = pudgy is inappropriate if you want to lose weight; it needs to be changed to something more in accord with your adult needs (e.g., healthy = trim, feel energetic, and able to do day-to-day chores without tiring). If a more useful criterial equivalence is not apparent, you can ask for this information from an acquaintance who already has as part of his or her ongoing experience what you want for yourself in the future. Suppose that when it comes to interviews, you are terrified before, nervous during and despondent afterwards. Your friend Nate, on the other hand, looks forward to the interview, and is happy afterwards. When you ask him about whether or not he cares about succeeding, he will answer, yes. Asking him how he knows when he is succeeding will get you the information that you want, namely, "When I am learning something." Proceed now to identify which of your criteria and criterial equivalences are appropriate for your goals in life and which need changing. For those that need changing, determine how you can change them such that they will be congruent with who you want to be and what you want to accomplish.

The purpose of the preceding sequence of steps is to allow you to get to know yourself in an especially useful way. You now know how to identify your criteria (indeed, you already have identified several important ones). You also know how to evaluate your criteria to make sure they are appropriate. And you have already begun to develop flexibility in how your criteria can be fulfilled. This know-how will facilitate your knowledgeable and effective progress toward achieving any of your personal or professional goals.

Relative Specificity

Fundamental to having a compelling future that is able, for example, to motivate you to eat properly, is a belief that your present actions largely determine your future well-being. We term this belief a *present-to-future cause-effect relationship*. Unless that cause-effect relationship is tangible to you, there will be no good reason to engage in (or avoid) certain behaviors *now* in order to attain (or avoid) certain futures.

Important in creating that tangibility is the relative specificity of your mental computations. Suppose that you want to lose weight and that the relative specificity at which you are operating is fairly general and, therefore, large. Accordingly, you might decide that you want to go from a size twenty-four to a size eight. Left at that, you are either at the desired size eight or you have not lost the weight you want to lose. The magnitude of the change that is required by an outcome specified this globally makes any relatively small reductions in your dress size (from size twenty-four to a tight twenty-two, for example) meaningless. It also makes meaningless any behaviors you may engage in while dropping that one dress size. In other words, the fact that you abstained from sweets for a week does not make tangible the cause-effect relationship between your eating patterns and weight loss since the week of abstinence did not cause you to go from a size twenty-four to a size eight. On the other hand, by organizing your experience in smaller pieces (specifying at a smaller size) you provide yourself with the opportunity to make the operating cause-effect relationships tangible. For instance, you could specify (or break down) the steps of your weight loss to the level of size-by-size (i.e., size twenty-four to size twenty-two, size twenty-two to size twenty, and so on to size eight) and then begin by losing enough weight to go down to a size twenty-two. In dropping that one size, you will have attained a specific piece of, and step toward, your desired future, from which you can identify (as you did earlier in generating a compelling future) the ways your behavior made it possible for you to have lost the weight (i.e., the cause-effect relationships).

The degree of specificity you use to organize your outcomes also interacts with your criteria. In the previous example, specifying the outcome at a relatively large magnitude made the criterial equivalence for successfully losing weight attaining size eight. The effect of keeping the outcome represented as one large chunk is that it precludes the possibility of ongoing, easily attainable experiences of success. Thus, going from a size twenty-four to a size twenty-two as the result of dieting for a week will not seem to be an accomplishment on the way toward your goal since you did not go from size twenty-four to size eight. Small steps, however, provide opportunities to experience ongoing levels of success. If you organize your experience at the level of size-by-size, losing the weight that gets you down to a size twenty-two becomes a success. That is, you have met the criterial equivalence necessary to have attained one of your small-stepped futures on the way to your larger, overall desired future. Similarly, be pleased that you are able to do thirty sit-ups today when last week you only did twenty-five, rather than evaluating whether or not you have lost the twenty pounds you want to lose; or be pleased that you have decreased the number of cigarettes you are smoking this week over last week, rather than evaluating whether or not you have quit smoking; or notice that there are nutritional aspects of food that you appreciate this week that you did not even know about last week, rather than evaluating whether or not you are completely healthy.

Let us use being attractive as another example. Evaluating attractiveness as a total or whole piece might lead you to want to match pictures in *Playboy, Vogue* or *Gentlemen's Quarterly*, absorbing those pictures as your notion (your criterial equivalence) of what represents attractiveness. The result would be an attempt on your part to become a clone of the model(s) you are using as the criterial equivalence of attractiveness. Specifying attractiveness into its smaller component pieces would mean identifying just what you think are attractive nails, hands, feet, hair, voice, gestures, jewelry, and so on. Looking at those same *Vogue* and *GQ* pictures and organizing your perceptions with respect to smaller and more detailed aspects will allow you to notice the particular aspects of the model's makeup, hair style, mannerisms, pieces of clothing, and personality qualities that you find attractive, and the particular aspects you do not find attractive. Again, these more specific details of what makes up the experience of attractiveness provide much greater opportunities for satisfying the criterion of attractiveness. It is more possible to wear your *makeup* like Brooke Shields than it is to be just like Brooke Shields (especially if you are 5′2″ and 44 years old).

In terms of health, some people organize their experience in such a general way that the criterion they are testing for becomes ill or not ill. As a result, these people do not engage in behaviors intended to keep or make themselves healthy until they become ill. They are either (fortuitously) healthy, or are *restoring* their health. Specifying the experience of health in more detail, on the other hand, accesses criteria that provide the opportunity to attend to the continuum of feedback that we all have available. This makes it possible to respond to those physiological signals that are informing us of the need for sleep, rest, activity, vitamins, sex, personal contact, fresh air, and so on.

We are not suggesting here that criteria that are specified in detailed pieces are necessarily the best criteria to have. Rather, our research has consistently shown that *flexibility* in how you organize your experience is crucial (you will be reminded of this when you read about James in the "Wishing to Having" chapter). It is best to have the flexibility of criteria fulfillment that comes with being able to vary the relative specificity you are attending to and using to organize your experience. With this flexibility comes the ability to affect your ongoing experience and behavior dramatically. For instance, above we gave the example of using the all or nothing approach to satisfying the criterion of attractiveness, as contrasted with breaking attractiveness down into its component pieces (Brooke Shields vs. Brooke Shields' hair style, makeup, nails, etc.). In that example, the flexibility to experience yourself as genuinely attractive comes from not necessarily having to match the whole person, but only certain aspects of that person's attractiveness.

1 Spend a few moments thinking about the goals you have
set for yourself, both personally and professionally. What are
some of the outcomes you want to achieve? Pick two of your
goals and identify several specific *and detailed* examples that
would be evidence to you that you were making progress
toward attainment of each of those goals. For example, if
financial security is one of your outcomes, the list of small
steps that indicate progress might include reducing the out-
standing balance on your charge cards, reading about in-
vestment choices, developing a budget, sticking to your budget, opening an IRA account, and maintaining adequate
insurance policies. Use the space provided below to make a
list for both of the goals you have chosen. And remember, now
is one of the times in life when it pays to think small.

Goal   **Evidence of Progress**

#1 _____   _____

                                           _____

                                           _____

                                           _____

                                           _____

                                           _____

#2 _____   _____

                                           _____

                                           _____

                                           _____

                                           _____

                                           _____

2 Now go through a similar process with two of the important criteria you identified in the previous section on criteria flexibility. This time, however, you will be identifying the
small, detailed attributes or behaviors that can be used as
evidence of that criteria being fulfilled. For example, if you
identified intellectual compatability as being important to you

in a love relationship, your list of specific criterial equivalences might include similar tastes in film, enjoys science fiction, reads and discusses the editorial page of the newspaper, and doesn't watch wrestling or bowling on TV. As you do this now for two of your important criteria, remember that what you are accomplishing is breaking an all-or-nothing-at-all requirement for your criterial equivalences.

Criteria   **Evidence Of Fulfillment**

#1 _____   _____

_____

_____

_____

_____

_____

#2 _____   _____

_____

_____

_____

_____

Default vs. Choice Responses

Now, does changing your criteria mean that you must go without satisfying those criteria that you have traditionally cherished (as in the pleasure example above)? Of course not. Eating rich foods is a *behavior* and certainly can be a way of giving yourself pleasure, but it is not the *only* way. By having a wide-ranging repertoire of ways for giving yourself pleasure (that is, a range of criterial equivalences) you make it possible to gratify your criterion of pleasure in ways that are congruent with your overall outcomes (losing weight, being healthy, etc.). It becomes a matter of selecting appropriate situations. Mealtime is an inappropriate time for an overweight person to employ the criterion of pleasure in choosing what food to eat. If you are really clever, of course, you will discover ways to give yourself pleasure at mealtimes other than by eating certain foods, such as finding pleasure in being leisurely, lively discussions, or watching the behavior of other diners. This is as close to having your cake and eating it too that we can imagine.

If you have only one way to satisfy a criterion of yours, then that way becomes a *default response* for you. That is, you have only one response and, so, no choice: If you want to feel pleasure then you have to eat; if you want to be uninhibited then you have to drink; if you want to relax then you have to take a Valium. In each of these instances, how the individual creates his or her experience is not a matter of choice. Whether or not they have the experience depends upon eating, drinking or taking a pill. By having more than one way of getting what you want you make it possible to do so even when the rest of the world is not cooperating as it should or used to. Even if you are overweight, there is no reason why being on a diet should necessarily mean that you have to forego pleasure as long as you have ways of satisfying your desire for pleasure that are in alignment with your need to control your intake of food.

So, how do you increase your range of choice? People get what they want for themselves through their behavior (which includes internal behaviors, such as daydreaming, imagining what other people are experiencing, reminiscing, listening to internally generated music, and so on). If you have only one way to get what you want within a particular situation, you can develop a range of choice simply by denying yourself that choice, and continuing to vary your behavior until you discover several other ways which are as effective in getting you what you want as was your original behavior. In other words, force yourself to experiment with other ways of satisfying your wants and needs by specifically denying yourself the one response you have always relied upon. For instance, if you need a couple of cups of coffee to get you going in the morning, deny yourself that coffee and try other things to get yourself going until you have found several that work. Maybe it will be yoga, a big glass of fresh-squeezed orange juice, vitamins, a short bike ride, a couple of phone calls to friends, or somersaults down the hallway. Whatever it may be, once you have several ways of getting yourself going in the morning, how you get going will become a matter of choice.

You might ask, "But why bother to try somersaulting down the hallway when coffee works fine?" There are two answers to this. The first is that it puts you at the mercy of circumstances if having coffee is the only way for you to get going in the morning. If you stumble into the kitchen expecting a cup full of Javan eye-opener, only to discover that you are groundless, you drag yourself to your car, and peering through half-lidded eyes you go scouting for some other source of coffee. If instead of being at home, you were camping and ran out of coffee, the situation might take on critical proportions (at least as far as you are concerned). As a case in point, we are familiar with one woman who literally felt incapable of getting out of bed in the morning until she had first smoked three cigarettes. So, having a range of behaviors capable of getting you what you want helps insure that you *can* get what you want, regardless of worldly capriciousness.

The second reason for having the behavioral range we are talking about is that it may at some point become prudent or necessary *not* to engage in a certain behavior that you normally rely upon. For instance, if you develop the jitters from all the coffee you are drinking in order to get going, you may be forced (or want) to cut down or eliminate coffee from your daily diet. But if coffee is the only way you have to get going, cutting out the morning cups will leave you listless and dazed (conditions which will, of course, make the resumption of coffee drinking very attractive). If, however, you do not need coffee for a lift, then the circumstance of not having coffee is neither a crisis nor a significant hardship.

1 Take the time now to identify a situation in which you use only one way to get what you want. Use your creativity to discover at least three or four other ways which would be equally effective in satisfying your wants and needs in that situation. List your new choices in the following spaces.

Situation

**New Choices for
Satisfying My Wants
and Needs**

_____   _____

                                 _____

                                 _____

                                 _____

The significance of having flexibility in satisfying what is important to you, then, is that it creates *experiential flexibility*. If you have only one way to satisfy your criteria, then the situation in which it occurs becomes a default response. There is no choice in the sense that if it is, for some reason, not possible to satisfy that criterial equivalence, then the criterion must go unfulfilled. For example, if your criterion of pleasure is satisfied only by eating, then you must either eat or go without the experience of pleasure. Whether or not you experience pleasure is a default response in the sense that you have no choice but to give up pleasure if you decide to diet. However, if you have a variety of ways of satisfying your criterion of pleasure (like eating, a warm bath, conversation with friends, and watching an old movie), then foregoing a bag of potato chips does not mean foregoing pleasure, since there are several other activities in which you can engage which give you pleasure. Having your ongoing experience made up of choice responses is, to our minds, a most pleasurable and sensual form of independence.

Cause-Effect

Certainly one of the values of having a rememberable past is that it can then be used as a tremendous source of information. As you move toward your goals, it is almost certain that some of what you do will seem to be appropriate, useful or representative of who you are and want to be, and some of what you do will be inappropriate, not useful or not representative of who you are and want to be. Few paths toward change traversed that there is no need to attend to where you are placing your feet. An ongoing assessment of how and what you are doing in relation to attaining your goal is essential to assure that you can keep going and that you will, eventually, reach that goal.

1   To this end we direct you to the following task: At the end of each day, take a moment to review that day's events. Specifically, how did your activities and behaviors of the day contribute toward attaining your desired future? How did your activities and behaviors fulfill you in the present? And, so, what will you want to be sure to do again? And, what will you want to be sure to never do again?

The purpose of these review questions is to provide you with filters capable of sifting from the day's events those activities and behaviors of yours which were the cause of your moving toward your desired future, and those which were the cause of your moving toward your *un*desired future. Being able to identify what activities and behaviors were in alignment with your goals and which were not is an important step in bringing the attainment of your desired futures into the realm of choice.

2   To insure that tomorrow you *carry out* the behaviors that are worth repeating and not the ones you have identified as nonuseful, take the time to make a mental movie of tomorrow's activities. Be sure to imagine carrying out the desirable behaviors in the approriate situations. You can do this effectively by either seeing yourself doing them or (better) by imagining actually doing them, seeing directly what you would be seeing, hearing directly what you would be hearing, and feeling the feelings associated with actually doing the chosen behaviors. If you imagine doing any of the undesirable behaviors, start over, making sure this time that this internally generated future is a full representation of *you doing what you want to do*. Take a step toward your desired future by taking the time right now to run that mental movie of tomorrow's activities. This form of mental rehearsal, or *future-pacing*, is a stunningly effective means of guiding yourself into being as you want to be.

In this chapter we have introduced you to the five fundamentals of success. These fundamentals are the key to the excellence and success of many gifted people. You have already taken the first steps toward your own mastery of the fundamentals of success, and you have gained some experience with the requisites for success in the areas of life discussed in each of the following chapters. We will now apply these fundamentals to one desirable project after another, guiding you to the results that are yours to enjoy when you have the know-how for personal and professional fulfillment.

4 Wishing to Having

Regardless of what you want for yourself—things (cars, jewelry), relationships (love, friendship), skills (math acuity, playing an instrument), or experiences (comfort, a strong will, sleeping beneath the stars)—actually getting what you want will be determined by what you *do* to have that thing, relationship, skill or experience. Many people, however, only wish for what they want, then wait to get it. Regardless of how ardently you want what you are wishing for, regardless of how creative you are about devising ways in which your want could eventually come to you, as long as you do nothing on the outside (in behavior), getting what you want remains solely dependent upon luck and the generous responsiveness of others. As long as all activity directed toward getting what you want remains inside you, it will be up to the often whimsical generosity of the world either to grant or deny your wish.

Thus, between wishing and having there must be *doing*. Furthermore, doing requires a *plan*—a plan which guides your activity along those paths which will (or are likely to) lead you to having what you want. Accordingly, we have identified five stages in the process of going from wishing to having:

Wishing ▶ Wanting ▶ Planning ▶ Doing ▶ Having

Bear in mind as we describe each of these stages that they are all parts of a larger, *interdependent* process, and that these five stages do not remain separate for those people who are characteristically successful at going from wishing to having.

Wishing

"I wish this light would change," Roy thought as he stood on the corner. Then, suddenly, he perked up. "There goes another one." He watched the Corvette make its shark-like way through the traffic. He sighed, then said aloud, painfully, "I wish I had one." "One what?" asked a stranger standing beside Roy. With a wistful "That," Roy pointed at the receding, fiberglass predator. The stranger shook his head and said, "I had one once. You have a lot of money?" Roy shook his head. "You have a lot of time?" Roy looked confused, then shrugged. "You got a family?" Roy nodded and said, "Three kids." The stranger wiped the air with his hand, saying, "You're better off without it," and then he walked off. Roy was trying to figure out what in the hell the stranger had been talking about, when suddenly another sleek Corvette slid before him. Transfixed, he murmured longingly, "Boy, how I wish I had one of those!" He watched it go, then turned back to face the crossing signal just as it turned from "walk" back to "don't walk". Roy wished that the light would change.

As Jimminy Cricket told us all in *Pinnochio*, "When you wish upon a star, It makes no difference who you are . . ." And as long as you are *wishing*, that is true. Roy has neither the money, the time nor a practical use for a Corvette. But none of those arguments really matter because Roy is not doing anything other than simply wishing for something. (For instance, he is not taking a night job in order to finance the car.) One of the authors' mother has a standard reply to people who while away their lives wishing and then complain about not having what they want. As she says, "Well, honey, if you wish in one hand and spit in the other, which one do you think is going to fill up first?"

Yet, people do wish for things all the time. You might wish you had a million dollars, that a movie star would call you up for a date, that people would get along better, that your kid would settle down, or that you didn't have to mow the lawn. What makes these distinctly *wishes* is that they *fail to engage behavior*. As an example of this, take a moment when you finish this paragraph to list three things you wish were true (or wish you had) and three things that you want. You will notice in comparing them that those goals that you *want* probably have stirred you to some kind of activity (even if only internal planning) intended to help make that want a reality. Those goals that are *wished* for, no matter how ardently, will be relatively unconnected to any personal behaviors intended to make those wishes come true. They remain, instead, as things that may some day be granted to you.

Use the space provided below to write down your list of three things you wish were true, and three things you want. Compare the differences in your response as you think about the items on the two lists. Do you have more action-oriented feelings or do you begin to do more planning in response to the items on one list more than the other? Be sure to develop and compare your lists before proceeding; you will be using your lists again in a few minutes.

Wishes   **Wants**

_____   _____

_____   _____

_____   _____

Though many people have no real separation between wishing and wanting, people who are consistently capable of turning their dreams into reality *do* have a separation between the two. During the process of interviewing successful people to determine the organization of internal processes that results in this talent, we found that each of them put their dreams through a qualifying process before taking any additional steps toward making them come true. If a wish didn't qualify as a full-fledged *want*, they didn't bother to act on it. The procedure for distinguishing a wish from a want that is presented in the "Making It Come True For You" section at the end of this chapter is a refinement of the qualifying processes we found in each of those talented people.

Your application of certain standards primarily determines whether a wish remains a wish or becomes a want (that is, a goal that compels you to some kind of action). We call those standards *well-formedness criteria*. Well-formedness criteria refer to those standards that have to do with such considerations as:

- Is it possible to have, or do, or be, or experience?
- Is it worth having?
- Will it get me what I *really* want?
- Is it worth what it will take to get it?

The first question, "Is it possible . . .?" should be answered with a yes if you or any other person you know of has ever attained your wish before, *or* if you can imagine the circumstances that could exist that would make that wish attainable. It is not necessary at this point to believe in the probability or feasibility of that wish coming true. As you will discover in the next section, there is a more appropriate time and way to focus on those considerations. If there is nothing you are wishing for (and you wish you had something), you can generate a list of candidates by finding answers to the question, "*What* is possible to have, to do, to be, and to experience?"

Asking yourself, "Is it worth having?" will lead you to consider the consequences of having your wish be realized. *Wishing* for a boat, or a dog, or horses, or a child, or more children, or a second home, or your own business can be wonderful. But some of the likely consequences of *having* those things—costly maintenance, frustration, loss of freedom, and added responsibility—can be less than wonderful. Also, it is wise to think about whether having "it" would be an appropriate expression of your personal values. It may be a sumptuous and sensuous fur coat you are wishing for; but, if you would never forgive yourself for contributing to an industry you sincerely believe to be unethical, it probably would not be worth having. And finally (for now), you can use this question to direct you to evaluate how having it would affect your relationship with, and the lives of, your family members, friends, and co-workers.

All too often, people yearn for something that ultimately turns out to be emotionally hollow and unfulfilling. By asking "Will it get me what I really want?" *before* you involve yourself in the pursuit of a wish, you will give yourself the opportunity to identify the desires, emotional needs, and yearnings that are most meaningful to fulfill. This provides you with the information you need to judge fairly the future worth of your wish. If what you are wishing for will not provide you with what you really want, it would be better to develop and consider other wishes that *do* hold the possibility of satisfaction.

In order to answer the fourth question, "Is it worth what it will take to get it?" you are required to anticipate what you will have to do (as well as the time, energy and cost) to pursue a particular wish. If you know ahead of time about the challenges, difficulties and obstacles you will have to overcome, and you are still convinced it is worth the effort, your desire and commitment will fortify you when the going gets tough.

The importance of these questions is that in order to answer them you will have to measure your wishes against who you are and your situation in life. As you will see in the sections to follow, who you are as a person—your personal needs, inclinations, values and desires—as well as the needs, inclinations, values and desires of those with whom you are involved, all become important when you start moving toward a goal.

Beyond the importance of answering these well-formedness questions in establishing appropriate goals for yourself is the change that comes when those questions can be satisfactorily answered: wishes become wants. That is, once wishes become possible to have and to get, are worth having, are worth the effort, and are in accord with your personal ecology, your response changes from passively waiting, to feeling impelled toward the planning and action which will make that wish come true.

We want to emphasize that we are not implying here that there is anything inherently wrong with wishing, but that (1) things left as wishes do not engage behavior intended to attain what you are wishing for, and (2) you should be aware of when you are wishing for something rather than wanting it, since being aware of the difference will make it possible for you to select those wishes that are important enough to turn into wants. As an example of this difference, apply the well-formedness questions to each of the wishes that you listed previously, noticing how your response changes when you are able to satisfactorily answer all of those questions with regard to any one of those wishes. It will only take a minute or two to do this, and you will be learning a process that will benefit you for the rest of your life.

Wanting

Sitting alone once again in his bedroom, Kenny just couldn't figure out what had gone wrong *this* time. This time it had been Alicia. Before her there was Barbara, Linda, Mae . . . too many. Alicia was so pretty, and they had seemed to have such a good time together in the beginning. Within two weeks, he had convinced her to move in. Later, as always, the disappointments started mounting. With Alicia there had been the squabbling over the kinds of food they ate and the fact that he liked to stay up late while she preferred to turn in early. Then there was the fact that she seemed to have no sense of humor at all (if she did, it was impervious to Kenny's kind of clowning), and she was *so* childlike and dependent! "But things seemed so right in the beginning," Kenny thinks as he shakes his head. He leans back on the pillow and muses aloud, "And to think, I was already planning our family. Maybe I'll get lucky with the next one."

It does not take long for Kenny to move from things being right in the beginning to making plans that go into the future—far into the future. It is obvious, however, that whoever the person was that he imagined living with and having a family with in that future, it was not Alicia, but only looked like her. Like everyone else, Kenny has criteria (standards) which characterize for him what he wants in a long-term mate. Kenny's mistake was in disregarding his criteria for a long-term relationship when considering a possible future relationship with Alicia. Alicia was *not* a vegetarian, late-niter, independent, or possessed of a good sense of humor—all qualities which are of obvious importance to Kenny. She did fulfill his criteria for prettiness and fun, but these criteria provide an insufficient basis (for Kenny, at least) upon which to establish a lifelong commitment.

In deciding that he wants to live with Alicia, Kenny ignores or forgets to attend to a great many of those criteria which are relevant to deciding what is worth wanting in the future for himself. In this way, Kenny succeeds in generating an attractive and seemingly real future for himself that is nevertheless inappropriate. Had he included those criteria in his musings about the future he would very quickly have realized that the person who was Alicia was not the person for him (though she may very well have fit his criteria for a friend, casual lover, and so on).

Betty felt almost destitute. There was so much that she wanted. She wanted a new car and a house of her own. There were so many nice outfits she would like to get for the children. Speaking of children, she would like to have another. And how about a vacation? She and her husband hadn't been on one for years. Betty would like to get a well-paying job, but she also wants more time for herself and to spend with the kids, so she is hoping to find a well-paying job that will leave her weekdays, nights and weekends free. She decides to speak to her husband (when he gets home tonight from his second job) about spending more time with the kids. Betty perks up when she remembers that she also has news for him about another part-time job he can take on the weekends. She leans back on the cushions for a few moments of satisfying reverie as she thinks, "With that job we can take that vacation!"

Unlike Kenny, Betty does not fail to take into account those things which are important to her when she imagines her future. She takes them *all* into account. What paralyzes Betty and effectively prevents her from satisfying most (if any) of her criteria is that she ignores the fact that there *are* certain facts of life (such as mortality, your height, twenty-four hours in the day) that must be taken into account. In general, money must be earned in order to purchase a car, house, or clothes; earning money involves time and effort; it is difficult to go on a vacation if you are working-—even if you can afford the ticket; it is difficult to work at one, two or three jobs without taking some time away from the family, and so on. The simple fact is that some of Betty's criteria are *simultaneously incompatible* (i.e., getting a job *and* having more free time), while others are *sequentially* contingent upon one another (i.e., work ▶ money ▶ house).

It is not the number of criteria that ensnares Betty, but the fact that they are not *prioritized*. Every one of us could easily list a hundred things that we want for ourselves. But we actually employ only a few of these in making evaluations about the future. The reason for this is that they are prioritized, making it possible for us to attend only to those which are of greatest importance or to those which must be dealt with *before* others on the list enter the realm of possibility. For Betty, the fact that she operates out of a choice response is of no help to her at all since her lack of prioritization keeps her from sticking to one aspiration long enough to make it happen.

> James had played music all his life. He loved it and for most of his adult life he had earned a living (though, admittedly, a tenuous one) as a musician. But then things changed—he married and had children. A family is fine if you are selling platinum records every month, but the bones they throw even an excellent club musician like James makes having a family all but impossible. Always a responsible person (he had never missed a single gig), James took seriously the care of his family. Looking into the future he realized that he would have to find a steadier, more lucrative way of making money so that he could support his family. He'd always been fascinated by technology, and everywhere he looked there were companies begging for computer programmers. He knew little about the field, so he started researching it by reading and talking with those in it. Armed with that information, he imagined himself working as a computer programmer, decided he would like it and, so, went back to school. While he worked hard at school he continued to play his music, but only for extra money and on weekends; after all, he had his studies and a family to keep up with.

There are several things to note about how James went

about deciding what to want. One is that, unlike Kenny, James includes in his deliberations the relevant criteria, namely, those criteria that will be significant in *both his short-run and long-run futures*. Being creative musically and being responsible are both criteria which have always been and (probably) always will be important to James. By including them both, he helps insure that the future that he ends up wanting for himself will be respectful of both of those criteria. Left at that, however, James could easily have ended up torn between the two criteria (as was Betty by hers). Instead, James prioritizes them, giving his responsibility to his family somewhat more weight than his need to play music. The importance of this prioritization is that it makes it possible for him to resolve any conflicts created by those criteria in the possible futures he is considering. Having specified and prioritized his criteria, James is then free to generate possible futures for himself and evaluate them with respect to those criteria. Taking his criteria with him, James steps into each of these possible futures, trying to find the one or ones that seem most satisfying and compelling. Whether he is doing it explicitly or not, he is, in this process, trying to get some general answers to the well-formedness questions we introduced in the previous section:

- What is possible to have, or be, or do, or experience?
- Is it worth having?
- Will it get me what I *really* want?
- Is it worth what it will take to get it?

Since James needed to generate new possibilities for earning money (as opposed to already having an idea that only needed evaluating), the first question he considered was "*What* is possible . . .?" instead of "*Is* it possible . . .?" This question presupposes that there *are* many possibilities and, so, as with James, orients you toward seeking alternatives. A yes to all three of the other questions identifies that the wanted future is one which is in accord with your criteria and whatever kinds of experiences and information you are using to evaluate the possible fulfillment of that criteria. (All human decision-making processes require information to refer to, and that data can include remembered and imagined experiences and present sensory input.) The memories and experiences that constitute the data base are then evaluated with respect to the criteria being used. For example, in this situation James uses a data base that includes his past experiences in the music business, his present family obligations, what other people he knows or knows of have done or are doing both inside and outside the music business, as well as information he has read and been told. He refers to all of this in his decision-making processes regarding his professional future. He experimented with various possible careers for himself, evaluating each of them with respect to his criteria and his priorities, as well as other considerations, such as the reeducation time involved, the cost, income potential, family arrangements, and so on. If he could not answer those questions from his personal experience, he would seek out sources of experience and information (people and books) which he could then use to enrich his representations of the possible futures.

Also characteristic of James's thinking is a presupposition that his destiny is his to *choose* and his responsibility to make happen. If there were (to his mind) only one way to satisfy each of his criteria, then the process of deciding what he wants would never progress beyond trying to figure out how to amplify what he already does in order to meet the needs of his family (i.e., try to work more gigs). James, however, is not constrained in this way and, so, looks for various ways to be responsible, various ways to satisfy his desire to play music, and even ways of simultaneously satisfying both of those criteria. Also underlying his wanting is a presupposition of *a causal relationship between what he does in the present and the future he will eventually have.* This means James believes and expresses in actual behavior his belief that what he does now will, to a large extent, produce his future. This is an important cause-effect presupposition since it helps ensure that he recognizes that the fulfillment of his wants is at least somewhat contingent upon his own present and future efforts.

The scenarios of possible futures are quite general at this point, as compared to a scenario that had every detail specified. It is essential to be able to break down an outcome into its component pieces, as well as specify the activities required to accomplish each piece. For instance, in the activity of cooking dinner, making the salad is a behavior that is a component of the overall activity of cooking dinner. It is, however, relatively more general than taking the lettuce from the refrigerator, washing it, breaking off leaves, etc., which are relatively smaller, more detailed steps. The relative specificity of behavior that a person uses to represent what it will take to achieve a desired outcome is a very important distinction in all endeavors that require planning and carrying out plans in a sequential fashion. As you will learn, success is largely dependent upon using the appropriate amount of detail at each stage in going from wanting to having.

When you are at the point of wanting in your decision-making process, the relative detail of your considerations can, and probably should be, fairly general. Attending to the very fine details at this point can lead you into tiny particulars that are only relevant if you are actually going to pursue that particular future. By considering only relatively large details, you can make relatively simple and quick evaluations of the potential suitability of a possible want. With those possible futures that seem to fit your bill, you move into the next stage in the sequence:

Planning

It is 1979, and Bill has decided that he wants to become a computer programmer. His wife thinks it's a great idea, and wants to know where he will be going to school. "I don't know yet," Bill replies, "but I'll start checking them out tomorrow." Bill began checking them all—even schools on the other side of the continent. When he could, he went to the campuses to talk with the people there. Soon he had mounds of information on each school and their programs. He also started gathering information about corporate needs and industry trends, both in relation to computers and in general. It was a very complex thing to plan. Each school had its advantages and disadvantages, which Bill weighed carefully. It was only with great reluctance that he would drop a possibility. After all, perhaps there was something about that particular choice that he did not yet know. Of course, the differences in the schools had to be correlated with the demands and trends of the industry, economy and society. Bill examined these thoroughly, devoting many hours to trying to evaluate just what those needs and trends were. Then, of course, there was the not inconsiderable matter of how to support his family and maintain contact with them while going through school. With every new piece of information or consideration, Bill would go back through his possible plans of action, adjusting and evaluating them for the weeks, months, and years that they would require and lead to. Bill was going to find the best way to get to be a computer programmer, and he spent all of 1979 figuring that out. And all of 1980, 1981, 1982. . .

Once you have a notion of what it is that you want for yourself, you must then formulate some plan of action that you think will get you where you want to go. For example, if you decided to go to Seattle, you must decide how to get there. Should you go by car, bus, airplane, boat, train, or combinations of them? Which routes should you take? When should you start and end your trip? And so on. In other words, having created an outcome for yourself, it is now necessary to break that outcome into the steps that must be taken in order to make that future possible. A plan is the recipe that delineates just how to make that mouthwatering concoction pictured on the cover of *Cuisine* magazine. That recipe will tell you just what ingredients you need, when you need each one and what to do with them. The recipe does not make the dish for you, it just tells you *how* to do it.

Bill certainly recognizes that achieving his goal of becoming a computer programmer requires that he organize that outcome into the steps he must take. After all, he can't simply walk into Honeywell, sit down at a console and declare himself a programmer. What paralyzes Bill, however, is that he breaks the activities into units that are *too* small. Driven by a criterion about selecting the *best* plan, Bill occupies himself with accumulating and sifting through mountains of information and possibilities. It may very well be that the plan that Bill ultimately formulates will be utterly comprehensive, explicit and all but foolproof, but it might also be that by the time he has made that selection, computers will be obsolete. Bill gets lost in the details.

In addition to the tremendous delays between wanting and getting that can be caused by such finely detailed planning, there is also the danger that such narrowly defined plans can later become the source of inflexibility and disappointment. The purpose of a plan is to guide your behavior toward some specific outcome. But since none of us knows the future precisely, the very best laid plans can easily go astray. The uncertainties of the world assure that there will be surprises: the school Bill chooses changes its entrance requirements; the teacher he was planning to work with retires; his wife becomes pregnant (and it's twins); he is offered a promotion in his present job, or he discovers that he hates computers. What then? The endless refinement of future possibilities that he pursues in the service of his outcome could very well keep him proceeding down a path which was no longer congruous with nor respectful of his present situation. Thus, as with Bill, if your plans become too detailed and require you to live them out exactly, your life becomes much like a paint-by-number picture. As you doggedly fill in the designated color in each numbered spot it is easy to lose sight of what the picture represents. You lose the opportunity to change the picture as you go on, and you may be halted completely if the makers of the kit neglected to provide you with enough paint of a particular color.

Marsha had been taken advantage of her whole life. In school she was the butt of an unending parade of pranks and belittling. Things have not been much different since she graduated from college and went to work as a secretary in a stock brokerage. She is thirty years old, has worked at the firm for five years, and has done a good job. Even so, either no one takes notice of her or (if they do) they take advantage of her. One day one of the junior brokers handed her a grocery shopping list and asked her to take care of it. He was sure that she wouldn't mind. But Marsha did mind, and anger welled up in her as she looked at the list. Marsha decided that she had had enough. She knew that she was at least as worthwhile and smart as anyone working there and, accordingly, she decided she wanted both their respect and to become a broker as well. Marsha relaxed once she knew what she wanted for herself. Already she could see how it would all happen: the people she worked with would suddenly realize that they had been taking her for granted. Some would apologize and want to make it up to her. "That's when I'll tell them to teach me to be a broker!" she planned. Others would simply be too embarrassed and quietly start treating her better. "And then they will start talking me up to the boss, he'll take notice . . . a promotion. . ." Marsha thought as she sat at her desk and grinned. Walking by, the junior broker quipped, "Well, if I'd known that shopping lists made you so happy I would have started giving them to you long ago." "That's OK," Marsha told herself as she turned back to her typing, "Soon you'll realize how valuable I am."

Marsha has organized her plan to become respected and advanced to the position of broker in a useful way, that is, according to the behavioral steps required. The problem is, however, that the plan is dependent upon *other* people's behaviors, rather than her own. That is, whether or not she attains her desired outcome is dependent upon, and determined by, what other people do. Of course you must take worldly possibilities, constraints and resources into account in your planning, but making your outcome solely or largely dependent upon the response of others (for Marsha, her co-workers and superiors) is risky at best. In Marsha's case, for instance, it is probably unrealistic to assume that her co-workers will spontaneously realize their crassness and make the particular amends she wants them to make. It may be that they are otherwise very good people who, if made aware of their mistreatment of Marsha, would try to change, but her plan does not even include some means of *her* making them aware.

The most conspicuous features of Marsha's thinking, then, is that for her the locus of control resides with the outside world rather than with her, and that she has little or no conception of the cause-effect relationship between her present actions and the attainment of her desire to be respected and advanced in her job.

James did not, of course, simply decide to go into computer programming and then, wham, he was a programmer. There were a number of steps that he had to take in order to make being a programmer possible. In general, he needed to get his degree and get a job in the field, but each of those larger outcomes was made up of smaller outcomes. In order to get his degree he had to get into a school, then get through that program. Getting through the four year program and then finding a satisfying position afterwards were certainly bridges that would eventually have to be crossed. But they did not have to be crossed now. James knew that he had worked out and overcome many obstacles in his life, so he felt confident that he would indeed be able—somehow—to cross those bridges when the time came. He kept them in mind, but instead of worrying about what classes to take, arranging his study space at home, and deciding how to organize his resume, James concentrated on the task of getting into school. He determined that what he needed to do was to gather information about various schools ("I'll go to the library, and call several corporations for their recommendations"), and from that information select those which offered the kind of program he was interested in, were within a commute, and that he could conceivably afford. He would then have to apply to those he was interested in ("I can phone in the request for the applications, and I'll have to borrow Bill's typewriter to fill them out"), as well as apply for financial aid ("I should ask each school about what's available, then I'll need that typewriter again"), and all of this would have to happen within the next four weeks if he wanted to start in the fall. Well, James picked a couple of schools and decided on the financial aid he would seek, but he had never gone to college before, so he sought out a couple of friends who had gone all the way through graduate school and asked their opinion of his choices and plans. The plans seemed fine to them. Relieved, James applied. Once he was accepted, James shifted to the next phase of his plan, that of getting through school. Now he figured out what courses to take, when to take them, how to shift his music gigs around to accommodate his school schedule; he began setting up a study space at home, and so on.

The journey from wanting to be a computer programmer to *being* a computer programmer is a very long one, requiring many small steps in between. James is going to have to take each of those steps eventually, but instead of paralyzing himself by having to define all of those little steps before he can act, he specifies only the first few in the sequence, leaving the subsequent ones relatively unspecified. He makes two kinds of evaluations, or tests: detailed future evaluations that range only into the near future, and less specified evaluations for everything beyond that relatively near future.

That he feels free to nail down only the first few steps in his plan is the result of the interaction of having personal experiences in his past of having met challenges, of operating out of a *choice response* (so his destiny is within his power to influence), and of a presupposition of present-to-future cause-effect (that is, that what he does now determines the course of the future). Additional reflections of the choice response include the fact that James's plans rely on himself, rather than others. For instance, he does not hope that someone will offer him a typewriter so he can complete the forms. Also, he generates more than one way of taking the steps that he needs or wants to take (for instance, finding schools by library search and contacting corporations), thus providing him with flexibility in attaining his outcomes.

In making his evaluations regarding how to proceed with the plan, James is trying to determine (from both general and detailed perspectives) which steps will be effective (get him where he wants to go) and whether or not those steps are worth doing. "Effective" and "worth doing" are the criteria. The first (effective) directs him toward those steps/behaviors which are likely to take him in the direction he wants to go. The second (worth doing) causes him to examine (using his entire personal data base) each step as to its effects on his personal well-being in all areas of his life. For instance, one way of financing his education would be to rob a bank, but to

James such an option would not be *worth* the risks involved and the assault on his self-concept that would necessarily follow.

And finally, James tests his plans by comparing them with any past personal experiences he has for that particular step or general plan. If he does not have an example in his personal history, he takes his plans to some expert external resource, such as a book or a person. If he uses a book, he can check the plan himself. If he takes his plans to a person, they can check over the plan and suggest revisions if necessary. (James had seasoned students review his plans.)

Now that plans have been formulated, it is time for:

Doing

The client that had just left Barb's office had given her a lot to think about. He was a giant of a man (he had once crushed another man's face with one punch), of low intelligence, hard-working, *very* serious and in need of help with his failing marriage. Barb decided that one thing the man needed was to lighten the unrelentingly grave seriousness with which he viewed his situation. Barb formulated a plan in which she would give him a new and lighter perspective on his situation by joking about it with him. She imagined herself joking and laughing at each and every one of his somber pronouncements until finally a smile cracks his hard veneer and he joins her in a more lighthearted appraisal of the situation. Satisfied with the plan, Barb called him in for another appointment. At their next meeting, Barb put her plan into action. With every serious nod, every grave statement that he would make, Barb would come back with a joke or parody of some kind. She was immensely pleased with her performance. What she did not notice, however, was that her client was becoming increasingly red in the face, his hands clenching and unclenching, and his breathing rapid. Before she knew what had happened, Barb suddenly found herself dangling a foot off the floor, her blouse clenched tightly in one of her client's big paws, while the other paw was doubled-up in a fist cocked to strike her.

We do not know whether or not Barb's *intended* outcome for her client would have been appropriate, but we can certainly say that her plan for achieving that outcome was *not* appropriate. Having established what she wanted in relation to her client, Barb developed a plan which she imagined would be effective in getting the man to take a lighter perspective on his situation. Barb's mistake was that when she acted on her plan she neglected to take into account the ongoing, present responses of her client. Instead, she continued to execute her plan as she had originally conceived it. That she responded only according to the plan she had already formulated makes her behavior a default response in this situation (since the *only* choice she had was to respond to the plan as it was). As it turned out, Barb's plan was not appropriate given the circumstances, and had she not been locked into rigidly playing out the steps of that plan, she might have had the opportunity to use her client's responses as indications that she needed to adjust her behavior, and her plan, accordingly.

Barb's mistake was to follow her plan without adjusting it according to *feedback*. By feedback we mean all of the responses that occur in a situation that could be used to inform and guide a person's thinking and actions. Another mistake that people sometimes make in acting on their plans is to neglect to follow the plan at all. If you've made a plan that seems probable to you (and perhaps to the expert sources we mentioned in the "planning" section) to be effective in making it possible for you to have what you want, then you should follow that plan. It is only in following your plan that you provide yourself the opportunity to get the ongoing feedback which lets you know whether or not the step you are taking is useful in moving you toward your outcome.[1]

James's original plan had been to go to school during the day and play gigs at night. He realized that it would be a hard grind, but he thought he could do it and, in any event, he needed the money to help support his family. By the end of the first semester, James was a zombie. Between pulling *A*'s in school, studying, working nights and trying to spend time with his family, he was getting little sleep—and less rest. James realized that he would have to change his work situation. He still needed to bring in money; but how? He realized that after his first semester he already had certain rudimentary computer skills. He went peddling those skills and eventually landed two part-time jobs doing data entry for a professor at the school and for a private accountant. He bowed out of the band. The money from the two jobs wasn't much, but it helped out, and they were somewhat flexible as to hours so that he could fit them around his school schedule. In addition, and perhaps most important, James now got to bed before two in the morning, which had not been the case when he gigged. His wife was concerned about him giving up something that had been close to his heart for so long, but James explained, "Listen, I do love the music, but my family and where I'm headed now are a whole lot more important to me. It's time to let that one go."

The usefulness of a plan is that it is a guide to behavior that will ultimately make it possible for you to achieve a particular goal. The plan that appears to be the best plan in the world, however, can be either inherently faulty or become inappropriate given changes in that world. Continuing to follow such an obsolete plan is folly. James would have liked to have continued with his gigs, assumed he could and planned on it. The ongoing reality, however, was that going to school all day, wolfing down dinner with the family, then darting off to play in clubs until two in the morning was more than he could do without jeopardizing his health, relationships, future, and so on. The single most important feature to note about James's ongoing pursuit (the doing) of his future as a computer programmer is that he is evaluating on an ongoing basis his behavior and experience with respect to their effectiveness in leading him to his outcome. This information, then, becomes *feedback that he uses to determine whether to continue what he is doing or to make changes in his behavior/plan.* Faced with the exhausting reality of early classes and late-night gigs, James realized that he would have to amend his original plan (taking him back into the planning computation described in the previous section).

The other ongoing evaluation James is making is whether or not his plan is worthwhile. It may be that an aspect of your plan is effective in taking you toward your goal, but you discover in the doing of it that it is not (to you) *worth* the doing of it. In James's case, the gigging was certainly not effective as a step in attaining his goal. James went beyond that, however. He decided that given everything else going on in his life the music business itself was no longer an inherently worthwhile pursuit.

Appropriate doing (that is, the playing out of a plan), therefore, involves making *ongoing* present evaluations of the effectiveness and worthiness of the steps/behaviors you are taking. This ongoing evaluation is made with reference to the past plan(s) you have made, and also with respect to your present experience and needs. Operating out of the presupposition that what you actually do in the present greatly influences what will be occurring in your future, and having specified the appropriate (and appropriately detailed) behaviors, you can then create the flexibility you need should you want to or have to vary your plan. Of course, the outcome of wishing, wanting, planning and then doing is:

Having

Dobie could see it all now: a garden—his garden—all green and burgeoning, rows of corn rustling in the breeze, juicy red tomatoes hanging like Christmas ornaments on a tree, glossy carrots, mammoth cucumbers. . . . Never having gardened before, Dobie had no idea whether or not his thumb was green, but he was determined to have the garden he had envisioned. He bought tools and seed, and discovered that he liked wandering around the nursery. Dobie worked hard at preparing the ground and sowing. It felt good to be out working, rather than inside living other people's lives through the magic of television. The sun burnished Dobie's skin to a nut-brown as he busied himself in the garden, watering, weeding and waiting—waiting for the faint popping he imagined he would hear as his rows of little charges burst forth from their confining hulls. One morning he was rewarded with the glorious sight of tiny green leaves breaking through into the sunlight. Neighbors stopped to ask after his plants and comment on the weather. In his head, Dobie was already calling on these same neighbors with baskets of surplus vegetables, proudly complaining, "I know I was here with a basket just yesterday, but (shrug) the stuff just keeps coming." A week later Dobie watched helplessly as his seedlings drooped and expired. Too late to save the garden, he brought over a green-thumbed friend for the postmortem. Dobie was agape at the depth of his own lack of knowledge concerning plants. Some he had planted too deep, others too shallow. Some he had overwatered, others he had not watered enough. The shade of an overhanging tree had killed some, while the unrestrained sun itself had killed others. The soil was anemic, the snails healthy. His plans dashed, Dobie turned his back on the garden, saying, "Well, *that* was one rotten idea. I wonder what's on TV?"

The garden that Dobie had wished for seemed worth having, and certainly his sincerity and devotion in his pursuit of that wish could not be faulted. As it turned out, however, he simply did not have the knowledge and experience he needed to make the garden successful, *this* time.

As with Dobie, after all your wishing, wanting, planning and doing, there will be *some* outcome. What you will have may be what you had originally wanted, in which case you can rejoice over the effectiveness of your plan, and enjoy the having of whatever it was that you wanted. As in Dobie's case, however, it may also be that you end up having something other than what you wanted. What then?

Dobie's response to not having his expectations met was to decide that a garden was not worth having in the first place, and so he gave it up as an aspiration. The ongoing evaluation of "Are my expectations being met or not?" oftentimes leads to dissatisfaction; anytime there is a difference between what is occurring and what was expected, disappointment is the natural by-product.

In addition to his present evaluation for satisfaction of expectations, Dobie operates under the presuppositions that his experience happens to him, and that the past determines the present. In this way Dobie leaves himself and his own actions out of what produces his ongoing experience. Looking back now with more information, he could see how it happened that his garden failed. But left as something that happened to him, it does not occur to him that that failure was simply a function of information and experience, both of which could be acquired so that he could indeed someday be reaping his own vegetables. Left as something that circumstances determined rather than something that was personally determined, gardening becomes just another one of those pursuits at which he was not meant to succeed. And, so, it's back to the TV.

James had had his diploma in hand for a couple of weeks. For some reason that had eluded him, he had been postponing daily his planned search for a position as a computer programmer. He assumed that his hesitation was based on fear of failure. One morning as he was trying to convince himself to start setting up interviews, he suddenly realized that he was not afraid of failing so much as he was of succeeding—he no longer wanted to be a computer programmer. Though he did very well in his classes, two years in front of a video monitor had not been the experience he had originally hoped for. He liked interacting with *people*, he realized, not random access memories. For a few moments this realization was a very bitter pill, given the past four years he had spent learning and earning the right to program. That diploma on his desk started to seem more like just a piece of paper than the symbol and passport that it was. But as James thought about it, he realized that a B.A. is a college degree, and he had always wanted a college degree. It was in itself something to be proud of. Also, nearly every professional position these days required a college degree anyway. With that degree and with the proliferation of computers, he would be very well-equipped to approach those same companies that he had originally planned to apply to, only now he would be interviewing for the people oriented positions, rather than the technological positions. James relaxed for the first time in weeks as the future once again held possibilities that he found compelling. He had made a lot of friends while in college, he had learned a lot, and now it was time to start yet another phase of his life. James looked up at the clock—it was ten in the morning. He sighed with relief and thought to himself, "Thank goodness I went to college; otherwise I'd probably be waking up right now from yet another twenty-five dollar gig."

Since we can not always end up with just what we want to have, what should we then do with unwanted outcomes? James hoped and expected to be—and to enjoy being—a computer programmer. Things did not work out that way. Instead of deciding that his original decision was wrong or that the four years in school were wasted, James starts generating ways in which what he has (that is, a B.A. in a field in which he is no longer interested) *was, is,* and *could be* useful, an opportunity, a blessing, and so on. Accordingly, he finds that having earned a diploma is in and of itself gratifying, that a diploma will in any case be a plus in starting a new career, that his computer training will also be a plus in almost any career pursuit, that he learned a great deal that he would not otherwise have learned, that he enlarged his circle of friends, and that going after becoming a computer programmer allowed him to step out of a career rut as a one-night-stand musician. In fact, James is able to combine the knowledge, experience and credentials he has earned in computer programming with his interest in people to create new career possibilities, such as working in sales, customer relations, employee relations, and so on.

The art in having, then, is in wanting what you get. *This does* not *mean giving up what you* originally *wanted.* The having that we are talking about here could be achieving one of the detailed steps along the way to accomplishing your overall outcome, or it could be achieving the overall outcome itself. The difference between James's and Dobie's responses to a mismatch between what they had wanted and what they got is primarily based upon how James is able to range through the past, present and future. By attending to what he learned in a single class or from a single interaction, as well as to what he personally acquired over whole semesters and even over the entire process, James varied the relative scope of what he was paying attention to in his evaluations. By way of contrast, Dobie held the entire desired outcome constant when evaluating his efforts. Flexibility in how his criteria could be fulfilled contributed to James's ability to utilize his experiences for personal satisfaction in the present and for continued personal success into his future. Dobie's inflexibility contributes only to his growing list of inadequacies and inabilities.

Congruent with James's flexibility is his presupposition of past-to-present-to-future cause-effect relationships. This provides him with experiential continuity and the continuing possibility of achieving his preferred outcomes. He also has the presupposition that outcomes are something that are up to him to achieve. This orients him toward determining how to change his behavior in accord with his outcomes.

Had Dobie used the above computations, instead of castigating himself for having been foolish and then turning his back on a dream of his, he might have been glad to have discovered a place that he liked (nurseries), cherished his tan, enjoyed the exercise, wanted more of the neighbor contact, and realized that his failed garden was a reference experience that he could now use to ensure that his next garden would be more successful.

And finally, when you do have what you once wanted, it is important to use it and regard it well. Part of *maintaining* an outcome is appreciating what you have and what it took to get it. The time and effort that you have put into making your body well or strong, advancing your career, getting and keeping up a car that you wanted, or forming and nurturing a relationship, are of great value. And, the fact that you *achieved* your outcome is, itself, something to cherish and be proud of. A taut body can return to flab without exercise; a job title can be lost; a car can be repossessed or decay into a neglected pile of rust, dirt and grease; a relationship can fade when it is taken for granted, its rituals and needs ignored or forgotten. Appreciation, however, helps ensure that you will continue to engage in whatever ongoing behaviors and activities are needed to maintain the having of what it is that you so much wanted.

As we said initially, those individuals who consistently do well at going from wishing to having use the five stages we have just described as an evolving sequence, rather than as discrete steps. As was probably evident from the discussion of those computations, it is not always possible to go in only one direction through the sequence. In fact that would certainly be the exception rather than the rule. The complexities involved in attaining most goals, and the often unpredictable variety of responses from the world, combine to virtually insure that at some point you will have to adjust what you want, your plan and your actions. These stages interrelate in the following way:

Wishing ▶ Wanting ▶ Planning ▶ Doing ▶ Having

In other words, if some aspect of your plan is unsatisfactory for attaining your goal, then you must either change the plan accordingly or go back to the stage/computation of wanting and change in some way just what it is that you want. If in the actual doing of your plan you get feedback that your behavior is either ineffective or not worthwhile, then you may either go back to planning and alter your plan, or it may be that you will have to go back and reassess your goal (want). And if what you get is other than what you wanted, you can make it something that you do want *or* step back and readjust your plan to bring it more into accord with the desired outcome, or perhaps go back even further and change what you want. What we have just described, then, is the way in which those individuals who are successful at going from wishing to having automatically move through and use these internal processes. This talent for converting dreams into realities is productive in any situation. The next section contains the EMPRINT format that will give you this valuable know-how.

Making It Come True for You

Wishing and Wanting

1 The first step in providing yourself with the EMPRINT format for successful wanting-to-having strategies is to separate those things you wish for from those that you want. At the end of this paragraph, take a moment to identify for yourself five things, goals, or changes you *wish* you had, then five you *want*. (Prompting yourself with the statement, "I wish I had . . . ," then "I want . . . ," will help you with this task.) Identify them now and list them here:

Wishes   **Wants**

_____   _____

_____   _____

_____   _____

_____   _____

_____   _____

2 Next, when you come to the end of this paragraph compare the two lists using the following questions: Are there any differences between your wishes and your wants in terms of how you think and feel about them? Do you make images of each of them? Do you describe them to yourself and have feelings that are either what you would feel if you actually had the experience, or feelings about the feasibility of your imaginings? How do you respond to them? Take the time you need to compare how you think about and respond to your wishes and your wants.

It is likely that those things that you wish for are only hazily represented, lacking detail and indistinct, compared to those things which you want, which tend to be represented in more detail and clarity. Perhaps the most significant difference, however, is in terms of response: *Wishing* tends to elicit passivity, while *wanting* is more active and intentional. If you take a moment to wish for one of the items on your list you will probably notice that, though you may really be happy to get whatever that thing is, you do not feel particularly impelled toward any activities involved in attaining it. This is in contrast with those things that you *want*, which, when you step into wanting them, probably engage feelings of motivation, need for action, planning, and other action-oriented responses.

The importance of this distinction lies in the fact that those things which we want tend to engage behavior intended to attain that desired goal, while wishes do not engage such behavior. If you are going to pursue a goal, you certainly want to be sure that it meets your criteria for what is important to you, what is worthwhile, who you are as a person, and so on. If you are not pursuing the goal, however, there is no need or reason to constrain your wishing with criteria since it is, essentially, an exercise in fantasy. Wishing is the realm of unconstrained fantasizing about what could be, and as such is a good way of generating new and creative possibilities. If you applied your criteria as a filter to the world of possibilities you would undoubtedly fail to recognize or consider whole continents of desirable goals because you would be blind to them. You can test the screening effect of criteria very simply by taking a moment to consider what you would do with the rest of your life if you had all the time, money and freedom to be able to do *anything* you wanted; and then compare those speculations with what you have already planned for your life.

In order to avoid excluding your wishes from the possibility of being pursued to fulfillment, we offer you the following steps for transforming a wish into a full-fledged and worthwhile want. The first step is to engage your behavior. This is typically achieved when you have a specific, detailed and vivid representation of a goal that you are wishing for.

3 At the end of this paragraph, select one of the wishes you listed previously, and make a specific, detailed and vivid mental picture of actually having what you wished for. Be sure to make your representation as real as possible. You can enrich it by adding color, movement, and sound, being sure to see, hear and feel what would be actually occurring if you were in this wished-for reality. Perhaps you wish for true love, fame, or a specific career. Whatever your wish may be, generate for yourself a richly detailed scenario in which you are directly experiencing having your wish. As you increase the reality of *having* your wish be true, notice what changes in your internal responses regarding that wish. Take a few moments now to create that scenario and fully imagine having your wish.

Are you strongly attracted to this imagined experience? If you are not, it is not appropriate to continue pursuing this particular wish. When you do become strongly attracted to one of your wishes after creating such an imagined experience, continue on to the next step.

4 The second thing that needs to happen in turning a wish into a want that is worth pursuing is for you to ask and answer the well-formedness questions. These questions should also be answered for each of your wants to make sure they are worth pursuing to fulfillment. Before you do this for each of your wants, however, take one of your wishes to which you are strongly attracted (after having completed the previous step), and evaluate it with respect to each of the following questions:

Is it within the realm of what is possible? That is, is there at least one other person who has achieved a similar goal, or are the necessary basic resources, body of knowledge, etc., available to utilize? In terms of possibility, there is a big difference between wanting to live on Mars this year and wanting to be an astronaut, or wishing your feet were two sizes smaller and wanting to be financially independent. While a goal may be possible in the world, existing factors may make it not possible for you. For instance, the possibility of your becoming an astronaut is greatly reduced if you are a paraplegic or seventy years old. Evaluate your wish using this question before you proceed.

Is it worth having? That is, is this goal that you want in harmony with those attributes, ideals, and predilections which are important to you and by which you define your self? For example, our would-be astronaut might conclude that participating in the space program is tantamount to giving approval to increasing militarization of space, something which he is very much against. Or perhaps the goal of being an astronaut is not worth having when the long hours away from home and family are taken into consideration. Now use the question, "Is it worth having?" to evaluate your wish.

Will it get me what I really want?   You have probably had the experience of really wanting something that looked, sounded and seemed worth wanting, only to discover once you finally did get it that it was not at all worth having (and perhaps even worth avoiding). For example, you might have wanted, worked for and acquired a large, lovely, prestigious home, only to discover that maintaining it and the grounds around it is a consuming and undesirable burden. Similarly, owning and running a business (long hours, unpredictable pay), or owning an expensive but delicate car (lots of shop time, expensive repairs), or having your own horse (daily care, vet bills), may seem like things worth wanting until you are actually faced with the perhaps unpleasant reality of having them. To determine if your wish will get you what you really want, you need to step into the vivid representation you previously generated of having your wish—step in so that it is as if you are there, seeing what you would see, hearing what you would hear and, most especially, feeling what you would feel. Is your experience what you would want it to be? If not, can your wish be adjusted or amended in order to make it satisfying? Step into that representation and make the evaluation now.

Is it worth doing what it would take to attain the outcome? Before devoting yourself to a goal it is important to evaluate whether or not it is worth the effort you will probably have to invest in pursuing it. For this evaluation, first imagine some of what is involved in making that which you are wishing for a reality (in our astronaut example, giving up a present job, moving to NASA in Houston, low pay, stretches of time away from home, etc.), then step into the undertaking itself and assess your feelings about it. Do you feel that it is worth doing what it will require? Make this assessment for your wish before you go on.

5   Having done that, you can now compare how you feel about the undertaking with how you feel about the goal itself, and then use that comparison to decide whether the goal is worth what it will take to attain it. Take the time now to make this comparison and decision for your wish.

To recap, the conclusions that you need to come to in order to usefully and appropriately want something are:

■ That you have a specific, detailed, vivid representation of the goal (what it is you want),

■ That the goal is something that can be achieved, even if you do not, at present, know how, and

■ That the goal satisfies your personal criteria (it is what you really want, and it is worth doing what is required to accomplish it), as opposed to externally imposed criteria (such as from advertising: "This is the car for the man of the 80's!")

6 When you finish reading this paragraph, take a few moments to run each of the several wishes and wants you previously listed through the above tests. You might also like to take one or two things that you *want* to want—that is, goals that you don't now want but think you *should* want (like quitting smoking, or obtaining a retirement plan)—and run those goals through this same sequence. You may find after taking those goals through this sequence of tests that they have qualitatively changed and it is now much more your experience that you *want* them, that your behavior is more engaged. Run the tests now and discover the changes that occur.

It is often counterproductive to your personal well-being to pursue goals that have not been subjected to the kinds of evaluations you have just learned to make. A person who pursues goals that have not first been thoroughly evaluated is not necessarily chasing rainbows, but oftentimes they do remind us of the dog that charges blindly into traffic to chase a car. Chasing after goals that stem only from whim and fancy is a generally unproductive and possibly dangerous pursuit. By applying a few moments of thoughtful consideration to your dreams, desires, wishes, and wants *before you act on them* you will be protecting and enhancing your personal well-being.

Planning

In planning you are essentially working out the sequences of actions and their subsequent results which will lead to the outcome you want. If the sequence you have planned is in fact capable of leading to the outcome, then following it will lead to attaining what you want (assuming, for the moment, that the world around you is not whimsical). Of course, there are very few sure things, and rarely does one know exactly what steps will necessarily lead to the desired outcome. So, it should be a feature of any plan that you make that it include *branch points*. Branch points are those steps in the sequence which, depending upon what has so far happened, will lead you toward one of several alternatives. For instance, if your plan is to become an astronaut, it is wise to have built into that plan what you will do if your initial application is rejected. (You could join a NASA affiliated company, apply to the European Space Agency, and so on.)

The purpose of branch points in your plan is to help insure that you can still continue toward your goal if part of your plan goes awry. Obviously, what underlies planning in general is the presupposition of present-to-future cause-effect: what you do now will determine your results in the future. Underlying the creation of branch points in the plan is the recognition of the importance of having a choice response rather than having only one, fixed sequence leading to your goal. Having only one, fixed sequence is a default response, and it makes it possible for just one unsuccessful step to scuttle your plan. Where does the sequence and its branch points come from? As we discussed above, developing a plan involves figuring out a sequence of steps which will lead to the attainment of your goal. This sequence of steps comes from breaking down (detailing) the pursuit of the goal with respect to various considerations. For instance, as an aspiring astronaut making plans, you might detail the process of becoming an astronaut with respect to the *activities* involved. The first relatively general steps that come to mind are that you have to apply and be accepted, and that you have to go through training. These can, in turn, be broken down further. As to the application, there is obtaining it, filling it out, making yourself attractive to NASA, and returning it. Each of these steps can then be further specified: filling out the application requires a type-writer, correction fluid, photocopying, and so on; making yourself attractive to NASA means making the application easy to read, telling them those things that they will respond to favorably, and so on. If you come to a step for which you do not know the details (e.g., what they will favorably respond to) then that is *feedback* that you need to seek some external source of information which is capable of giving you the detailed information you need. In our example, information sources might be books and articles about astronaut re-cruitment, contacting the NASA personnel office, or talking with an astronaut.

When do you stop going for more detail by breaking down the steps? In general, you have broken the pursuit of a goal down into enough steps when you have gotten to a specificity which requires knowledge, abilities and behaviors that you have and are familiar with. In planning to apply to be an astronaut there is no need to detail the step of filling out the application if that is a skill with which you are already famil-iar. Also, in general, it is usually not necessary to specify the entire sequence from where you are now to that time in the future when you have attained your goal. It is usually suffi-cient to specify only those steps which are necessary to start moving toward your goal. The subsequent steps need be spe-cified only far enough such that you are able to fully imagine what it would be like to actually take those steps. Thus you begin by imagining yourself as thoroughly as possible doing the sequenced steps to your outcome, feeling what each in turn is like. By generating an imaginary experience of carry-ing out the necessary behaviors to achieve your outcome you gain the opportunity to check out the feasibility and worth of each step before you commit yourself to it. This is to insure that as you make your plan you do not build it around steps that are not worth doing or are not congruent with your self. (For example, you determine that one step involves living in an urban environment and that this will in some way wreak havoc with your personal values.) You then specify the ac-tions and considerations needed for the first step and begin to carry that step out. Once you are engaged in carrying out the initial step, it is time to fully specify and evaluate the details of the next required step or two in the sequence, and so on until you have made your way to having what it is you want.

The example we have given above is one of breaking down an outcome in terms of the *activities* required to accomplish it (getting and filling out the application, training, finding out what NASA will respond to favorably, and so on). There are other ways of detailing an outcome, including the following ways which we have found are important in generating a plan which is effective:

■ **Activities**   What are the behaviors, tasks, and procedures which must be done?

■ **Information**   What are the things you already know, and what do you still need to learn in relation to attaining the outcome?

■ **People**   Who is, or might be, involved in attaining the outcome, who can you count on to help (or hinder) you, and how might they help (or hinder)?

■ **Resources**   What abilities, skills, and tangible assets do you have that will help (or hinder) you, and what external sources of assistance could or must be utilized?

■ **Time**   How long will various steps take, and when should they be taken?

■ **Stages of progress**   How and when will you know that you are moving toward your outcome?

1   At the end of this paragraph review your list and select one of your wants. Break the pursuit of this goal down to a level of detail appropriate for you in order to generate a plan. To do this, use the planning frames listed above, taking them one at a time and in turn. Once you are familiar with planning with respect to each of these frames, you will find that it is no longer necessary to restrict yourself to them, and you will find that you naturally include information pertinent to each of the frames in your planning. Spend a few minutes now going through this planning process. Doing it now will help insure that you will do it in the future.

A final point needs to be made about exiting from planning. It is possible to continue breaking down possible sequences for achieving a goal *ad infinitum*. We know of individuals who so thoroughly specify the various possibilities and procedures that they often fail to get around to *doing* anything to attain the goal. It is therefore important to arrange for yourself an exit from planning. This is at least partly taken care of by noticing when you have specified thoroughly enough. That is, when you have broken the initial stages of the plan down to behaviors and abilities with which you are familiar, you can then leave off further planning and start taking those steps toward your goal. It is *also* useful to set some kind of external limitation on your planning, such as one hour, one week, one year, until Debbie comes home, until it is time to leave, and so on. If when the time is up you still have not satisfactorily completed your plan, you still have the choice of setting yet another exit time. The usefulness of having the exit time, however, is that it may motivate you to be decisive in your planning and, at the very least, will act as a reminder that some time has past without your having taken action toward your goal.

Planning is a significant step in the overall process of attaining what you want. The elements of planning you have learned here are essential to your future success. Use these strategies and you will enjoy an improvement in your effectiveness. If what you are after is worth wanting, it is worth the planning it takes to determine how best to achieve it.

Doing

There comes a point when you have planned your sequence of steps and it is time to engage in the behaviors that the plan specifies (whatever they may be). Perhaps what is most important about the doing of your plan is to view it as an opportunity for *feedback*, rather than failure. It is often the case that people consider a lack of success at a particular step in their plan as a failure. They become disheartened, feel inadequate, become pessimistic about being able to continue, and give up.

It is, however, much more appropriate and useful to view those failed steps as valuable *feedback*. Specifically, the feedback that you have just received when you fail at a step in your plan is this: *You need to break that step down fur-*

ther, and you probably need more information as to how to do that. Perhaps a skill, behavior or procedure that you thought was familiar to you was, in fact, unfamiliar or rusty. For example, as an aspiring astronaut you may discover upon looking over the application that you had forgotten how to appropriately fill out such forms. Or it might also be that you discover as you proceed through your plan that there are required skills, behaviors and procedures that you had not anticipated and which require additional information and learning. In either case, you need to gather the information to further specify this forgotten or novel step to a level at which you can master it.

Sometimes further specification will not make it possible to continue with the plan the way it is. For example, having your astronaut application rejected is an eventuality that is essentially out of your hands (discounting, of course, bribery or powerful contacts), and any further specification of the steps that will lead to that particular outcome is not going to bear fruit. It is at this point that the previously considered and planned branch points become important, for they will allow you to continue toward your overall goal (albeit by a different path), or perhaps to another, equally attractive, alternative goal.

Whatever happens, be sure to put your plan into action. Act on it. *Do* it. Left as a mental exercise, a plan can never bear fruit. Commit your plan to action and you will get *some-*where. And, if you remain flexible and respond to difficulties and stumblings as opportunities to learn, you will probably get all the way there.

Having

Eventually you attain your goal (or an acceptable alternative). That is, you have what you wanted. *Appropriate* having is not quite the passive experience the word "have" seems to imply, however. It is important to value that which you have attained with the appreciative regard that it deserves. To disregard or dismiss your achievement with, "Oh, it's alright I suppose," or "Naw, anybody could have done it," is not only dis-respectful of your own efforts, but it also jeopardizes both the attainment of the outcome in the first place and the pursuit of future goals. If having results is not valued, then the motivation to do what is necessary to achieve additional results is not likely to be stimulated. This is not only true of the overall goal that you are moving toward, but of the planned steps along the way. Each of those steps are themselves (smaller) goals, and should be cherished as such.

1 Select for yourself several instances in your personal history in which you attained a goal and, as a consequence, experienced some degree of pleasure. The goals you select can be major ones (getting your college degree, raising a child, maintaining loving and caring feelings for someone who hurt you, losing thirty pounds) or minor ones (cleaning your room, buying a present, washing the car). As you compare those examples, identify what was being satisfied in the attainment of those goals that made them pleasing. In this way you will be identifying the criteria by which you either value or devalue attaining goals. Accomplishment, perfection, learning, accolades of others, thoroughness, to the best of my ability, and done quickly are all examples of criteria by which the attainment of an outcome could be evaluated. Once you have identified yours, however, you should take the time to evaluate them with respect to appropriateness. Using the criteria listed above as examples, such evaluative standards as perfection, accolades of others, and done quickly are likely to lead to disappointment, and devalue having that which you have achieved: *perfection* is hard to measure, harder to attain, and easily thwarted; the *accolades of others* depend upon others being there to congratulate you, and upon their agreement with you in the first place that what you have done is praiseworthy; *done quickly* often runs up against a world which is not as responsive as you might want it to be, and is easily hamstrung by the emergence of obstacles that you did not foresee. The other criteria listed, on the other hand, are more appropriate simply because they depend only upon your own efforts and experiences. The experiences of having accomplished, learned, or done to the best of your ability are all criteria which are evaluated and satisfied (or not) by you alone. It will be worth your while to take the time to assess the criteria you presently use to value attaining an outcome, changing any that depend upon external factors that are relatively beyond your influence. By doing so you insure that you will continue to enjoy and appreciate your achievements in the present, as well as value and regard your abilities for what they can be—the basis of confidence in your ability to achieve future success.

You now have the strategic know-how to go from wishing to having. The choice is now yours. This EMPRINT format is a vehicle that will transform your experience from dreams to reality. True, it relies on you to provide the energy. Your efforts fuel its momentum, but its structure insures your efficient and effective progress to chosen destinations.

5 Eating

Everyone knows that personal health should be very high (if not first) on one's list of priorities since ill health can so severely limit the expression and blunt the enjoyment of everything else on one's list. Even so, many of us ignore our personal health until we are faced with an illness or the frailty of old age. It seems remarkable that there are those who, though already overweight, continue to overeat, that there are those who knowingly eat unhealthful foods or smoke cigarettes despite unquestionable proof of their injuriousness, shun exercise even though they are winded after walking up two flights of stairs (their muscles occasionally aching from non-use), and so on. What is remarkable about all of these people is that most of them want to be healthy and most have made many attempts at emulating those that are able to maintain an appropriate weight, exercise, and avoid indulging in injurious substances. But they have also often failed. And having failed enough times, many of them have given up the hope of being the way they want to be.

But there are those who eat appropriately, who shun substances they know to be harmful (or at least use them in moderation), and who get enough exercise. It is doubtful that these people were born with brains already wired for dealing appropriately with the health implications of gooey pies, tobacco, and office jobs. As we are about to discover in this chapter, and in the two chapters which follow it, what makes it possible for one person to overeat, lay about, or smoke while another person eats appropriately, exercises, or shuns cigarettes, can be found in the differences in how these individual's use their internal processes.[1]

> Wilma is out to lunch with some friends and having a wonderful time. One of her friends admires Wilma's new dress. With a grin, Wilma proudly sits up to show her dress off to better advantage, then starts waving her hands in the air as she blushingly confesses that she could ill afford it. "But it was just so right for me," Wilma explains, "that I had to have it. My husband will probably hit the ceiling when he sees the bill!" There is no argument from Wilma's companions regarding her choice of dress style, as the dress does a creditable job of hiding a figure that has been steadily swelling over the past year or so. Wilma has enjoyed her meal and is sated, but the meal, it seems, is not over. The waitress is asking Wilma's party about dessert. As the waitress recites the list of cakes, pies, and custards of the day, Wilma imagines tasting each one. She knows she should forego dessert, but the selections seem so delicious that she decides to make an exception this time, and orders the chocolate fudge cake. Later, at home, she is bustling about the house, taking care of small chores, when she notices a box of See's candy. Lunch is still with her, and dinner is not far off, but those caramels and nut clusters look so good. So, having first set her mind at ease with a promise of eating a light dinner, Wilma opens the box of candy.

Wilma is not ignorant of consequences, but is actually rather well-informed. Based on past experiences, she knows what she can expect the result of her behavior to be. She already knows that her husband will rail at her for the extravagance at the dress shop, that dessert will make her uncomfortably full, that the candy will ruin her appetite for dinner, and that both the dessert and the candy will bloat her body. She knows all this, and yet none of these very probable futures is as compellingly real to her as the sensual presence of dress, cake or candy. For Wilma, it is the satisfaction of the pleasures of the moment that must be responded to, and her experience, rationalizations, and behavior are bent to the service of present satisfaction.

Wilma *subordinates future* health and comfort *for present* sensual pleasure. By subordinates we mean that she finds her evaluations about the present *more subjectively compelling* than her evaluations about the future. We do not need to specify other variables of her experience because the fact that she subordinates the future for present sensual pleasure is sufficient to determine the behavior of overeating. If you take a moment to imagine yourself in an eating situation (or any other situation for that matter) *and* using as the basis of your decisions *only* what will bring you sensual pleasure *now*, you will discover that overeating is easily done, and that any other considerations are easily overwhelmed and set aside.

> Mae is one of the people having lunch with Wilma. As the waitress reels off the menu of sugary charms she wants to sell, Mae finds herself tempted by several of the selections. But she knows that the dessert will just be something she will have to work off later, and so she declines. Her friends all beg her to join them in having dessert, reasoning with her that she is not overweight and (unlike them) can afford to indulge. But Mae is unmoved, saying, "No, I'll regret it if I do. I'd rather save my moments of indulgence for something really special. Besides, how do you think I've kept from being overweight in the first place?" Later, at home, Mae comes across a box of her favorite—English toffee. It looks good, but she doesn't want to spoil her dinner, so she sets aside the box, promising herself one if after dinner she is still hungry.

Like Wilma, Mae is able to consider the immediate gratification of some pleasurable possibility, but whether or not Mae actually indulges depends upon the congruence between the satisfaction of the moment and resulting consequences of the future. For Mae those future consequences are compellingly real and so must be responded to. Accordingly, while Wilma finds it foolish to give up an indulgence now because of some *possible* (i.e., non-compelling) future consequences, Mae finds it foolish to indulge now only to *have to* pay the price later. In this situation, Mae has a compelling future.

Mae, then, subordinates the gratifications of the present for the gratifications of the future. Also of importance is her recognition of how her present actions are connected to and lead to those future gratifications (present-to-future cause-effect relationships), as well as having choices about how to satisfy her criteria of both the present and future.

Sharon closes the door behind her and, leaning up against it, breathes a sigh of relief. It has been a long, hot, frustrating day at work. Gratefully, she turns on the air conditioner, then peels off her sticky pantyhose and damp dress. But her clothes don't come off easily. The dress and pantyhose are tight and binding. "Oh damn, I still haven't lost any weight!" She shakes her head ruefully and promises herself to start dieting again. Cooler and more relaxed now, Sharon begins wondering what she should do, but soon realizes that there really isn't anything at home that she wants to do. This depresses her until she remembers that she has not yet checked her answering machine for messages. She is excited to see that there is a message, but it turns out to be a reminder from the phone company to pay her bill. "Why don't my friends ever call me?" she wonders. Lonely, adrift and a little depressed, Sharon soon finds herself ransacking the refrigerator. She hauls out some cheese, peanut butter and a diet drink, grabs a box of crackers, then aims herself for the sofa. On the way, for company while she eats, Sharon scoops up a back issue of a magazine she has already read, then flops down on the sofa with her plunder. A half an hour later she is full, but not satisfied. Setting aside what is left of her crackers, cheese and peanut butter, she goes back to the kitchen to raid the freezer. The prize this time is a half-gallon of ice cream, which she spoons right from the carton. Halfway through the carton of ice cream, the telephone rings. Sharon sets the carton aside and goes to answer the telephone. It is (Sharon rejoices) a friend! Sharon and her friend trade the day's horror stories and a few inside jokes. By the time Sharon hangs up she is feeling light-hearted, connected with people and cared for. She clucks her tongue reproachfully at herself when she discovers that she has left the ice cream out to melt, then is startled when she realizes that she did not crave it in the slightest while she was on the telephone. This triggers a string of memories, and Sharon recalls that just last weekend she had spent an entire day at a barbecue—a wonderful, friend-filled day— and had hardly eaten (and had hardly wanted to eat) a thing all that day.

Like everyone else, Sharon has good times and bad times, a good time being one that engenders a pleasant emotion (such as loved, hopeful, secure, and important), and a bad time being one that engenders an unpleasant emotion (such as lonely, unattractive, worthless, and useless). The events of the day have made Sharon feel the way she feels now, but the day has not, as yet, provided the stimuli she needs in order to feel better or differently. In an attempt to fill the emptiness that she feels, she eats. And while the emptiness of hunger can be satisfied by a full stomach, the emptiness of her highly valued emotional states of being connected and being cared for are not so easily satisfied. However, since for Sharon fulfilling those highly valued emotional states is not a matter of choice but of worldly happenstance, she does the only thing that she knows to do to change the feelings that are roiling inside her: she eats.

Sharon's ongoing evaluations are primarily about how she is feeling now. They are present evaluations about her emotional states. Preoccupied as she is with her ongoing emotions, Sharon will quickly come to value anything which makes her feel good (such as phone calls, parties, food, etc.), and want to avoid anything that makes her feel bad. Of course, no one wants to or enjoys feeling bad, but many individuals are willing to endure unpleasantness in order to reap some compellingly important future. Such individuals have compelling futures and are able to subordinate their present desires in order to attain future desires. They also manifest a belief in the cause-effect relationship between present actions and future experiences.

What we have just described of Sharon's internal processing is, however, not enough to create her behavior of overeating. Attending to and valuing your emotional states, as

well as valuing those things which give you satisfying emotions, is important and useful. Everyone deserves the opportunity to experience gratification. What makes her internal
processes a problem for Sharon, however, is that she is operating out of default responses, rather than having choices
about her responses. By this we mean her experience is
something that happens to her rather than being under her
control. She has only one way to relieve her unpleasant
emotions—eating—and it does not work well. Having only
one way to respond is not choice. Governed as she is by
default, she automatically turns to that which gives her even
an approximation of the emotional states that she values. In
her case, the internal states that she values (connection,
cared for) are marked by feelings of emptiness when they are
not satisfied, and by feelings of fulfillment when they are
satisfied. That is, the feeling of fulfillment is part of the
criterial equivalence for those internal states. Food is a
readily available way of relieving emptiness, though it does
not really give her the feelings she desires. If, instead, she
sought out and nurtured other choices for herself in this
context, she would be in a position to generate many ways of
having the internal states that she so highly values.

Carol closes the door behind her and, leaning up against it,
breathes a sigh of relief. It has been a long, hot, frustrating
day at work. Gratefully, she turns on the air conditioner,
then peels off her sticky pantyhose and damp dress. After
cooling off in front of the air conditioner for awhile, Carol
starts to plan what she will wear on her date later that
evening. Only two hours into her work day she had realized
that it was going to be a day she would want to forget, so
she had called one of her friends and had made a movie
date with him for that evening. She informed her date that
her only stipulation was that whatever they saw that evening had to be amusing, if not utterly ridiculous. It would
be a warm evening, so Carol got out some loose, light
clothing. That done, she made herself some dinner. Carol
was half way through a chicken salad sandwich when she
discovered that she felt full, so she wrapped the remaining
half in cellophane and stuck it in the refrigerator. She still

had two hours before she would leave for the theater, so she sat down with a magazine, but she soon started to feel lonely. Tossing the magazine aside, Carol snatched the telephone receiver from its cradle and called a friend, who was glad that she called. They traded the day's horror stories and several inside jokes. Before hanging up, Carol made plans with her friend to get together the next evening. Her conversation reminded Carol of another old friend whom she hadn't contacted in a long time, so she spent her last hour before the show writing that person a letter.

Carol may have the same situational problems as Sharon, but her way of responding to them is very different. Although both of them share the same criteria (cared for, connected), they make distinctly different evaluations regarding those criteria. Sharon's evaluations compel her to respond to changes in her emotional states almost from moment to moment. Carol, however, makes rich internal representations of the future and evaluates her present actions in relation to that future (based upon cause-effect), all of which compels her to make plans about how she is *going to feel* at various times in the day. Thus, Carol makes *plans* about how to organize her situation and behavior so that she will be able to have the kinds of experiences she wants to have, when she wants to have them. If and when things do not work out the way that she planned them, she continues to generate choices by breaking down her goals into useful and effective behaviors that provide her with other ways of meeting her needs.

Consequently, while Sharon arrives home with no intentions beyond satisfying the present need to cool off, Carol arrives home having already made plans for the evening, plans which are intended to provide her with the emotional state(s) she thought she would be wanting. And as is demonstrated by Carol's multiplicity of ways of generating her desired emotional states (making a date, calling a friend, writing a letter), Carol's emotional states are to a very great extent a matter of her own choosing, while Sharon remains dependent upon eating and the largess of the world for any satisfaction of her need for connection and caring. Carol is not likely to overeat because (1) she generates many ways to meet her emotional needs and, so, does not come to imbue eating with special properties beyond its connection with satisfying physiological hunger, and (2) as someone who makes evaluations about, and is compelled by, the future, Carol will consider and be guided by her projections about the heavy consequences of inappropriate eating.

> When he was a kid, George weighed forty pounds and he expected a lot of things. He wanted a bicycle, he wanted to be class president, and he wanted Sylvia to like him. When he did not get any of these things, he was mystified and angry at his parents, his classmates, Sylvia, and the world for depriving him. George is now a grown man, weighs 250 pounds, and still *expects* a lot of things. Sitting in front of the television and munching a bowl of popcorn, George watches the svelte leading men dashing across the screen and imagines himself as one of them, with a lovely lady sitting beside him, sharing his popcorn. He wants to be attractive, but when he realizes that he still is not, and that the starlet is not sitting beside him, he feels sad and deprived. "I wish I was thinner," George later tells his friends over some beer and pretzels. When they suggest that he go on a diet, George shakes his head and snorts, "Diet! I don't want to diet. I want to be thin like you lucky bastards!"

George does a curious thing with his futures—he makes them the present. Like anyone else, there are things which George wants that he does not at present have (such as being thin and attractive), which would normally relegate them to either the past or the future. But George represents his desired goals in the present, that is, he imagines already having what he wants. Left as daydreams, this would not be a problem.

But George *really* wishes he had these things. By representing his goals as being the present, George erases the time between not having the goal (which is the reality) and *achieving* that goal (which is the possibility). It is during that interval between wanting and getting that a person takes those steps which make *getting* a reality. By not representing that interval, George robs himself of the opportunity to figure out the sequence of steps he needs to take in order to lose weight, be attractive to another person, and so on. The way he thinks about what he wants makes the attainment of his goals default responses, since whether or not George gets any of those goals will be due to fortuitous circumstances, rather than any efforts on his part to create the necessary circumstances and carry out the required steps.

Organizing his experience in the relatively large units that he does (having the goal), George has no conceptual access to the steps that will lead to his valued outcomes. Being successful for George, then, is having *already* achieved the goal in its entirety. In the case of being svelt and attractive, George does not make those cause-effect relationships which will demonstrate and convince him of the cumulative impact of his eating habits, and so he can continue to eat inappropriately. In this way, his eating habits never become compellingly connected to the experience of being thin.

A day came when Martha tried slipping into an old pair of pants and discovered that she could no longer zip them up. Obviously she had gained weight, and she imagined herself several years down the road, bloated, ungainly, and shunned. As someone who values being trim, healthy and attractive, the prospect of being overweight was unacceptable to her. While wriggling out of the pants, Martha imagined how she did want to look and feel, then sat down on the edge of the bed to figure out what she would need to do in order to look and feel the way she wanted. She realized that she would have to change some of her eating patterns and would have to start exercising, and made the necessary plans to implement those changes. That night she went out to dinner with friends. When it came time to order, Martha selected a fish dish and a salad. Later, when the waiter was flaunting the dessert cart in front of her, Martha ignored the proddings of her friends, passed on dessert, and felt very proud of herself. Each day brought new challenges and opportunities to feel pride in herself as she selected the foods and did the exercising that she knew would make her healthy and attractive. Her own renewed energies and the ardent attentions of others testified to the fact that she was indeed heading toward her goals. When she discovered one day that she could once again zip up that old pair of pants, she was elated and proud. But she knew what would happen if she were to now give up her regimen, so Martha experimented in order to find out just how much exercise and food she needed to maintain her present good health.

Unlike George, Martha evaluates and is compelled by a *remote future*. This makes it possible for her to consider what will be occurring between her present experience and that imagined future. Martha's considerations turn to what she is going to do in order to attain, or avoid, that future. This is due to interaction between her detailed degree of specificity (designating specific behaviors), choice responses (she will *do* the behaviors), and present-to-future cause-effect (she believes her actions will produce results in the future). This is similar to her belief that what she has done in the past produced the existing results. In addition to these computational elements which compel her to make behaviorally oriented plans, Martha also uses pride as a highly valued criterion, and defines success as engaging in purposeful behavior (rather than as having achieved the goal). The effect of the criterion of pride is to give Martha a way of feeling good even when there is deprivation involved; for instance, she can be proud of herself for refusing dessert. Similarly, defining success as doing the steps allows her to feel successful every time she exercises or eats properly.

Martha's ongoing experience, then, is not that she is wading through the swamps of deprivation and effort in order to attain her desired goal, but that she is continuously enjoying successes (even if small) and satisfying internal experiences (pride). In other words, for Martha, *getting there* is a rewarding experience in and of itself.

From Knowledge to Experience

In the previous section we presented the specific ways of thinking (internal processes) which can be significant in transforming inappropriate eating patterns into appropriate ones. Likewise, subsequent chapters on exercise and substance abuse will specify the differences in internal processes which make possible shunning exercise and exercising regularly, smoking and non-smoking, abuse of drugs, and so on. Whether it happens suddenly as the result of one compelling experience, or over time as the result of repetition, if you do become someone who eats appropriately, does not smoke, and so on, it will be because you have changed the perceptual and conceptual filters through which you perceive the world. You now have descriptions of the internal processes that underlie inappropriate and appropriate eating patterns, but not the means for going from one set of processes to the other. In this section we will be guiding you through the EMPRINT format intended to provide you with what you need to make these internal resources available to you and (if they suit you) a part of your *ongoing* processing and experience.

If you look back through the different examples we have presented in this chapter, you will notice that common to all of the examples of appropriate (healthy) eating is a *compelling future*. Without a compelling future the long-term effects of sloth, overeating, drinking, and drug indulgences become mere pieces of unaffecting information, rather than an upcoming reality. So the first question is, do you have a compelling future in relation to your health? And more specifically for this section, do you have a compelling future in relation to your eating habits and weight? If you do not, the first step is to generate for yourself a compelling future with respect to your weight. This compelling future is the foundation upon which all that is to come is built.

1   To begin, identify whether you are presently overweight and, if so, by how much. Take note of the criteria you are using to evaluate this. Is it attractiveness in the visual sense, or the effort it takes to climb stairs, or the counsel of your doctor, or some combination of these? Would you care to be seen in a

bathing suit, or would this be a source of shame? If any of these or similar circumstances are true for you, it is time to realize that unless you act now to change this you will only be older and fatter in the future. This, then, needs to be the harsh reality of the future that you are avoiding. If you are presently at a desirable weight but are concerned with your eating habits and would like to maintain your present weight or eating habits (and, perhaps, even improve your overall appearance, fitness and health by motivating yourself to *improve* your eating habits), then do the following steps also. But first, take the time now to determine if you are overweight, and, if you are, by how much. Remember also to identify the criteria you are using to make this determination.

I am overweight by _____ pounds. I know this because ___

_____.

2 There are several ways to begin building your compelling future for healthy eating habits. After you have read the instructions in this paragraph, imagine yourself six months in the future suffering from the results of overeating, and most especially from overeating fat-producing foods. You can imagine seeing yourself in the mirror, nude, looking at yourself from the front, side, back, seeing the tone of your flesh as well as the overall configuration of your body. Using this future body, imagine touching your toes, doing some sit-ups and leg lifts, feeling the effort and exertion these small tasks require of your abused body. Hear your future self say, "If only I had the body that I *want* now instead of this. Instead, now I am even deeper into the hole of my own indulgence." Do this now.

3 If that is not real enough for you, spend some time doing the following, then repeat the steps above. Look for fat people of your own gender wherever you go. Watch them climb stairs, squeeze into chairs, maneuver down airplane aisles, and struggle in and out of cars. Imagine being them as you watch, feeling the additional flesh straining your heart, draining your vitality and spirit. Watch how others respond, how they look at these people and what they say as that very overweight person walks by. It's a cruel reality, but the unpleasantness serves to make that reality compelling.

4 Enough of that. Now at the end of this paragraph imagine yourself six months into the future after having carried out impeccable eating habits. Look at your future self in the mirror again from the front, back and side. *Be sure to compare this future self with both your previous dire projection and your present appearance,* and *only* with that previous dire projection and your present appearance. In this way you will be comparing the best *you* can be with what is, for you, less than acceptable. Note that your skin and hair has also benefited from your changed ways. Feel the ease and joy of movement this thinner, healthier, cared for body can experience with movements like toe-touching, sit-ups, and walking up stairs. Review these instructions, if necessary, and complete this step before proceeding.

5 If you have trouble making this projection of your future self seem real, then take the time to do the following: Recall a time in your past—even back as far as your teen years—when your body was at a weight and tone you appreciated. Recall how this felt and looked. Step back into some pleasant memories of the ease with which your body moved at that weight, possibly including the freedom from concern about your weight at that time. Having recalled that past self, transfer those weight and vitality characteristics out into your imagined and desired future self. In making this transfer, be sure to keep characteristics of your actual age, but change the weight and vitality you experience having. And especially keep your wisdom, that which you have gained in life experiences and worthwhile criteria since those earlier years.

If you have never been at what you consider a desirable weight and level of vitality it is essential for you to begin by imagining a childhood and adolescence at a more ideal weight and level of vitality, and then carry that imagined history into your future. If this seems difficult, go out into the world to gather your examples. Watch people of all ages who are at an appropriate weight. Identify with them. Imagine moving within and along with your chosen example's body. (Remember: Only learning, behavior and a little time stand between you and what you want.) Translate these examples from others into your own representation of your future self. If this step is appropriate for you, now is the time to engage in this interesting experiment.

6 Regardless of how you went about creating this compelling, desirable future, feel the pleasure of being this future self by first stepping into the picture you have made, seeing everything as you would from your future self's eyes. Then feel yourself move, beginning with how it feels to walk, bend, and dance from within this desirable body. Feel the sensual experiences of vitality and grace this future self offers. Be sure to hear yourself say, "I'm so glad I changed my ways, and I'm so proud." Once you have accomplished this, slowly step back into the present.

7 With your two possible futures clearly before you it is now time to examine your criteria. Upon what basis do you choose *to* eat and upon what basis do you choose *what* to eat? Are your criteria going to support your desired behaviors, or undermine them? Let's contrast two possible sets of criteria, and how these criteria could be fulfilled:

Set A

Nutritious = nutrients, vitamins, protein

Light = not filling, not feeling heavy or full after

Fresh = not frozen, canned or processed; raw fruits, vegetables

Full = no longer hungry

Set B

Pleasure = sweet, rich, creamy

Reward = sweet, rich, creamy

Available = packaged food; no preparation required

Full = can't eat another bite

Obviously one set of criteria will support accomplishing the goal, whereas the other will not (that is, unless the means of fulfilling the criteria are changed). Examine your criteria and the evidence you use to fulfill those criteria. Are your criteria appropriate and supportive of your desired future? Is the evidence you use to determine whether or not your criteria are being fulfilled appropriate and supportive of your desired future? Knowing if your criteria is helping or hindering you is a key to success in this area, so be sure to complete this evaluation before going on.

If your criteria and the evidence for their fulfillment are inappropriate for your goals then adopt others that are appropriate. This will seem artificial only for a short time. Since you will be getting what you want on a larger scale (progress toward your desired future) these new criteria will become integrated with your success. To become familiar with the process, practice choosing meals from menus using your appropriate criteria. For example, using the previously defined criteria of nutritious, lightness, and fresh, choose meals from the menu on pages 104 and 105.

Having created a compelling future for yourself with respect to your weight and examined your criteria (and the evidence you use to know when those criteria are fulfilled) for appropriateness, you now need to specify the steps necessary to attain your desired future. You also need to make sure that the steps you choose are in accord with satisfying your criteria and attaining that future.

8 This next step involves making sure that you have organized your goal into small enough steps to provide adequately rewarding feedback. The details you need to attend to should take three forms: (1) Your size, attending to your clothes going from fitting tightly to fitting looser, then tight again at the next smaller size, and so on; (2) on a daily basis, attend to your ability to carry out your chosen behaviors (for instance, attending to the fact that today you avoided sugar and hydrogenated fats, and ate two kinds of fruit and vegetables); and (3) attend to your health and changes in vitality. Noting changes in vitality is probably best attended to on a weekly basis. Be sure to exclude any week that includes any passing

APPETIZERS

Fresh Oysters on the half shell - ½ dozen
Fettuccini Alfredo
Lamb Turnover with Cumin
French Onion Soup under Puff Pastry
Mixed Green Salad
Vegetable Consommé

LIGHTER FARE

BLUE CHEESE SALAD (Oregon Blue)

SPINACH SALAD
*topped with fresh mushrooms, our own garlic croutons,
hard-cooked egg, bacon bits, other goodies and dressing*

CHICKEN SALAD
(different versions created in our pantry)

GOLDEN OMELETTE
spinach, fresh mushrooms, jack cheese, served with fruit garnish

MONTE CRISTO
*a delicious 3-layer turkey, ham and jack cheese sandwich,
dipped in egg batter, deep-fried to a golden turn,
sprinkled with powdered sugar and served with strawberry
preserves and sour cream*

HERB ROASTED TURKEY BREAST SANDWICH
*turkey breast roasted with herbs, served on local bakery bread,
garnished with lettuce, tomato and cranberry on the side,
served with fruit garnish*

SIRLOIN BURGER
*tender ground sirloin mesquite broiled to order
served with sauteed mushrooms on onion roll
with lots of garnish*

NEW YORK STEAK SANDWICH
*tender cut of steak mesquite broiled to order
with sauteed fresh mushrooms and
served on onion roll from our local bakery*

MESQUITE BROILED HALF CHICKEN

ENTREES

NEW YORK STEAK
mesquite grilled to order with garlic butter,
bearnaise or green peppercorn sauce

SADDLE OF LAMB FLORENTINE
wrapped in puff pastry and served with green peppercorn sauce

RACK OF LAMB
roasted to order and served with rosemary lamb sauce

CHICKEN TROPICA
chicken breasts sauteed and served with
a mango, ginger buerre blanc

ROAST HALF CHICKEN
roasted with garlic and fresh mushrooms, or creamy brandy sauce

MESQUITE GRILLED FILET OF BEEF

GRILLED SALMON
mesquite broiled and served with a dill buerre blanc

MESQUITE BROILED SWORDFISH OR ALBACORE
served with fennel sauce

FRESH TROUT
poached in sonoma valley chardonnay

PRAWN BROCHETTE
served with orange buerre blanc

FETTUCCINI ALFREDO

DESSERTS

Fresh Berries
Pineapple Sorbet
Hazelnut Torte
Chocolate Mousse
Chocolate Decadence Cake

illness since it is unreasonable to expect your new eating habits to protect you from *all* viruses, etc., though it is reasonable to expect an improvement in your vitality over several months time. Thus you might notice *fewer* colds, flus, and so on this winter, as opposed to last. Before moving to the next step, use the following space to list the small, short-term goals you will use as evidence of your continuing success. By writing them down you will be creating a permanent reminder for yourself.

Your Short-Term Goals for Successful Eating

_____

_____

_____

_____

_____

9 With these short-term goals identified (which are evidence that you are approaching your desired future), you can now begin to specify which behaviors will bring them into being. Here you establish the cause-effect relationships between your present actions and future results. By keeping in mind both your next immediate goal and your compelling futures (the one you are avoiding as well as the one you yearn for) you will give a sense of purpose and meaning to your individual actions that will sustain your success over time.

Be specific about *what* you will and will not eat, including *quantities*, and *when* you will and will not eat. Be realistic. If all the pieces we have described are in place you will experience satisfaction, not deprivation. *If deprivation is there it is a signal that an adjustment is needed,* probably with respect to the criteria you are using, but possibly in the range of behaviors you are expecting or demanding of yourself. Take the time now to identify the behaviors that will lead you toward your goals. Write them down in the following space. In this way you will be developing a list of effective means to which you can refer anytime you need to rekindle your commitment.

What I Won't Eat _____

_____

_____

_____

What I Will Eat _____

_____

_____

_____

How Much I Will Eat _____

_____

_____

_____

When I Will Eat _____

_____

_____

_____

When I Won't Eat _____

_____

_____

_____

You now have a compelling representation of your future self having lost weight; you have specified your actions to a level that provides ongoing feedback; your actions are subject to appropriate criteria; and you have identified those behaviors that will either hinder or lead you to your desired future. According to our research, another important aspect of weight/eating control is your belief that your eating patterns and weight are a matter of choice—*your* choice. Until your weight and eating habits become a choice response for you, whether or not you eat appropriately and control your weight will be determined by circumstances, rather than by you.

Refer, for a moment, to the possible future fat/unhealthy you, and to the possible future trim/healthy you. The difference between those two futures is what you *do* (and don't do) now. The difference between choice and default responses is the difference between the activity of choosing and simply responding.

You need, then, to have personal experiences for the following:

■ Weight is a choice response.

■ What you eat is a choice response.

■ How much you eat is a choice response.

10 You can provide yourself with these experiences by deliberately choosing and behaving (for one meal) in accordance with some explicit choice of your own, in the following way: Choose to accompany friends out to eat but choose not to eat anything yourself while still having a good time (if necessary for your comfort, eat before going out with them). Or, choose to eat and enjoy exclusively vegetables for a dinner (if necessary, creating the enjoyment from, perhaps, the surroundings in which they are eaten, an in-depth exploration of their textures and flavors, experimentation with ways of preparation, or any other arrangement that makes it possible for you to have at least one experience of enjoying a chosen meal of vegetables). Each experience of the kind we have just exemplified will provide you with meaningful reference experiences capable of positively influencing you in the future as you progress toward your desired goal.

As we have noted several times (and illustrated with respect to eating) it is often the case that people eat, drink, smoke and take drugs in order to satisfy important criteria, such as pleasure, fulfillment, control, and confidence. But how many ways are there to satisfy any one of these criteria? Pleasure may indeed be the result of chocolate fudge melting in your mouth, but it can also come from:

■ your body gliding through warm, silky waters

■ bounding lithely up the stairs

■ clean, crisp sheets on a muggy evening

■ hot cider on a cool evening

- powerfully racing down a ski slope

- great music on a fine stereo (or in person)

- a good cup of coffee and the Sunday paper in bed

- the multi-hued greens and browns of a forest on a warm afternoon

- listening to your own footfalls as you stroll under the evening stars

11 And, of course, the menu goes on. What could your list of pleasurable experiences include? Taking each of your criteria for losing weight, make up a menu of possible ways of satisfying those criteria, other than eating.

Menu of Satisfying Experiences

_____

_____

_____

_____

_____

_____

12 Because you are acquiring new strategies for yourself, it is necessary to rehearse them internally, practicing by placing them in the situations in which you want those programs to function in the future. For example, when we ask you to, rehearse (internally) arriving at a party and asking for mineral water instead of beer or champagne—hear yourself ask for the mineral water. If, for instance, you overeat when you are tired, rehearse (internally) coming home tired and climbing into a warm bath or a comfy chair with a favorite magazine (or whatever behaviors you have determined will satisfy the need created by being tired), instead of making a snack-laden beeline from the fridge to the TV.

In rehearsal it is important that you represent to yourself only what you _will do_, rather than what you no longer want to do. The reason for this is that we respond to imagined experience, and even negations must still be represented in order to be negated. (It is like European road signs, which picture some possibility, such as walking, passing, or bringing your dog in, then put a big slash mark across the picture to inform you further that it is *not* to be done.) For instance, say to yourself, "I won't eat the piece of chocolate cake." In order to comprehend the meaning of that injunction you probably made a picture of that piece of chocolate cake. Perhaps you imagined the taste, smell and texture of the cake as well. The richer the representation, the more irresistible it becomes. The words—or a slash mark across a picture of the cake— simply can not compete with the responses elicited by that sensory rich representation of the cake. In terms of the goal of losing weight, then, it is more useful to say, "I will eat the fresh, juicy nectarine" than to say, "I won't eat the New York cheesecake."

In short, as vividly and thoroughly as possible, imagine yourself behaving and responding in the ways that you want to in the situations in which you need those behaviors and responses. Try it right now. Spend a few moments rehearsing your new strategies.

Each day, or as the occasion arises, assess which of your behaviors are leading toward your desired future. Any changes that you find you need to make as a result of this evaluation should be checked for appropriateness, then future-paced into your subsequent behavioral repertoire in the way we have just described. By following these pro- cedures, and repeating them on a consistent basis, you can use this EMPRINT format to adopt the strategies of the suc- cessful people you have met in this chapter. Practice them often; they will feel more natural and more your own each time you do.

6 Exercise

> Fran stood there naked, looking at herself in the mirror. "Too flabby," she sighed as she patted the toneless muscles on her arms, abdomen and thighs. "I wish I were in better shape." Fran considered starting some kind of exercise program that very day, but she still had dinner to get on the table. And tomorrow she would be at work, so she would be too tired when she got home. And the day after that they were going on their vacation. "Oh well, I'll just have to wait until things settle down around here."

Two things are striking about Fran's approach to exercise. The first is that she does not approach it, but waits for it to approach her. She is kept from exercising by dinner, work, vacations, and anything else that does not seize her by the hand and say, "Now you will exercise!" Secondly, like George in the section on overeating, Fran represents her desired goal of attractiveness in the present and, so, limits her ability to identify the sequence of steps that she needs to take in order not only to become attractive, but to arrange for exercising-time as well. As a result of these two factors, Fran can neither specify a reasonably sequenced plan for exercising, nor will she make arrangements for those broadly conceived exercise plans that she does make.

For Fran, then, what evaluations she does make about the future are about inconveniences that may arise because of exercising, while her present evaluations are devoted to assessing whether or not and in what ways she is attractive.

What is more, a future of exercising is not compelling to her. Rather, what she does is (in her mind) determined by what the world makes possible for her to have happen. And so she is left thinking of herself as unattractive, and feeling helpless to do anything about it. It is precisely because of these considerations that health and exercise spas are doing so well and proliferating in this country. They provide complete environments in which their clients have little to do but diet and exercise, and are told when to do what and how. The problem with such spas for the person who uses them, however, is that there comes a time when he or she must leave and reenter a world which demands that personal decisions be made and carried out.

> Sally came puffing upstairs carrying a large box of clothes. Once in her bedroom, she let the box fall onto the bed, then sank down beside the box to rest. "Whew!" she panted. "Why am I so winded?" She looked down at her arms and legs. They not only felt weak, but looked weak, and her skin seemed unnecessarily loose in places. Sally stood up and went to stand in front of the mirror. For a moment she was transported to some years before, when playing tennis, riding a bike and doing her own yard work were a part of almost every day; and she remembered what it was like to take stairs two at a time and to move with limbs that were sleek and trim. When she looked back at the mirror, she suddenly saw herself, only a couple of years away, unable to even make it up the stairs without being out of breath, and wearing clothes intended to hide skin that had lost its resilience. "No," she found herself saying aloud, "Not me." Then and there, Sally decided on times, places and means of exercising, and got to work.

When Sally compared her earlier vigorous years to what she was experiencing now, it was obvious to her that the inactivity of the last several years had taken its toll, and that it would continue to sap her of strength and vitality if she did not do something about it. The wan and wrinkled future that she imagined for herself was so compellingly real and so awful that any present inconveniences or impediments to exercising that she might encounter were petty by comparison. And, of course, of great importance is the fact that she believes that whether she shrivels or thrives is up to her.

Sally's past, present and future experiences of herself form the basis of a cause-effect relationship attributing her present poor physical shape and future horrible physical shape to the care she takes of her body. Exercising kept her body toned then, and if she wants to experience that again, she will have to exercise. Coincident with the cause-effect relationship is the fact that the future is compelling for Sally; so that to her both the abhorrent toneless future and the attractive robust future are real, and it is up to her to decide which one she is going to make for herself (choice response). The other important distinction to note about Sally's internal processes is that she organizes her thinking according to *behaviors* — riding a bike, playing tennis, doing her own yardwork. Unlike Fran, whose thinking is organized according to the whole goal, Sally provides herself with representations of the behaviors which will take her from the present into the future that she wants for herself.

What we have just described of Sally's internal processes is enough to get her to exercise, but it will not insure that she exercises *regularly*. Each time she steps into that way of thinking she will be motivated to exercise. However, as it stands now, her motivation is linked to being attractive and strong, and, so, is likely to be elicited only at those times when the situation causes her to take notice of her muscle tone or strength. That is, she will be motivated when she is somewhat out of breath after walking up a flight of stairs, or when she can't keep up with her children while bike riding, or when she puts on her bathing suit and notices that her legs don't look as sleek as they could.

Exercising becomes a part of one's regular routine when the fruits of exercising become the fulfillment of important criteria. For instance, as things stand for Sally, being strong will make it possible for her to do more in situations that require strength, and those situations are the only times strength is relevant. Suppose, however, that Sally also values independence *and* operates out of the criterial equivalence that being independent at least partly involves being physically strong (independent = physically strong). Being independent, unlike physical strength, is a criterion that can overlap almost every situation, making being strong of ongoing importance. Similarly, while muscle tone is a criterion Sally is likely to access only occasionally, attractiveness is a criterion she is likely to be aware of often. By making good muscle tone at least partly satisfy her with regard to attractiveness, Sally connects exercise to a meaningful part of her life. These more generalized ways of fulfilling criteria make exercise more important, more prevalent, and more a part of her ongoing awareness.

Putting Some Muscle Into It

In this section we will guide you through an EMPRINT format that will provide you with the skills, perceptions, and internal processes that lead naturally to making exercise a regular part of your life. You are about to receive the know-how that will allow you to establish appropriate criteria, generate a compelling future, adopt useful present-to-future cause-effect relationships, specify *when* you will exercise (as well as what kind of exercise is appropriate for you), and develop goals that orient your success around useful steps and stages of progress. The following EMPRINT format is designed to organize your internal resources in a way that makes exercise a natural and enjoyable, if not effortless, part of your daily routine.

In order to be motivated to exercise, exercise itself must become the way to satisfy some criteria which are important to you. If you normally operate under such highly valued criteria as wealth, efficiency, ease, and witty, you will probably not find exercise appealing simply because it does not seem to satisfy any of those criteria which you deem important. If this is the case, you need to establish criteria for yourself that will lead you to prefer walking up two flights of stairs rather than taking the elevator; criteria that make seeing others engaged in activities such as swimming, playing tennis and bicycling look fun to you; criteria that make moving and exerting yourself feel good to you. Examples of criteria which lead to valuing exercise include:

health

stamina

physical flexibility

strength

attractiveness

well-being through time

longevity

1 Criteria such as these make exercise valuable, since it is exercise that will (at least in part) make the satisfaction of those criteria possible. When you have finished reading this paragraph, use your imagination and adopt—one at a time— each one of the listed criteria (*and any others you may have come up with*) and take yourself through time into the future using a selected criterion. To do this you will imagine going through time always behaving in ways that fulfill your chosen criterion. For instance, if you are using stamina as the criterion you are consistently fulfilling, your actions will be congruent with getting and maintaining stamina. This would lead to such behaviors as taking the stairs instead of elevators, choosing active vacations over sedentary ones, as well as active leisure activities in general instead of watching TV, etc. It may even extend into career choices (at least to the extent of not participating in a career that would directly diminish your stamina). Notice whether or not going through time with the selected criterion takes you to a possible future that you like. Those criteria which do lead you to the kind of futures that you want for yourself are worthy of being adopted. Enrich your representation of the future that those criteria create until it becomes, for you, a compelling future. If you need assistance, review the procedure for creating compelling futures presented in Chapter 3. Spend several minutes on this exploration. Do it now, before you move to the next step. It will be time well spent.

2 The reality that exercise will lead to the fulfillment of the criteria you have identified for yourself must be based upon personal experiences. This step is intended to give you those kinds of personal experiences. Acquaint yourself with the instructions, then follow the instructions when we ask you to.

Supposing again that one of your criteria is stamina, go back through your personal history until you find an example of your having the kind of stamina you would like to have again (or preserve). From there, work backward through time from that point, farther into the past, noticing how your behavior and activities made that stamina possible. If you do not have such experiences in your personal history, you can get vicarious examples of them from other individuals who do have stamina. Then step into what you believe their ongoing experience is. That is, imagine what it must be like to be them. This gives you the basis of a cause-effect relationship between actions and results regarding stamina. Now carry this into the present and future by creating a you in the future that has your desired level of stamina. (You can choose several ages of self, from the near future on into old age.) Work backward from each future to the present, identifying what you *will have done* to have achieved that desired future. In this way you will build a set of cause-effect relationships between what you do now and the future physical shape you want for yourself. Go ahead and build those cause-effect relationships now.

3 In determining what kind of exercising leads to the kind of shape you want to be in, you should include possible times for exercise, as well as generating specific kinds of exercise and their typical settings. Bike riding and swimming are specific exercise contexts, which means that a time must be set aside for them (a decisive drawback for many people). However, walking to and from work, or taking stairs instead of elevators or escalators, are examples of taking the opportunity to exercise in everyday contexts. Given your criteria and daily wanderings, what are ways in which you could exercise within the various situations in which you normally find yourself?

In addition, you can discover or create exercise contexts that fulfill other, otherwise unrelated criteria such as going to a gym for contact, running for solitude, walking to sightsee, exercising while listening to a radio to keep current on music or events, playing handball for competitiveness, and so on. Use the following space to jot down ways you could exercise within the situations you normally find yourself. Also include ways of exercising that would satisfy other important needs or desires.

Attractive Forms of Exercise

_____

_____

_____

_____

_____

_____

4 Regardless of the ways you discover to exercise, it is important that the process of exercising and/or the learning of the sport which is intended to give you that exercise be broken down into stages and steps. There is no need to start out by trying to meet an ultimate goal of working out for a full hour. You are more apt to succeed over time by starting out with a ten minute segment and adding more time as it becomes familiar and comfortable. Move your body, discovering as you go what movements feel good to you now, and use that feedback to increase your movement repertoire. For example, we know of an avid tennis player who severely injured his knee. He continued to play as much as ever, but he stayed at the baseline when he played, since he could not move very much or very quickly. As he healed, he rated his progress not in terms of his before-injury-prowess, but in terms of his day-to-day improvement; and he always responded to his body's signals for the need to maintain his physical well-being. By organizing your experience into small steps, you ensure that you move toward your desired future only as fast as is appropriate given your present shape and the exercise activity. And you provide yourself with the opportunity of having the satisfaction of attaining many continuous goals along the way toward becoming the future you that you have set as your goal.

With this in mind, consider each of the ways of exercising you listed above, breaking each one down into steps and stages that are easily attainable and sustainable, as well as respectful of your present physical condition and well-being. Be realistic. Let your bias be directed toward brevity and simplicity. Detail those steps and stages now, before reading any further.

5 You are acquiring new strategies for yourself, and further practice is necessary to insure that these new ways of thinking and behaving work effectively in the future. Fortunately, this kind of practice is as easy and enjoyable as it is profitable. When you come to the end of this paragraph, mentally rehearse how you will be exercising during the next two weeks. Imagine the events of each of those upcoming days—where you are, what you are doing, who you are with—from the time you wake up in the morning to the time you retire in the evening. Feel the flow of time and activities, making sure to participate in your chosen exercise program in a way that makes your exercising a natural part of that flow. Be sure to include any necessary preparation or travel time. Feel the movement of your body and the attendant sensations as you carry out the steps or stages of your exercise program. If at any time you imagine yourself thinking or behaving in an undesirable way, back up and adjust your mental rehearsal until it is in keeping with your exercise goals. For instance, if you imagine coming home from a tiring day at work and plopping down in front of the TV and staying there until it is time to get up and go to bed, you might want to start over and imagine how glad you are that you took a brisk and refreshing walk around the block (or to that evening exercise class). Take a minute or two right now to mentally rehearse your new exercise habits.

A common problem with exercising for some people is that they want to *be runners*, rather than *learn to run; be skiers*, rather than *learn to ski; be tennis players*, rather than *learn to play tennis*. While these individuals may acquire very satisfying outfits and equipment, they will probably be disappointed in their desire to become proficient and healthy as a consequence of running, skiing, tennis, or what have you. If you want to achieve goals, the right shoes, poles and racquets will not make you strong or flexible, nor will they increase your stamina or longevity. What *will* make it possible for you to develop strength, flexibility, and stamina is having a strong enough belief in the benefits of exercise (compelling future), a pervasive connection between your self-image and the act and results of exercise (satisfaction of criteria), and a sufficiently incremental approach (specified small steps). All of these combine to make exercising a part of who you are as a person, rather than something to be applied—like a Band-Aid—when you suddenly need to fix your body.

You are now familiar with the know-how for evaluating, planning and carrying out an exercise program. If there is something that currently prevents you from making a commitment to an exercise program, remember to return to these pages whenever you are ready. If now is the time for such a worthwhile commitment, this know-how will carry you from good intentions to beneficial actions.

7 Temperance and Temperaments

Appropriate eating and regular exercise habits are two important aspects involved in reaching and maintaining a state of physical and emotional well-being. But they are not the only aspects involved. The benefits of nourishing food and hearty exercise cannot compete with the damage that can accumulate if you impair your well-being by abusing harmful substances. The substances we are referring to are all of those naturally occurring and manufactured drugs which are known to threaten one's physical or psychological well-being. These substances include such things as cocaine, amphetamines, Valium, depressants, coffee, cigarettes, and alcohol. Because all of these substances *are* drugs, abuse of them occurs when, despite their known cumulative dangerous effects, a person nevertheless habitually uses one or another of these substances. This abuse is marked in almost every case by a degree of acquired psychological and physiological dependency on the substance. The health risks of these substances, as well as the problems associated with dependent use of them, has been documented well in many other places and will not be repeated here. In fact, over the past decade the short and long-term effects of these substances has become a matter of common knowledge for everyone over the age of twenty-one (and often much younger). Even five-year-old children now know that the cigarettes that their parents are smoking are bad for them. These days, few people can shield their various drug habits beneath the armor of ignorance. And yet there continue to be millions of individuals who either drink coffee by the quart, snort cocaine, smoke three packs of cigarettes, or become intoxicated daily. How is this possible?

Drugs

Like many people today, we have witnessed the often tragic consequences of drug dependence and abuse. Drug dependency and abuse is obviously in conflict with the most important intended outcome of the concept we have been presenting, which is to make it possible for individuals to interact with the world on the basis of choice, rather than default responses. Though we do not condone the use of drugs, we also recognize that many people take drugs as a part of being in a certain subculture, partaking in rituals, and so on. We hope that what follows will help provide many people with the ability to keep drug use a choice response, rather than a default response.

Hooper had been very impressed with cocaine by the second or third time he had used it. After a couple of lines he was so full of energy, so sharp in his perceptions, so brilliant in his reasoning that he could scarcely believe it. Hooper *liked* being brilliant and one up on those around him, and here was a white powder that made him that way whenever he wanted it! Things were not so good at work now, however. People that Hooper worked with were complaining about his touchiness and unpredictable moods. "They're just envious," Hooper reassured himself. But then there was his boss who was not happy with Hooper's work on some recent projects. Now, sitting in his office, Hooper gets a call from his boss demanding better performance. This is a bad day for Hooper, since he has had another restless, sleepless night during which he came up with a number of dynamite ideas. Unfortunately, he can't remember any of them now, and here is his boss giving him deadlines. "But," he thinks to himself as he locks his office door, "I know what to do about that." Hooper snorts a couple of lines, but his brain doesn't respond, continuing to limp along at its usual plodding pace. So Hooper does another set of lines. After a while he can begin to feel its effects. He feels more alert now, but where is the brilliance? Where is the rush of ideas? Where is the feeling of control? Hooper does two more lines, and soon is electrified by his own brilliance and feelings of self-assurance. Later that day he hands in his work. A short time later, Hooper's boss calls him in to the office to discuss it. The boss is confused by Hooper's work, and is unable to tell whether or not it is worth anything because it is so jumbled and disjointed. Hooper is ready to meet his boss's onslaught, however. Before meeting with him, Hooper, expecting trouble, had done a couple more lines of cocaine.

Experiences which Hooper highly values are being brilliant and in control, and cocaine gives him the feelings and emotions he associates with those experiences. That is, on cocaine Hooper experiences the perceptual acuity, feelings, kinesthetics, internal imagery, and internal dialogue that he associates with being brilliant and in control. How can a drug that does all that be a bad thing? Having discovered an easy way to generate these highly valued experiences in himself on demand, Hooper starts using cocaine regularly. But with continued use comes a physiological accommodation to the effects of the drug. This acquired tolerance of the drug means that the line that used to get him high a couple of months ago no longer has much of an impact, and forces him to keep doing lines of cocaine until he finally achieves the feelings and emotions he is after. It also means that when he does not use cocaine, he experiences a lack of control and brilliance which is more severe than he knew before the days of cocaine. This experienced lack of control increases the attractiveness of the drug, and so the spiral continues.

Hooper's behavior with regard to cocaine use is shaped by the interaction of three things. The first is that he seeks certain emotional states and abilities (brilliance, control). The second is that he has only one way (cocaine) to get the emotional states and abilities he seeks, which means that the availability of cocaine determines whether or not he gets to have experiences of being in control and brilliance. And the third is that his concern is for the present (measured in hours), rather than for any consequences which may be lurking in the future.

For Hooper, how he meets his criteria of brilliance and control is a default response, since he operates out of the belief that the only way to satisfy those criteria is through cocaine. Even with taking cocaine being a default response, however, if he was compelled by the future rather than the present, then Hooper might refrain from indulging out of fear of future consequences. But compelled as he is by the present, and attending primarily to his emotional states (limiting the duration of time he considers to perhaps a couple of hours), Hooper finds the present need is much more substantial than any future complications. Unfortunately for him, although the cocaine generates the emotional states (that is, the *feelings*) that he wants, it does not necessarily also give him the perceptual distinctions, internal processes, and behaviors which make control and brilliance a behavioral reality.

Chloe had been introduced to cocaine by Hooper, and she had to admit that she enjoyed it. She suddenly discovered that she had a million things to say, most of which impressed her as being very witty and perceptive. Though she enjoyed its immediate effects, she was concerned about the long-term effects as well. Last year she got a call telling her that her friend had been committed to a detox center. His career had been destroyed by that time, and now, a year later, he was still spending half his time in such centers. It was obvious to Chloe that even Hooper had become gaunt and moody during the past year, and she did not want that to happen to her. At work she found herself under the gun. The boss wanted the material she had been working on, but she had not as yet come up with an approach that she would consider worthy. Because she could no longer wait for inspiration, she tried taking a walk to relax her mind, which often helped her to think more lucidly when she returned to her desk. This time it didn't work, however, so she turned to reading articles and thumbing through books on related areas. Still not satisfied with what she was coming up with, Chloe got a couple of her colleagues together and started talking with them about her project. This worked. Soon Chloe was excited about her project, generating new ideas, and with her colleagues' help, refining those ideas.

Like Hooper, Chloe likes being brilliant and in control, but she also highly values her physical and psychological well-being. Based on the past and present experience of others, and the futures she can imagine, she *knows* that if she gets into cocaine she will eventually jeopardize that well-being. It may be that Hooper also values his own well-being, but any cocaine-related futures jeopardizing that well-being that he does imagine are thin and unimpressive and are not real to him. However, Chloe's determination that the immediate effects of cocaine are not worth its future side-effects does not make her desire for control and brilliance go away. Instead of using the drug, she has developed several *other* ways of generating in herself those emotional states and abilities. Walking to clear her mind, relevant reading, and talking with associates are several of the ways she has of stimulating brilliant thinking in herself. Whether she is brilliant or not, then, is not determined by the availability of cocaine, but by her own behavior, which is something about which she has some choice.

What makes it possible for Chloe not to use (or use only on highly circumscribed occasions) cocaine is that her imagined futures are *compelling* with respect to well-being, and she has other ways to generate those emotional states and abilities which cocaine also seems to give her. (It may very well be that Hooper considered the future consequences of using cocaine, but those future consequences were not real to him in the sense of being compelling enough to motivate his behavior.)

Of course, many other drugs besides cocaine are used abusively. There seems to be no shortage of demand for uppers, downers, heroin, marijuana, and so on. The patterns of internal processing that characterize the repeated use of each of these drugs is in most cases the same as that described for cocaine. What makes these drugs initially (psychologically) addictive for a particular individual is that the drug provides that person with some highly valued emotional state; the future is subordinated for present gratification; and there is no perception of choice about alternative ways of generating the highly valued emotional state. What does vary from individual to individual are the criteria which the drug satisfies.

For the Sake of Your Future

The following EMPRINT format is based on the internal processes of those people who have never been susceptible to drug abuse. This format is useful for preventing a problem from developing, for redirecting someone who *is* susceptible to having such a problem, and for correcting a problem in its early stages. Treatment of a long-term addiction is not within the scope of this book, although the following steps do address the elements that are essential for drug independence: compelling futures, present-to-future cause-effect, criteria flexibility so that the taking of drugs becomes a choice response, and a contextualization of behaviors.

Like over-eating, the abusive use of drugs involves taking them to satisfy immediate needs *without compelling regard for their long-term effects*. Therefore, you need to generate both a compelling representation of a future you suffering physical, emotional and social problems as a result of continued drug use, and a compelling representation of the future you enjoying physical, emotional and social well-being as a result of your independence of drugs.

Perhaps you have no substance abuse problems and these patterns seem personally irrelevant to you. Even so, if you take yourself through them you will be inoculated against ever having such a problem. Also, you might choose to assist a friend or youth in altering their drug related behaviors, in which case your familiarity with the following sequence will be helpful.

1   So, even if you are not bothered by substance abuse problems, take the time to call up visions from your past—

memories of yourself or others—and identify people who have drug related problems. Then answer these questions: How do you know that they do have a drug problem? What are the ways in which they act and respond that are indicators of a drug problem? You will use this information in the next step, so explore your memories and find answers to these questions before going on.

2 Once you have identified the manifestations of a drug problem you are ready to take the next step. When you reach the end of this paragraph, imagine actually having that drug problem and its attendant manifestations and symptoms. Make this scenario as real as possible by paying close attention to who you are with and what you are doing, how your vision is affected, how your sense of hearing and taste are altered, and how you feel. Include in this future possibility that other people, people you care for and respect, recognize that you have this out-of-control drug problem. Your evidence that you have done a sufficient job of stepping into this problem is the degree to which you experience this possibility as devastatingly unpleasant. While still within this awful, projected future, picture the drug that is its cause. In this way the unpleasant future is associated with the drug that is its cause. Do this now, and then be sure to free yourself from that terrible future and come back to the present.

3 Now generate a future reality of yourself being in control of your own well-being, confident and secure in your independence. Looking back from this future, find examples of saying no to the opportunities for using the drug, examples which have contributed so greatly to this desirable future. Take all the time you need to fully imagine being in this desirable future. (If you would like more help in generating these compelling futures, review the procedure for creating compelling futures in Chapter 3.)

4 The evaluations of the future which support the attainment of a desired future need to be based upon criteria that focus your attention upon your physical, emotional and social experiences. Criteria that we can suggest include:

Criteria	Criterial Equivalences
Independence from substances	You do not *have* to have a drug in order to satisfy your needs
Well-being	Your body is healthy, your mind is lucid, and your relationships are satisfying *now and into the future*
Regard for self	You would not intentionally do things to hurt yourself
Limits on quantities	If you decide to continue to use the drug *recreationally*, you have established appropriate consumption levels (that is, levels which relate to *independence* from substances, well-being, and regard for self)

We suggest these criteria because we have found them to be almost universal among those individuals who either do not use drugs or who use them only for recreation (and even then in moderation). Regardless of what you select as your criteria, be sure that they will naturally induce you to engage in the kinds of behaviors which will lead you toward your desired future of drug independence. (Remember that the formats in Chapter 3 will help you in accomplishing this.)

5　We want to say a little more about the fourth criterion listed above, limits on quantities, since it involves another means of gaining and maintaining flexibility in avoiding drug dependency. This is done by *contextualizing* the intake of substances that are considered by some to be recreational drugs (such as alcohol and marijuana). By contextualizing we mean the limiting of the use of these drugs to specific situations (as defined by when, where, with whom, and for how long). It is important, however, that this contextualization be done with regard to your desired future and your other well-being criteria in order to insure that what you define as appropriate, recreational situations is still in accord with your desired future. For instance, in deciding that *home from work* constitutes an appropriate recreational situation for taking drugs you may be neglecting to make other evaluations about the future in relationship to that situation. Making those evaluations about the future will take you into the next day *at work*, trying to cope with drug-induced hangovers and fuzziness, thereby jeopardizing your well-being. Again, in making these future tests, you must make the strung out, weary, bleary jitters that follow indulging in for example, alcohol, at least as compelling as the more immediate pleasurable high you are anticipating from indulging in alcohol. In this way you will be able to establish more informed and appropriate (in terms of your desired future) situations for drug indulgence. Examples are "In the evening when I have the next day off," and "Early in the day when I have no further responsibilities." Before proceeding to the next step, identify a few situations that seem appropriate for limited use of recreational drugs like alcohol and marijuana. After writing them down, review each of those situations in light of future consequences, and make any changes required to bring them into alignment with your concern for your future well-being.

Appropriate Situations for Recreational Drug Use

_____

_____

_____

_____

6 Establishing narrow situations for drug use, or eliminating drugs altogether, does not mean that the needs that those drugs fulfilled must now go wanting. As we have noted several times, it is often the case that people drink, smoke and take drugs to satisfy important criteria, such as pleasure, control, and confidence. But there are many ways to satisfy any one of those criteria. As described in the previous section on eating, you need to *create for yourself a menu of behaviors capable of satisfying the need(s) that the drug was intended to meet.* To do this, first identify the needs and desires that you presently satisfy by taking drugs. Then make up a menu of possible ways of satisfying those criteria, other than taking drugs.

Menu of Satisfying Behaviors

_____

_____

_____

_____

_____

_____

It is from such menus of behavior (and the responses those behaviors will generate) that you create for yourself the independence of experiential and behavioral response that comes with being able to choose. This is certainly preferable to the slavish dependence of having your experience and behavior determined by the availability of a drug.

7 To insure that you will select from your new menu and behave differently in the future, you now need to mentally rehearse how you will be satisfying yourself in the future. When you finish reading this paragraph, close your eyes and imagine being in those situations in which drugs are a temptation. Imagine them one at a time, and in each situation experience yourself feeling and behaving in ways (other than using the drugs, of course) that satisfy your needs and desires. As vividly and thoroughly as possible, imagine behaving and responding in ways that are congruent with your desired future. For the sake of your future, take a few moments and do this now.

8 If drug abuse is a personal concern rather than a curiosity, we suggest you support what you have learned and acquired in this section by repeating the exercises and explorations in Chapters 3 through 6. You will also benefit from the EMPRINT formats in the following sections on smoking and alcohol. Substitute your drug concern for the topic of cigarettes or alcohol as you go through the steps in those sections.

Throughout this section you have been creating for yourself a set of valuable resources. Rather than listening to a sermon informing you of the effects of drug abuse, you have organized your perceptions and internal processes in a way that will naturally lead you away from drug use and toward more useful means of personal fulfillment.

Smoking

John is glad to be home, glad to be back with his wife. She tells him about a funny thing the kids did today, and John starts to laugh—he *wants* to laugh—but what starts out as a guffaw rapidly degenerates into a coughing spell. By the time he's done hacking, his children's latest antics are forgotten. "Are you alright?" his wife asks. Wiping his hand across his mouth, John growls, "Ah, it's these damn cigarettes!" John has been through all this before. He knows he shouldn't smoke, and wishes he didn't, but he has never been able to quit. John started smoking when he was a teenager, partly as a rebellious statement of independence, and partly as a way of feeling included among his peers. Of course, that was nearly twenty years ago. Feeling the need to take a break, his wife lights up a cigarette. There she is, smoking, and he isn't. It makes John feel uncomfortable to have his wife smoking while he sits there, doing nothing. He wants to *be* with his wife, so he lights one up too. As he exhales a cloud of smoke, John relaxes, feeling like he and his wife are sharing something. "Maybe you shouldn't just yet, John," cautions his wife solicitously. I'll do what I want to do, was John's first thought to himself, then he replied aloud, casually, "Ahh, another coffin nail or two isn't going to make much difference."

Most people who smoke started smoking when they were young. And none of them started because cigarettes tasted good or made them feel good. Dizziness, nausea, and coughing are the rule rather than the exception for the novice smoker. Once past those hurdles, the young smoker has a raw throat, burning lungs, lack of wind, lousy breath, yellow stains, added expense, and the specter of lung cancer and heart disease to . . . look forward to? At least when people start smoking they do not do it for the pleasure inherent in smoking cigarettes. They smoke because of the associations that go along with smoking. For instance, like most teenagers, John placed great importance upon being accepted by his peers. He wanted to feel a part of the group; he wanted to be liked, respected and wanted by them. Also, like most teenagers, John was intent upon asserting his independence from parental authority; and there were his friends, defying their parents by smoking. John did not start smoking because he liked the taste of cigarettes, but because it made him feel independent of his parents and included with his peers.

It did not take long for John to take the next step. Through association with the criteria of his youth, smoking a cigarette changed how he felt (making him feel independent and included). In addition, John became physiologically dependent upon the nicotine. Consequently, smoking actually generated emotional states of well-being, comfort and calm in him. A certain amount of time after finishing his last cigarette, John would begin to feel irritable, uncomfortable, out of sync with the world and himself; but all he had to do was light up, and within moments those feelings of well-being were his once again. Soon John was associating smoking with being able to *control how he was feeling.*[1] Years later, while sitting at the kitchen table with his wife, John feels separated from her, oppressed by his own body and the surgeon general, uncomfortable and edgy. He then lights up a cigarette, and with that simple behavior evokes those old, familiar feelings of inclusion, independence and well-being.

Most people who smoke started smoking as a way of satisfying certain highly valued criteria. (As we pointed out above, virtually no one starts smoking because cigarettes taste good.) These criteria can include such things as distancing, coolness, suaveness, toughness, relaxation, maturity, potency, and audacity. Three of the most common are inclusion, independence, and sophistication. Even many years after first starting to smoke, the act of lighting up a cigarette accesses those old experiences in which this criteria was seemingly fulfilled. (A client of ours told us, "When I light up a cigarette, I get a flash of myself in high school, leaning up against

my car with my arm around my girl.") The associations between smoking and valued criteria that were formed in adolescence may have been appropriate at the time, but are no
longer appropriate when those people emerge into the adult
world. The inappropriateness of these associations comes
from the fact that they are *from a past time frame that is no
longer relevant to present and future well-being.*

While smoking may have been a way of having the experiences of inclusion and independence when you were sixteen,
it is no longer appropriate at the age of thirty. In the adult
world, lighting up a cigarette is rarely an entree into a group
(except, perhaps, one made up of other smokers), nor is it a
sign of independence. Those are the chronic criteria of adolescence. If they were all that was operating to make smoking
a criteria-satisfying behavior then there would probably be
many fewer adult smokers than there are. Left on their own,
the anachronism and inappropriateness of those early associations would in most cases succumb to the non-supportive
feedback of the adult world and our own bodies. The advertising industry however, has not forgotten our adolescent criteria and our efforts to fulfill that criteria, and continues to
pander to them. Almost every cigarette ad is directed toward
stimulating in you the notion that cigarette smoking will fulfill
criteria either of inclusion, independence or sophistication.
The Lark campaign ("Show us your Lark!") was designed to
tap people's notions of *belonging* to a select group (Lark
smokers). The Marlborough Man is for people who want to
think of themselves as evidencing the *independence* of the
cowboy. And have you "come a long way baby?" That is, have
you turned in your milkmaid naiveness for the business-
woman's *sophistication* that comes with smoking Virginia
Slims? A sample of others: (photo of a happy party of smokers)
"Players go places" (*inclusion*); (man alone in woods)
"Camel—where a man belongs" (*independence*); (two pilots
lighting up) "Winston—join the first team" (*inclusion*); (an
elegantly dressed couple at the theatre) "Benson & Hedges—
The Deluxe 100" (*sophistication*); (solo vibes player) "Kool
Lights—there's only one way to play it" (*independence*); (a
nattily dressed couple strolling) "Pall Mall—a step ahead"
(*sophistication*).

In addition to such constant media reinforcement of those adolescent identifications, smoking is reinforced by associations acquired in adulthood as well. One of these is the important, pervasive criterion of *control*. *Every* smoker we have talked to has told us that smoking gave them the experience of control, by which they meant the ability to influence their own experience. Over time, as a smoker has repeated experiences that smoking changes his or her emotional state (often in satisfaction of the criteria we described above), a new, special association is generated: smoking = experiential control. In addition, smoking is (again) reinforced by advertising that creates those special associations (criterial equivalences) which are evocative of *adult* concerns: smoking Camels = *man;* smoking Winstons = *first, best;* smoking Pall Malls = *stepping up;* smoking Vantage = *success.*

Quitting smoking involves several variables, two of which are absolutely essential to *lasting* success. The first involves generating the motivation to quit, based on present-to-future cause-effect, with evaluations of a compellingly real future. Individuals for whom the future is compellingly real, with regard to health at any rate, will (these days) not start smoking in the first place. For virtually everyone who does smoke, the future is not *compellingly real.* In almost every person we have interviewed who quit smoking, the motivation to actually quit (not *want* to quit, but *quit*) came as a result of some experience which suddenly made some awful future consequence of smoking compellingly real. By awful we mean that the future jeopardized some highly valued criteria. Here are three examples:

> Liz started smoking in her late teens in an era when people were ignorant of the harmful effects of cigarettes. Smoking was the IN thing to do, and Liz wanted to be IN. She had been smoking regularly for nearly fifteen years when the media began publicizing the connection between smoking and cancer. Liz shuddered when she imagined dying so horribly, so she quit smoking.
>
> Jerry took up smoking when he joined the Air Force at the age of sixteen. All the guys smoked—it was part of being a man. When (fifteen years later) Jerry got the news

of the link between smoking and cancer, he believed it, but did not feel compelled to do anything about his own smoking. Several years passed. One day Jerry put down his cigarette to go play with his children. Within a couple of minutes his lungs started burning and he suddenly found himself coughing and wheezing. Jerry realized that the cancer warnings meant *him*, and he quit smoking.

Naomi had smoked for twenty-eight of her forty-five years. Her nearly grown children often urged her to quit, but each time she tried she became panicky and went back to smoking. "Alright, I'm a weak person," she would explain to her family, then shrug. "What can I say?" Eventually her doctor said plenty. After a thorough examination, he told Naomi that if she did not quit smoking she would not live to see her grandchildren. Naomi was shocked. Coughing, aching lungs, and being a smelly pariah in public she could endure. But not seeing her grandchildren? No. Naomi quit smoking.

In all three of these examples, what led to quitting cigarettes was that *the future became compelling*. That, in turn, was a function of imagining the future in a great deal of detail. Invariably, people who smoke will use relatively specific and detailed representations of the experience they desire in the present (some emotional state), and vague, unspecified representations for their future experiences (e.g., being healthy). The lack of detail makes the future seem unreal and non-immediate, or, in other words, unrelatable to yourself in terms of what you will see, hear, smell, taste and feel.

Being healthy goes across so many areas of life that when most people contemplate a healthy future, all they will get are some vague pictures of themselves looking healthy and perhaps a flickering of robust feelings. However, by building a more specified representation you can be more easily drawn inside the experience by virtue of having been provided with not only what will be felt, but what will be seen and heard as well. Naomi *knew* she should quit smoking, that it would lead to health problems. But it was not until the doctor created a future for her which she could readily step into that she was compelled to actually quit. She could see that there were no grandchildren standing around her deathbed; she could hear herself castigating herself for her foolishness; and she could feel the pain and regret. Similarly, Liz was transported to being in a hospital (with all its attendant *sights* and *sounds*) and dying in *pain*. The only difference between the two women's experiences was the highly valued criteria which was being jeopardized by the smoking. (No matter how real the detailed representation makes that future seem, if Naomi places little importance upon seeing her heirs, it will not motivate her to quit smoking.) What brought the specificity of the future down to compellingly real proportions for Jerry was not external information (as in Liz and Naomi's case), but the personal experience of feeling debilitated by smoking. When that happened Jerry suddenly had all of the experiential pieces he needed to fabricate a compelling future.

In summary, then, motivation to quit smoking comes from finding highly valued futures which will be jeopardized by smoking, and then specifying those futures down to the point that the person can step inside them (that is, they become compelling). The effect of this will be to make the future far more compelling than the present and, so, lead to the subordination of such present considerations as discomfort, lack of manliness, lack of sophistication, and so on. These real future representations are connected to smoking by present-to-future cause-effect such that smoking or thinking of smoking reaccesses the real, unpleasant future. The discomforts that come with withdrawing from nicotine are temporary. But what of those considerations of manliness and sophistication?

Dan smoked as a teenager. When his father (who also smoked) found out, he hit the roof. Dan was too young to smoke, his dad decreed, and warned him that he had better not catch him doing it again. Several weeks later, Dan was injured during a ball game. His father rushed him to the hospital emergency room. While waiting for the doctor, his father lit up two cigarettes, and handed one to Dan. Even now, twenty years later, Dan remembers that moment of adulthood that he shared with his father. Of course, now Dan was a smoker. He knew he should quit, but then everyone in his family had been smokers. He was just one of those people who functioned better with a cigarette in his hand. When Dan's father died of emphysema, Dan thought of his own future, but could only sigh, saying, "Well, as a smoker I may not live as long as others, but I can't help that." His despair prompted him to light up another cigarette to calm himself down.

As millions of people know, quitting smoking and becoming a nonsmoker are two different things. Many people who quit and successfully get through the initial period of physical discomfort during which their bodies are readjusting nevertheless find themselves smoking again within a week, a month, or six months. For many of these people, the behavior of smoking fulfills positive, gratifying criterial equivalences. In the example above, for instance, as a teenager Dan had a very positive and gratifying experience with his father that associated smoking with being a man (man = smoking). In time, Dan developed additional criterial equivalences which led him to identify himself as a smoker (smoking is not something he does, but is part of who he is: self = smoker), as well as criterial equivalences which support that identification of self (smoker = comes from a family that smokes, enjoys smoking, functions better with cigarettes).

If it does happen that Dan has some experiences that make the future that he is warned of on every pack of cigarettes suddenly compellingly present (such as being told that he may have lung cancer), he may consequently quit, but that does not necessarily change either his criteria or what he uses as evidence of fulfilling that criteria. A week or month after quitting, he is still identifying smoking with being a man, still thinking of himself as a smoker who is merely trying to fight his natural tendencies. He experiences a discontinuity between the *evidence* he uses as fulfillment of his criteria for being a man and for being himself (namely: man = smokes; self = smoker) and his *behavior* (not smoking). As a result, the discontinuity builds, becomes unbearable, and finally is resolved by going back to smoking.

The second essential step in quitting smoking, then, is to make sure to change the means by which highly valued criteria are fulfilled, so that criteria and concepts of self are in accord with, and supportive of, not smoking. For instance, had Dan changed his criterial equivalence to *being a man = meeting responsibilities to others*, or *not NEEDING anything*, or *willpower*, then all sorts of behaviors other than smoking would suggest themselves as ways of satisfying his criterion of being a man. In addition, it is important to separate smoking from experiences that are used in defining self. It is much more appropriate to perceive those smoking-related associations in terms of cause-effect (family smokes ▶ makes Dan want to take up smoking; nicotine dependence ▶ creates a desire to smoke, and so on), thus making them potentially subject to choice and change. In this way, Dan (or anyone) can go from being a smoker to being a kind, hardworking man who happens to presently smoke. This makes it much easier ultimately to reach the point when definitions of self may include *nonsmoker*, as well.

To a Breath of Fresh Air

The EMPRINT format for becoming a nonsmoker includes the essential components of our successful five week treatment program. The experiences created by the following steps are beneficial for everyone because they deal with aspects of the *whole* person, not just the behavior of smoking. Even if you are a nonsmoker, this section provides much of value that is not repeated elsewhere in this book. Read through each step before following the instructions, and, if you are a non-smoker, substitute other unwanted behaviors in place of smoking cigarettes.

There is a special emphasis in this section on developing a strong and positive self-concept. You will benefit from this portion of the sequence whether or not you smoke. If you do smoke, this self-concept sequence will help insure that after you quit smoking you *remain* a nonsmoker. In addition to connecting useful behaviors to a strong and positive self-concept, you are about to develop a compelling future, adopt beneficial present-to-future cause-effect relationships, identify the needs that smoking presently fulfills, find new ways for satisfying those needs, and learn how to break down success into easily attainable steps.

As you may have already discerned, one of the significant differences between the smoker and the nonsmoker (or ex-smoker) is that for the smoker, the negative consequential effects of smoking remains sterile information, rather than a very real personal possibility. This is demonstrated by the fact that it is often the case that giving up smoking is precipitated by some compelling *personal experience*, such as coughing up blood, being winded after climbing one flight of stairs, being told by the doctor that they have (or are going to have) cancer, or by having one of these kinds of experiences happen to someone close to them. The effect of these experiences is to transform mere information regarding the harmful effects of smoking into personal experience. Everyone knows that smoking is bad for them, but for some people, the possibility of heart disease, high blood pressure, or cancer remains distant and sterile information, unconnected with *their* personal experience. Obviously, then, if you want to quit smoking you need to generate for yourself a compelling future in which you are ill—desperately ill—as a consequence of smoking. This compelling future will definitely serve to motivate you toward giving up smoking.

1 To this end you need to imagine your own experience in the future to be devastatingly bad as a direct result of having smoked cigarettes on a habitual basis. You can start with any memory of having been confined to a hospital (or a bed). If you don't have a memory like this, remember visiting someone confined to a hospital (or a bed) and how good it was when you left. Locate this memory now so you will have it to use in the next step.

2 Now imagine that you are the patient instead of the visitor. You need to include in your projections the desirable experiences that your smoking will have robbed from you, such as not seeing your grandchildren (as with Naomi, above), not making love, not being able to smell a spring morning, not being able to take that special trip, and so on. Get in touch with the feelings of sadness, regret, pain, longing or disappointment that belong in this reality. It will be challenging for you to make this real, because as soon as it is you are going to be very uncomfortable when trying to smoke a cigarette. Thus we suggest you begin to make this compelling future real enough to motivate you now, and return to it again after doing the upcoming steps. (Refer to Chapter 3 if you need more help in creating this compelling future.) In this way you will be fully compelled into action when you have more of the other necessary steps in preparing yourself to comfortably become a nonsmoker. Take the time now to complete this step.

3 In addition to being unconnected to compelling personal experiences of the kind we have discussed, smoking is also (unfortunately) the source of primary pleasure for many people. For them, smoking has become a means of controlling their experience. Smoking makes it possible for them to relax, to think, to pause, to become isolated, to feel contained, to become energized, to reflect, and to know that something has ended (such as a meal). Identify what you get from smoking in terms of controlling your experience. And, having done that, identify the situations in which those experiences are important to you.

What I Get from Smoking   When It is Important

_____   _____

_____   _____

_____   _____

4 In addition to what you have already identified, and to accomplish this more thoroughly, keep a diary for two weeks in which you note when, where, and with whom you smoked each cigarette, and what it was you wanted or hoped to get by smoking that cigarette at that time (such as relaxation, time to yourself, something to do with your hands, making the time pass easier, or perhaps for no reason other than habit and availability).

5 Once you have identified the situations in which you smoke, deny yourself cigarettes in *one* of those situations (at the end of a meal perhaps) for one week, meanwhile continuing to smoke at other times. During that week, experiment with other behaviors until you find *several* that make it possible for you to have the same kind of experience in that situation without smoking. (This will provide you with a personal experience for turning a cigarette-determined default response into a choice response in at least one situation.) You can then start to snowball the process by discovering other ways of satisfying your needs in other situations as well. The question you will need to be asking yourself throughout all of this is, "What can I—*will I*—do *instead* of smoking that will work as well in this situation?" And, consider it for what it really is—a process of discovery rather than denial.

6 The next step is to identify the criteria you have connected to your self-concept. How would you describe your qualities and attributes? What are the traits and characteristics that you would like others to see in you? What kind of person do you want to be? For example, do you consider yourself to be nice, giving, caring, mature, intelligent, curious, vigorous, cool, unflappable, independent, proud, stubborn? Do you want to be more considerate of others, more attractive, self-reliant? Identify at least five of your valued qualities and list them in the space provided below.

My Present and (hopefully) Future Qualities

_____

_____

_____

_____

_____

7 Now that you have identified your self-concept criteria, you need to evaluate them. Do this by answering these three questions: Are they representative of who you are, or are they left over from a previous, now inappropriate time in your life (for example, looking cool, looking mature, and so on)? Are they representative of who you *want* to be (for example, do you want to be considerate of others, independent, vigorous)? What criteria might you add that would be in accord with your desire to quit smoking (for example, independent, healthy, proud)? Take the time now to make these evaluations for each of the qualities you listed.

It is possible that after evaluating your self-concept criteria you found that smoking is in conflict with who you want to be. If so, the following sequence will be especially useful.

8 Recall what you were like five years ago. Fill in as much detail as possible: what you were doing, what was important to you, what dreams and yearnings you had then, and so on.

9 Next, identify two significant changes that you have made since then, and notice exactly *how* you made those two changes. That is, specify for yourself what *you* did that contributed to those two changes and made them possible. (By doing this you will be establishing your own positive past-to-present cause-effect relationships.) Be sure to complete this step before proceeding.

10 Now imagine yourself in the future, five years from now, as a longtime nonsmoker. Enrich your representation of your future non-smoking self as fully as possible; see what you would be seeing then, hear the differences in your voice, and sense how differently you feel as a long-term nonsmoker.

11 In your own mind, ask your future self to act as a resource for the present you by encouraging and supporting your efforts to become a nonsmoker. Because no one will pay more dearly for your smoking than your future self, you have someone important to quit for. Once your future self has agreed to encourage and support your efforts, comfortably return to the present.

12 Orienting yourself all the way back into the present, write down your answers to the following questions. By answering these questions, you are setting behavioral *limits* that are useful in maintaining your well-being. For example, knowing that you would not deliberately eat something that could be poisonous and that you would not willingly allow another person to physically abuse you permits you to know that you are caring for and insuring your well-being.

■ What are examples of behaviors (actions, thoughts, or things that you could say) that you would *not* do?

Things I Would Not Do

_____

_____

_____

■ What are examples of behaviors you would not do to another person?

Things I Would Not Do To Others

_____

_____

_____

■ What are examples of behaviors that you would not let another person do to you?

Things I Would Not Let Others Do To Me

_____

_____

_____

■ What are examples of behaviors that you would not do to yourself?

Things I Would Not Do To Myself

_____

_____

_____

Can you now (without qualifications or hesitation) place smoking into the category of things that you would not do to yourself? If not, then you do not *yet* have a representation of smoking as something damaging that you are doing to yourself, *something destructive for which the future you will have to pay dearly*.

Remember that you can always move toward your goal in stages. If you are now smoking a full pack a day, for instance, you could set a limit—in the wouldn't-do-to-myself-category—of no more than sixteen cigarettes a day. The limit can then be lowered to fourteen a day, then twelve, and so on, *one step at a time* until you have successfully eliminated smoking from your life. To make sure you abide by each limit, you will need to continue to use the future you as a resource, encouraging and supporting you as well as reminding you of the terrible future consequences of *not* quitting smoking. Your future you can help insure that you do not violate limits that you have identified as being vital to your well-being.

13 The next step in this sequence is to identify five existing behaviors that you carry out on a daily basis, behaviors that you know will lead to a desirable future. These behaviors can be as seemingly insignificant as brushing your teeth. It might seem like a small thing, but brushing your teeth *does* contribute to a desirable future, one in which you have your own teeth as well as healthy gums. Another behavior might be expressing some kind of affection to your loved ones on a daily basis. This contributes toward a future of meaningful and significant relationships. You will probably be able to identify many of these beneficial behaviors, but five will do for now. Identify them now and jot them down below.

Things I Do that Lead to a Desirable Future

_____

_____

_____

_____

_____

14 Once you are aware of these useful behaviors, determine how each one of them is evidence of a particular attribute. For instance, brushing your teeth could be evidence that you are conscientious or well groomed or responsible. Expressing affection could be evidence, of course, of your being affectionate. It could also be evidence of being loving or even a different kind of being responsible. Make this determination now, before proceeding.

15 What is common to all five of these behaviors is that they all carry you toward desirable futures. Take a moment to imagine the positive futures that you are creating by manifesting each of these behaviors. Make sure these futures are ones that your future self also wants and appreciates. Now determine how *not* doing these behaviors could lead to *un*desirable futures. Imagine the futures that will greet you if you fail to carry out the five behaviors. Be sure to finish this step before going on to the next.

16 Now identify four behaviors that you do *not* engage in and, if you did, would result in you experiencing terrible consequences. These could be behaviors like stealing, lying, abusing others, not paying taxes, or ignoring the needs of your loved ones. Perhaps you do not drink alcohol, eat red meat, or cheat on your spouse. These are all examples of behaviors that could result in you feeling bad about yourself, or other dire consequences. So for this step, you need to specify four behaviors that you do *not* do—behaviors that you are *glad* you refrain from doing.

Things I Don't Do (and I'm Glad I Don't)

_____

_____

_____

_____

_____

17 Now add a fifth behavior to this list: either *smoking*, or smoking *as much* as you presently do.

18 Imagine the positive future that you are headed for by *not* participating in these five undesirable behaviors. Imagine moving into that positive future a day at a time, a week at a time, and a month at a time. Take the time to make each of the stages real. In this way you can know and appreciate that for *each day you do not engage in those behaviors you move one step closer to realizing your desirable future,* and one step further away from an unwanted and unpleasant future. Before reading any further, spend a few minutes making each of these stages of your future real and compelling.

19 After you have explored the stages of your progress, identify the attributes you are manifesting by *not* engaging in those five behaviors. How are you demonstrating attributes such as faithfulness, honor, caring, responsibility, competence, wisdom (and any other attributes that fit for you), by not doing the behaviors you identified as potentially harmful or self-defeating?

These behaviors that you do (and do not do) on a regular basis can provide you with the evidence of your being the kind of person you want to be. Be sure occasionally to add to your list of things that you do and don't do. Add them one at a time. By adding them one at a time, you will assist yourself in setting goals that can be planned for and achieved. Each behavior you add to your list gives you a means for monitoring your progress. It also gives you a verifiable basis for feelings of self-worth. Review your list of do-and-don't-do behaviors as you drift off to sleep tonight, and reward yourself with personal satisfaction for how you are acting in the present, as well as for taking yourself into a future worth having.

We do not expect you to become a nonsmoker as a result of having read through this section only once (although you may surprise us). Becoming a nonsmoker takes strong motivation and a commitment to action. If you are ready to pursue the goal of becoming a nonsmoker then you need to take the time to repeat this entire sequence. You also should reinforce its effects with the EMPRINT formats in Chapters 3 through 6. You will then have the complete know-how of those who have never been attracted to smoking as well as the know-how of satisfied and successful ex-smokers.

Alcohol

As usual, Gus was a little nervous and more than a little self-conscious. The first few times he went out with a woman were always like that, and this time was no exception. He really liked the young woman he was with, Sophie, and already had high hopes for the evening. He didn't want his nervousness to show, so at dinner he had a couple of cocktails and the lion's share of a bottle of wine. By the end of dinner he was lit just enough so that he no longer felt jumpy. Rather, he thought he was warmly suave. But then Sophie had wanted to go dancing, and dragged Gus off to a nightclub. Gus was not too hot on dancing. He always felt intimidated by the uninhibited exuberance of the other dancers. And to make matters worse, the liquid ease of the dinner drinks had ebbed by the time he and Sophie reached the nightclub. She wanted to dance immediately, but Gus held her back for awhile while he downed a couple of drinks. Gradually his fears were replaced by that familiar, intoxicated warmth, and Gus led Sophie out on the floor. Gus enjoyed himself. He kept the barmaid busy with a steady order of cocktails, and with every additional drink, Gus's behavior became more and more abandoned. By the time Sophie wanted to go home, Gus was reeling. She suggested that he was in no shape to drive, but he assured her that he was "fine . . . great!" Gus wove his way down the (fortunately) nearly empty streets and dropped his date off at her home. His alarm clock split his head open at seven the next morning, reminding him that he had to be at work in an hour. "It's going to be a long day," he muttered quietly to himself as he gently swung his legs out over the edge of the bed. "But it was worth it," he thought. Meanwhile, Sophie was lying in her bed, thinking, "There must be a way to weed out the losers *before* I go out with 'em."

Alcohol is, of course, used by many millions of people as a way of altering their emotional states.[2] For Gus, as for many people, the effect of alcohol is to make him feel relaxed and uninhibited. Different individuals will characterize their personal experience under the influence of alcohol differently, citing its ability to make them feel comfortable, bold, gregarious, powerful, amorous, nostalgic, and so on. But the purpose of drinking is always the same—to change their emotional states.

In and of itself, there is nothing wrong with using alcohol to attain these emotional states. It is a *limitation*, however, if alcohol is the only way that you have to feel the way you want to feel. In that case, being uninhibited, for instance, will be determined by outside factors, as it is for Gus. Gus *needs* those drinks in order to feel uninhibited. So, he will keep drinking as long as he is in a situation in which he wants to be uninhibited. The problem with drinking himself into abandonment is that when the situation changes (to driving, for example) and it is no longer appropriate to be uninhibited, Gus is under the influence of a drug which he can't just turn off. In addition, there are the morning-after effects of drinking that Gus fails to take into account when he is tossing them down the night before.

What makes it possible for Gus to abuse alcohol is that (1) he drinks to attain highly valued emotional states of abandonment and relaxation (rather than for the taste of the wine, or to satisfy thirst, or be sociable, and so on); (2) whether or not he has those emotional states is a default response as he has no other means of inducing them; and, (3) he does not make future evaluations about limiting his drinking in order to avoid jeopardizing his needs in future situations (e.g., driving, working, being healthy). Given these parameters, when Gus is in a situation in which he wants to be relaxed and uninhibited, he will drink if he can, will continue to drink as long as he wants to be uninhibited, and will probably fail to limit his drinking with respect to any future consequences of being intoxicated.

Sophie accepted Gus's dinner offer because he seemed like someone she would like to know better. She enjoyed dinner and his company. The bottle of wine he ordered was delicious, and she loved the warmth that it lent her limbs. She wanted to dance, so she suggested they go to a nearby club. Gus didn't want to dance right away, making Sophie cool her heels while he had a couple of drinks. She wanted to relax, not lose control, so she drank mineral water after her first cocktail. She didn't want to get drunk because she had to work the next morning, and she also thought she should be sober when they left since Gus would obviously be too drunk to drive. When finally she did dance, she had a wonderful time. By eleven the alcohol buzz was gone, but Sophie still wanted to feel close to Gus. While they sat out a couple of dances, she started asking Gus some things about his personal life and past that she knew nothing about. Between sips of his drink, Gus recounted and confessed little pieces of his life, and Sophie was soon feeling a little closer to him. Later, Gus was adamant about his ability to drive, and the trip back to her house was tense for her. At her house, she accepted Gus's off-center kiss, and thanked him for a nice time. Once back inside her house, though, she wondered if there was any way to weed out the losers *before* she went out with them.

Sophie enjoys the buzz and warmth she gets from drinking. Unlike Gus, however, she is not dependent upon alcohol to feel close. She has at least one other way of creating for herself the experience of closeness, and it is a way over which she has behavioral control (i.e., asking personal questions). In addition, knowing that alcohol will cloud her perceptual acuity and physical responsiveness for awhile, and that beyond certain levels it will leave her hung-over tomorrow, Sophie evaluates her possible future experience with respect to what her emotional state will need to be both when it is time to go home and time to wake up in the morning. She then adjusts her drinking according to her evaluations about the future.

Being able to drink appropriately, then, requires that you make evaluations of possible future experiences that are real and compelling enough to motivate your behavior regarding any up-coming situations for which being intoxicated (or hung-over) will be inappropriate (e.g., in a couple of hours you will have to drive, do some work, be making love and not want to have your senses dulled; or the following day you need to be clear-headed for some task). It also requires that you have other ways besides alcohol of inducing those emotional states that you do want in the present. This allows you to respond to concerns about your future well-being without the competition of unfulfilled and presently important desires.

A Toast to Moderation

The following EMPRINT format is designed to provide you with the know-how for a significant talent: Moderation. Although there are similarities among the steps in this section and in the sections on eating, drugs and smoking, here we offer a method for acquiring new behaviors as well as the specific know-how for converting drinking into a choice response. Read all of the instructions and explanations for each step before participating in the exercises and explorations. By doing so you will learn how to take care of yourself in ways that satisfy and delight.

1 As we stated in the section above (in footnote #2), this format is not appropriate for dealing with the interactional and physiological complexities of alcoholism. There are, however, a great many people who drink excessively on occasion. If drinking is, for you, really a potential problem, the first step is to generate for yourself a compelling future of yourself as an alcoholic. It is important that when you do this you create a future you that reflects the actual long-term consequences of excessive drinking. The future alcoholic that you need to imagine is a real down-and-out one, desperately covert (hiding bottles of booze), and disgusting and pathetic to everyone around you. If you do not already have memories (of yourself or others) that provide the necessary elements to build such a representation, you can use the vicarious experiences offered to you by the drunks weaving down city streets, or the self-cheapening elbow-benders in bars. Or perhaps somewhere within your own family there is someone in whose alcoholic footsteps you would rather not follow.

One purpose of creating this compelling future of alcoholism is to provide the basis for motivating you *away* from alcohol indulgence *now*, long before it becomes necessary to cure yourself of alcoholism. Another purpose for creating this representation of future alcoholism is for you to have the opportunity to identify those behaviors which are likely to lead you to that undesired future. You will want to keep that information for a later time to use in evaluating whether or not you are behaving in a way consistent with your desire to be free of alcohol dependency. So take the time now to create that compelling future of yourself as an alcoholic.

2 If generating a future self as an alcoholic is too unreal for you (that is, you steadfastly believe that such a reality is in no way a real possibility for you), do the following: Imagine problem situations where a single occurrence of over-indulgence causes very unpleasant consequences (like being arrested for drunken driving, or worse, causing an accident and injuries to others as a result of drunken driving; or behaving in ways that bring you much personal shame while drinking). These should be specific, likely situations that you can imagine occurring to you. While we realize we are directing you to imagine very unpleasant experiences, we also know that they are better imagined and used to avoid the behaviors which cause them, rather than experienced directly, along with their attendant feelings of grief, remorse, guilt and shame.

To create these avoidable future experiences follow the same sequence as you have in previous sections *with one exception: Be sure to* see yourself *in these experiences*. The reason for this is that if you fully step into these imagined experiences you will be stepping into the numbing, blurred perceptions of the drunk. In dealing with excessive drinking, it is better to see yourself from an outside point of view that definitely motivates you to avoid such experiences.

3 If excessive drinking is presently a problem for you, a question that must be asked is, "What makes that possible now?" One possiblity is that your criteria are out of date: they might be from the past and need to be updated. In social drinking situations, do you return to the teenage days of chug-a-lug contests? Is a man someone who can hold his liquor, no matter how much? Is getting drunk still an assertion of your daring, maturity or independence? If so, evaluate your present criteria with respect to their appropriateness for who you are now and the world you are now living in. This re-ordering of criteria should include not only eliminating those which are no longer relevant, but adding those which you think more appropriate. For instance, do you want a person to whom you are attracted to know *you*, or to know you drunk? Perhaps in social drinking situations you will want to continue to treat yourself and others with respect and integrity. As you did before, prepare for yourself a menu of possible criteria, then imagine what, how and when you would drink in a social situation using each one of those criteria in turn. For example:

drunkenness

good time

escape

taste

health

my well-being tomorrow

being in control of my behavior

respect of others

pride

In applying these different criteria pick a situation, such as a mid-week evening after a particularly grueling day. It is evening and you are on your way home after this exhausting day. Now consider how you will spend your evening with respect to drinking. Try applying the criterion of *escape*, letting it become the experience you want. How do you plan and anticipate getting it? After doing this in relation to escape, return to the beginning and reorient yourself to your journey homeward after that grueling day, considering how you will spend the evening, this time applying the criterion of *well-being tomorrow*. The contrast of experience and effect between escape and well-being tomorrow will bring into sharp focus the behavioral differences made by such criteria considerations. Try this now for the criteria of escape and well-being tomorrow, imagining as vividly as possible actually being in this situation and using these different criteria.

4 Run through the above situation (or one of your own choosing) again and again, each time changing the criterion you are using (taken from the list above or from your own list). How does your experience and behavior change as you apply each of those criteria? Which criteria naturally lead to the kinds of experiences and behaviors which are supportive of your determination to be free of alcohol dependency? This is an important step, so take all the time you need to make these evaluations. Be sure to complete this step before proceeding.

5 As was the case with drugs, the use of alcohol needs to become a choice response rather than a default response. This requires the interaction of two things. The first is the acquisition of personal experiences that you can refer to for having choice within drinking situations. This is done by arranging the elements of a situation so that it is possible for you to respond differently than you ordinarily would. For instance, if one of the attractions of drinking for you is that it makes you uninhibited, arrange to have an interaction in an environment which you have set up such that you will be able to be more uninhibited without the use of alcohol. You can vary who you are with, how many, where, when, for what purpose, and so on. Control as many elements in these situations as you need to in order to feel comfortable. With each additional experience you will be building confidence in your ability to have the experiences that you want, without using alcohol.

6 The second thing needed to make the use of alcohol a choice response is the flexibility in behavior that will ensure that you have several ways of creating for yourself the experiences that you want to have. Specifically, now that you have examples for being able to have the experiences you want without alcohol, deny yourself alcohol in situations in which you would ordinarily drink, and then experiment with other ways of generating for yourself the experiences you want to have. Experiment with these behaviors while in the company of different individuals (both acquaintances and strangers), varying your behavior until you have no doubt about your ability to be poised, friendly and comfortable without the use of alcohol.

To acquire such new behaviors you can utilize the procedure known as the *new behavior generator*, presented in steps 7 through 11:

7   To begin, identify someone who manifests the behavior (or significant aspects of the behavior) that you intend to acquire, and does so in the appropriate situations.

8   Now run a short movie inside your head in which you watch and listen to your role model. Pay attention to how they use their body (the way they move, how they position themselves in relation to others, the gestures they use, their facial expressions, and so on) as well as what they say and *how* they say it (the tempo of their speech, the tonality and timbre qualities of their voice, and so on). Evaluate carefully whether or not you are satisfied with what they do and how they do it. If not, pick someone else and repeat these initial steps. (If no acquaintance comes to mind you can use movie or literary personalities in your movie.)

9   Having experienced someone else in detail doing what you want to be able to do, mentally replace that person with yourself and run the movie again. Be sure to adjust any undesirable aspects of your behavior until you are satisfied with what you see and hear. (While you are watching yourself in this movie, if you have any internal dialogue telling you, "That's not me—I can't do that—I'll never be able to do that, really," be sure to start over, making adjustments until this movie of you is at least as satisfactory as the movie of your role model, and then replace such dialogue with, "That looks good—I can do that—If he/she can do it, so can I—I'm going to really do that.")

10   Now imagine actually behaving in this way by stepping into the movie, being there and seeing what you would be seeing, hearing yourself talk, noticing how others respond to you, and, most of all, feeling how you would be feeling as you carry out this behavior naturally and congruently.

11   Finally, identify a future situation where you want to be sure to manifest the behavior. Imagine being there within that situation with whoever you anticipate will be there. First see yourself doing the new behavior there, then step inside your movie and imagine carrying out the behavior directly. Use this as an opportunity to make any further desirable refinements in your actions.

12 Having updated your criteria and made alcohol a choice variable through your behavioral flexibility, you may want to be able to resume drinking in certain situations, such as a party. Doing this in such a way as to preserve your desired future requires some future-pacing. In order to get to work or to an engagement on time you plan ahead, allotting the necessary time for travel, showering, breakfast, and so on. Do the same kind of planning for drinking. Before going to the party, assess for yourself the amount of time between the first drink and its effects, the amount of time between the second drink and its effects, the third drink, and so on, keeping in mind the time when you plan to leave and the amount of time it will take to sober up prior to leaving. In this way you can preset yourself for how many drinks to have, how far apart, and when to quit in time to leave sober. The effectiveness of such future-pacing was demonstrated by an acquaintance of ours who had set six o'clock as the time at which she would stop drinking champagne at an afternoon party. She forgot her resolution. At one point, while standing in the kitchen, she inexplicably let her full glass of champagne drop from her hand. When she bent to clean up the broken glass, she suddenly remembered her resolution and, looking up at the clock, noticed that it was precisely six o'clock.

So, take a social evening and plot it out for yourself as to time and experience in relation to alcohol intake. And be sure to take into account how far beyond that social evening the effects of drinking (including a hangover) extend. Any plans to get drunk should include considerations that go through the entire day/evening (i.e., driving home), as well as through the following day (i.e., having a hangover at work).

Once you know that you can and will be different in the future, you can begin to enjoy the pride and satisfaction that can result from taking control of a previously frustrating and perhaps self-destructive aspect of your life. Making this kind of change is a significant personal accomplishment, and as such it deserves to be enjoyed and appreciated by you at every opportunity.

8 Sex

Sex is an inherently sensual experience, a feast for the senses. Sexual behavior can convey passion, intimacy, love, tenderness, and much more. Though words may enhance, the vitality and depth of feeling of what is conveyed during sexual contact is expressed through immediate sensory experience. The touches, smells, tastes, sounds, and sights of lovemaking are profound and beautiful communications. Lovemaking is a natural and poignant human experience, and everyone should have the choice to experience its inherent pleasure and emotional fulfillment.

Despite this, few people are educated as to how to create the kinds of satisfying and fulfilling sexual experiences they desire. The EMPRINT format that we present in the "Arousing Your Interest" section of this chapter is intended to provide you with some of the fundamental elements of that education. But first, in the following vignettes three individuals exemplify three of the ways in which some people organize their internal experience so as to have *less* than satisfying sexual experiences. The description of internal processes which characterize satisfying sexual experiences will be presented after the three examples have been discussed. As you will discover, the patterns in each of the examples is distinct. The remedy, however, is the same for all three cases.

Tim's first sexual experience was arranged for him by his older brother and his brother's friends. One warm desert evening, they drove Tim to a Nogales cathouse, where they had arranged and paid for a prostitute to initiate him into manhood. Tim was unsure and embarrassed, but his brother shoved him forward, the lady took Tim's hand, and before he knew what was happening, he was in her room and she was shutting the door. Outside, Tim's brother and friends were laughing and pounding each other on the back as they congratulated themselves on their good deed. Tim was scared and was repulsed by the sordid environment. Naturally, he had difficulty getting an erection. The prostitute spent the next half hour humiliating Tim for not being able to get it up. The good deed was compelling. Now, ten years later, Tim flushes with embarrassment at the mere possibility of being with a woman sexually. And when he *is* with a woman, he worries about not being able to get an erection, and is often unable to. In fact, sex is such an embarrassing, fearful prospect for Tim, that he now often considers simply giving up the whole notion of his ever having a fulfilling relationship with a woman.

When she was twelve, Norma's mother sat her down to explain about men and sex. She revealed to Norma that although sex was dirty, unpleasant and disgusting, it was an obligation that a woman owed to her husband. The day eventually came when Norma married and, so, fell under that obligation. Considering the fear, pain and mess she experienced making love on her wedding night, Norma realized that her mother had been right. From then on Norma did oblige her husband when she had to, and tried to ignore the unpleasantness as much as possible.

Trudy has a lot to figure out when she is making love. While enfolding and being enfolded by her lover, she wonders: "When will he ejaculate?" "Will I have an orgasm this time?" "Will I get pregnant?" "When will we be done?" "How should we make love next time?" "What should we do when we finish making love?" Despite all her planning, it isn't often that Trudy has a satisfying sexual experience.

Whenever Tim is in a sexual context he is experientially transported right back to that humiliating first time in Nogales when a prostitute taught him that sex was about getting it up, and he couldn't. Whether or not he consciously remembers that unfortunate initiation, Tim is plunged once again into the feelings and perceptions that consumed him ten years ago. When it comes to sex, Tim is not with his partner, but is *in the past*. Similarly, Trudy is not with her partner, but instead of the past, Trudy is in the future. By occupying herself during lovemaking with considerations about what *will* happen a minute, an hour and a week in the future, Trudy misses much of the sensual experience *presently* available to her. Neither Tim nor Trudy are mentally or emotionally where there bodies are during lovemaking, but are immersed in the criteria (and their personally significant associations), memories and possibilities of the past and future. Norma, on the other hand, *is* in the present and wishes she were not. As a function of the beliefs she has, making love is the fulfillment of an obligation, a humiliation, and something dirty. Thus, she can take little pleasure in it.

For Mark and Maggie, making love is one of those special times when, through the giving and receiving of pleasure, they can let each other know how loved and important they really are. Lovemaking is an opportunity to experience pleasure, and everything that Mark and Maggie do when making love is done in the service of creating, exploring and enjoying the sensual possibilities of the moment. At times this enjoyment may even include imagining the sensations and pleasure that the other person is experiencing. Like everyone else, Mark and Maggie have had their share of unhappy or unsatisfying sexual experiences, but to them those were incidents from which they learned about satisfying their own sexual needs and the sexual needs of their partners. Having been together for years now, Mark and Maggie each know a great deal about what the other finds sensual and exciting. Even so, there are times when transient changes in mood blunt the ability of one of them to take pleasure in the kind of lovemaking that he or she normally (or used to) find sensual. Their response to such

159

moments is to explore for themselves and with each other novel sensual possibilities until they are once again sharing pleasure.

Sex is inherently (and certainly most enjoyable and satisfying as) an experience for the senses. As such, it is most appropriately an experience of the ongoing present. Lovemaking should be oriented toward giving and experiencing pleasure *now*, rather than being occupied with pleasure that has been or might be given and experienced. Whatever awareness you devote either to the past or the future is that much less available to you for the enjoyment of the pleasurable sensations of the ongoing present. In addition, if you lose yourself into that past or future, you will (as did Tim) be operating out of a set of beliefs and criteria which may be irrelevant to, or destructive of, the enjoyment of sex.

The appropriate experiences to refer to regarding sex are those past experiences which inform you of what you and your lover find pleasurable in your ongoing (present) experiences. These references form the basis of an interaction which makes it possible for you to satisfy yourself and your partner's ongoing needs for pleasure, stimulation, affection, and appreciation. In addition, there are times when imagining your lover's ongoing sensual and emotional experience is both appropriate and pleasurable (while orally stimulating your lover, for instance).

In addition to applying the criterion of pleasure while using present ongoing experience as a source of information, motivation and feedback, there are three other elements which are important in making satisfying sexual experiences a reality. The first, unlike the associations Norma has, is that the fulfillment of your sexual criteria (your criterial equivalences) should be congruent with the enjoyment of it. Such criterial equivalences as sex = *expression of love*, sex = *natural*, and sex = *pleasurable*, are associations which imbue sex with qualities of importance for you, your lover and your relationship.

The second important element is an operating presupposition of choice, so that if your and your lover's criteria are not being satisfied, you will try to change both your experience and behavior in order to fulfill those desires.

And the third is that your attentions should be at the level of sensation. It is the relatively detailed specificity of sensation which provides the flexibility you need to satisfy your criteria and sensual desires. It is from sensations that emotional states, self-concept, and so on are built. Whereas satisfying a globally represented criterion such as self-concept is likely to involve relatively many sets of behaviors and experiences that express to you the kind of person you are (making it difficult to achieve whenever you make love), only a shift in position, a certain kiss, a touch, a sound, or a smell is required to attain a pleasurable sensation.

Arousing Your Interest

The following EMPRINT format will provide you with a measure of useful know-how for sexual fulfillment—a measure of know-how that is often overlooked or unknown. Read through each step and then enjoy your experience as you carry out the instructions. The steps direct you to your own presently occurring sensual experience. You will focus your awareness on pleasurable sensations, as well as accept and appreciate your own inherent sexuality. Finally, you will learn how to make discriminations among several desirable emotions and how to choose satisfying ways to express those emotions. As a result, you will have acquired both the ability to elicit desirable responses in others and the know-how for experiencing your own sexual fulfillment.

As described above, sex is essentially a present, sensory-based experience. Occupying your consciousness with the past or the future during what is intended to be a sensual experience is certain to diminish and dissipate that experience (as you saw above). Since sex is an inherently sensual experience, the most fundamentally important change in internal processes involves attending to sensations.

1 Begin with external stimuli. At the end of this paragraph, close your eyes and feel various objects which are similar but still different. For example, you could use an avocado, an orange and a lemon. First, using your hands, feel the differences between them in texture, in moisture, in firmness, weight, warmth, and so on. Second, smell each one, comparing their odors and pungencies. Then feel and taste each one with your lips and tongue, using your lips and tongue to feel the same textures, temperatures, firmness that you felt with your fingers. Do this now, before you go on to the next step.

2 Next put your consciousness out to your extremities. Hold out your arm and move it back and forth until you can feel the air passing around it. Tap the table with a pencil, then tap it with your finger. What is the difference in how each feels? How much sensory information do you get from using the pencil compared to using your own finger? After answering that question, repeat the exercise (tapping first with the pencil, then with your own finger) attending this time more to the *range* of information that is available from each. (Often people use their bodies as if they were pencils, passive objects to be manipulated, rather than the responsive and interactive creatures that they are.) If you sort through the people you know or have known, you can probably find someone who does have a great deal of their awareness in their bodies. Perhaps you have been touched by someone with the wonderful hands of a healer, an expert masseuse, or a sensitive lover. Take a moment to remember how that person used his or her hands to gently pick up information about you as they touched you. As another reference experience for the kind of sensitivity and responsiveness we are describing here, you can also think of and compare acquaintances who hug well and acquaintances who don't. Now spend a moment or two for this exploration. Finish this step before proceeding to the next.

3 Pet a cat or a dog with a wooden spatula, then with your hand, and *remember the differences* in the sensations that you experienced with each, as well as noting differences in the animal's responses to your stroking. With your hands, explore your hands, feeling for areas of roughness, smoothness, hardness, softness, warmth, cold, and so on. Then use your hands to explore the rest of your body, discovering differences in sensitivity, texture and temperature on different portions of your skin.

4 Next, with a partner or friend, pick some communication to give that person but do not tell them what it is. Any communication such as affection, passion, concern, caring, or trust is appropriate. Take hold of that person's hand and using *only* your hand, communicate to them the message you have selected. Ask your partner what he or she understood the communication to be. Continue using just your hand to convey your message until the meaning that your partner is receiving matches the message you are intending. Having done that, expand the range of touch to include hugging, caresses and so on, using each to experiment with conveying other messages to your partner.

5 Now let's consider internal experience. This involves bringing the associations between specific experiences and their meanings into alignment with the fact that *sexuality is sensory experience*. Drop your awareness internally down through your body. As you go through your body, feel the mass, the substance of your physical being. From inside this living cylinder, feel your left arm, your right, your left and right thighs, your heart beating and your lungs expanding and contracting within your torso. Once you are aware of these sensations, identify just where you interface with the nonliving world— that is, your clothes, shoes, the chair, the floor, and so on. In doing this you are identifying the evidence of being *alive*. Continue to concentrate on those sensations which allow you to *know* you are alive. Be sure to take all the time you need for this step.

6 Next, without looking at or touching yourself, become aware of the internal sensations that let you know that you are a man or a woman. If you are a man there is the feeling of hair on your face, of your testicles, penis, the awareness of changing pressures in your penis and in the pelvic muscles that attach to it. If you are a woman, there is the presence and weight of your breasts, your vaginal lips and orifice and the muscles

surrounding this sensually rich opening, your uterus, and ovaries. Feel your body completely. Next, direct your consciousness into feeling your lips, teeth, and tongue. Touch your tongue to your lips, feeling their warmth, moisture, softness, and surface texture. Then take your awareness through the rest of your body—the evidence of your sexuality is on the same level as those feelings that lie within your body that are evidence of your being alive. At this most basic level of sensory experience, your sexuality can no more be separated from you than can your breathing or your heart beat. You may not always be aware of those sensations that are evidence of your sexuality, but they are nevertheless always there, part of your being, part of your well-being.

One of the most important outcomes of this sensory level of experience is that it separates sexuality from criteria; there is no right, wrong, pretty, ugly, big, small, bad, good, pride or shame. There is only experience. Everyone has had imposed upon them criteria (and the criterial equivalences for those criteria) regarding sexuality. Your parents, peers, institutions and the media have all extensively influenced your notions of what constitutes attractiveness, appropriate sexuality, and appropriate sex. The sequence of experiences described in the previous paragraph can take you back to an innocent awareness of your own sexuality, and in that way provide you with the opportunity to experience sexual sensations without the burden of imposed criteria. It also provides you with the opportunity to generate your own criteria based upon those experiences. This is a significant step in any adjustment toward fulfilling sexual experiences. It is part of the process of bringing into alignment pleasurable physiological responses, emotions and mental processes inherent in satisfying sexual experiences.

7 As you did before, direct your awareness to your sensory experience and notice what of a *pleasurable* nature you are presently experiencing, including emotions and places of comfort, warmth, and stimulation in your body and at the surface of your body. For instance, the emotion you are experiencing right now as you read this sentence might be one of curiosity, with the lower part of your face relaxed, the muscles around your eyes and in your torso pleasingly tense, and warmth in your mouth and in your hands. Before reading any further, explore your sensory experience to discover those pleasurable emotions and sensations.

8 By attending to sensations you can make discriminations in your own emotional states, making it possible to choose behaviors that are most appropriate for the expression of those emotional states. As was done in the sections on health, you need to make sensory discriminations between the various emotions that you have and those that are possible within the context of sex. Such emotional states include:

Lonely

Bored

Horny

Loving

Aroused

Powerful

Affectionate

Romantic

Tender

Take a moment to consider what emotions you experience or want to experience, then list them below.

Emotions I Want to Experience During Sexual Moments

_____

_____

_____

_____

9 Now, how do you know, *in terms of sensory experience*, one emotional state from another? When you reach the end of this paragraph, select one of the emotional states on your list and identify for yourself the sensations that combine to make up your experience of that emotional state. For example, *affec-*

tionate could be smiling with your mouth and eyes, relaxed face and torso, warmth throughout your body, feeling in your arms and hands the desire to reach out and touch your lover, and so on. Identify those sensations now.

10 Once you have done that, identify at least three behaviors that are appropriate, useful and fulfilling in the expression ᴏf that emotion. Using *affectionate* as our example, such behaviors might include gently stroking or patting your lover, surprising your lover with a strong hug and a smack of a kiss, complimenting your lover on a special quality, and telling your lover that you love him or her. Before you go on, identify and list at least three of the behaviors that express the emotion you have chosen.

Appropriately Expressive Behaviors

_____

_____

_____

_____

11 Next, future-pace those behaviors for yourself by finding an appropriate situation and imagining that you are doing each of them with your lover. Make this imagined experience as real as possible by paying attention to the sights, sounds, smells, tastes, and sensations which are a part of your actually being there with your lover. If you feel uncomfortable or fearful when you imagine engaging in these new behaviors, readjust the behavior (or what has led up to the behavior) in your image so that you are comfortable with it. Be sure to make any adjustments that are necessary in order to be able to behave in your chosen ways while maintaining the desired emotional state. Imagine engaging in your new behaviors while having your desired emotional state now, before reading any further.

12 Having done that with one sexually-related emotional state, go through the rest of your list, identifying for each emotion the subjective personal sensations that characterize it and at least three behaviors which are expressive of it. Then future-pace each one of those behaviors as you did before by imagining in as rich a fashion as possible actually doing your chosen behaviors. Doing this now will help insure that you will reach and maintain your desired emotional states and use appropriately expressive behaviors in the future.

The purpose of the experiences we have taken you through is to orient you toward a present sensual awareness during moments of sexual expression, and to bring your behaviors into accord with appropriate criteria and criterial equivalences for sexuality. The processes we have introduced to you here are intended to act as a foundation of personal experience to which you can always refer. While we have given you exercises intended to orient you to your ongoing sensory experience, the ultimate goal (as far as sexuality is concerned) is *automatically* to attend to your present ongoing experience for immediate sensual information. This immediate sensual information should be used as feedback for making immediate adjustments in moving toward greater pleasure. This will come with practice. In the meantime, you have gained new experiences, understandings, and perceptual and behavioral choices by going through the above sequences. Therefore, until you automatically orient to the present in sexual situations, use what you have gained through the above sequences to direct your awareness to those portions of your present experiences that are sensually pleasing. As you increase the range and intensity of your sensual pleasure, you will be moving toward the kinds of satisfying and fulfilling sexual experiences you desire.

9 Loving

Even if you have everything you want in terms of career, wealth, health and possessions, life can still seem empty if you have no significant, meaningful, loving relationships with others. Even a brief glance at literature, movies, television, and your own experiences will reveal that the striving for love and satisfying relationships is one of the most compelling forces forming our lives. Indeed, the need for love and attachment often underlies the striving for career, wealth, health and possessions.

Each of us has personal yearnings to fulfill, and many of these yearnings revolve around our relationships with others. Some of those relationships are a part of our birthright—we are sons and daughters, brothers and sisters, and grandchildren. Other relationships developed as we ventured from home, exploring life. In this way and in time we become neighbors, classmates, business partners, friends, dates, lovers, spouses and parents. However, despite the many relationships possible and experienced, those relationships involved in love and marriage stand out as perhaps the most important.

Unlike people in earlier centuries, in our culture at this time we include romantic love as an essential prerequisite to marriage. Romantic love has, in fact, become an important pursuit for almost all age groups in this society. Furthermore, the presence or absence of mutual love has become the test for whether or not two people should get married. One of the most obvious byproducts of this test has been our country's high divorce rate. As most people over eighteen probably know, an ongoing relationship is much more complicated and more demanding than is the pulse and embrace of love. The lack of education regarding love and marital relationships seems to betray a culture-wide assumption that we are all somehow supposed to know how to do these things well. Well, we don't.

When Marilyn Monroe first married Joe Dimaggio, she told reporters that nothing in the world made her happier than bringing Joe beer and sandwiches while he watched sports on TV. She filed for divorce ten months later, and the reason that she reportedly gave was that all Dimaggio wanted to do was watch TV and drink beer. She decided that she had better things to do with her life than putting up with that. What happened in those ten months?

How do people fall in love? How do people fall out of love? How do people *stay* in love? What makes a marriage satisfying? What makes it possible for a marriage to last? The answers to these questions lie in the changing requirements of the phases through which relationships pass.

■ First there is *attraction*, that phase during which you discover that the other person stirs and satisfies certain yearnings within you.

■ Then follows a period of *appreciation*, during which this person becomes the focus of your attention and affections and, seemingly, can do no wrong.

■ If, in time, your experience with this person continues to satisfy, you come to want a long-term commitment so that your moment-to-moment existence becomes lengthened in time to include not only the past and present, but also a fulfilling future. This is the *security* phase.

■ Now that you are going into the future together, the *expectation* phase begins, during which the foibles and transgressions that were ignored or tolerated before become irritating and unacceptable. It is now time to come through on the expectations that each of you has generated about the lives you will lead together.

■ If you both are able to fulfill those expectations, then all may be well. But if it is not possible (as often it is not) to fulfill the hopes and promises upon whose crests you originally rode into the relationship, then the disappointments start *stacking* up.

■ Should these disappointments reach a critical level, then a final phase of the relationship may begin: *threshold*. Once over threshold, suddenly there seems to be no possibility of going back to the intense loving feelings and relationship you once had. Not only is your partner forever seen as hopelessly unsatisfactory, but the history that you have shared becomes tainted as well and is now filled with nothing but bitter memories, regret and shame for wasted time and affections.

The relationship phases that we have just outlined usually end in disappointment, anger, regret and so on. Of course, relationships do not have to end up that way, but (as we noted above) the extremely high divorce rate in this country testifies to the unpleasant fact that many relationships do end up dissatisfying and unendurable. What can be done on a personal level?

Attraction

As Jill and Sam would often tell their friends later, it had been love at first sight. Jill's flowing red hair, green eyes, willowy figure and the coltish way she flirted with him was just what Sam had always wanted in a woman. The idea of being with her, of kissing her, making love to her, thrilled him. For her part, Jill found Sam not only handsome, but easygoing; and with his position as junior executive, financially well-off and secure. Before they had finished their first drink together, Jill was imagining how great it would be to be married to Sam: the parties, the traveling, the nice home, kids.

For most people, attraction begins when another person matches some visually based standards that have been established for attractiveness. Sam took one look at Jill and *wham!* Not only was she a match for the girl of his dreams, but instantly he was imagining how wonderful it would be to be with her. She was fulfilling his criteria for a woman to love.

By the time he finished fantasizing and came back out to notice what was actually occurring around him, he was already feeling feelings that he identified as love. And he hadn't even spoken with her yet.

In working with couples and individuals concerning relationships and the yearning for relationships, we have found that their strategies for being attracted make it far too easy to *be* attracted. Generally, their strategies involve being attracted to certain external, visual manifestations. Attraction that is based on such evaluations frequently leads to two less-than-useful consequences. The first is that they suddenly have a stake in the outcome of the relationship that is completely inappropriate and unwarranted, given the actual situation. As in Sam's case above, he and Jill are still *strangers*, and yet he already has his emotional well-being tied to and dependent upon the responses of this other unknown person.

The second thing that often happens is that even if two people are attracted to each other and do well at first (probably by matching one another's superficial, external criteria), there is still no basis for a lasting relationship. There is little for them to do other than look at one another or be seen with one another. This is fine for mannequins but ultimately is not so good for people who are hopeful of establishing relationships which bring them love, friendship, respect, stimulation, and so on.

In the example above, Sam flirts with these two problems when he becomes enthralled with Jill simply on the basis of how she appears. Because she fulfills his visual standards regarding what is an attractive and lovable woman, that is enough for him to step into the emotional state of love. All at once, Jill is elevated from the status of a pretty stranger to that of someone who, with a word, can inflame or pierce his heart.

The other common mistake in being attracted is made by Jill. Although she notices whether or not Sam fits her notions of handsomeness, her attraction to him is primarily based upon her relatively vague assessment of possible futures with him. That is, she imagines what it would be like to be married to him, the home they would have, the children, and so on. (We know a woman who tries to figure out *on a first date* if her escort is the kind of man who would keep up child support payments!) Deciding in the first twenty minutes of meeting whether he will make a good husband and father, or whether she will make a good wife and mother, is inappropriate. Such evaluations about the future are demeaning and inconsiderate to those being evaluated, shortchange those doing the evaluating, and turn the pursuit of relationships into a marketplace.

In being attracted to Sam, Jill is not responding so much to Sam as he *is*, but as she thinks he *could* and *will be*, and as they could and would be together. Jill's imagined future with Sam may, of course, have little to do with what is really possible. This lays the groundwork for disappointment. Furthermore, Sam deserves to be responded to and either loved or spurned for who he *is*.

If your attraction to another person is based upon evaluations of the future which lack adequate present and ongoing experiences, then you may not respond to that person as he or she is, but rather to how that person *could be*. This may seem like a compliment to them, and it is often intended that way ("But he/she has the potential to be so fine, so smart, so productive, so good-looking" and so on). However, no matter how well-intentioned, the clear and lethal message is that the person is not fine, smart, and productive now. In other words, they are not presently good enough. In this way, all concerned are cheated of the opportunity to experience loving what *is* there now.

The first thing that really caught Frances's attention about Ian was that he shook hands with her when they were introduced, unlike the other men who simply nodded and leered a little. She liked being treated as a person, rather than as an object—even an admired object. Later in the evening, when she was casting about for a change in conversation, she remembered that handshake and went looking for Ian. As they chatted away, she discovered that he was good humored and seemed to be genuinely interested in her and her work. He was modest about his own, and she had to ply him with good-natured threats in order to get him to talk about himself. The enjoyable time that Frances was having with him began to change in quality, however, becoming something more precious, more endearing, as she began to notice that Ian treated everyone with the same respect, cheerfulness, and sincere interest that he had shown her.

In contrast to Sam, Frances chooses who she wants to be with based upon qualities of personality, rather than physical characteristics. Unless all you want to do is look at your partner, the quality of a relationship is going to be determined by the quality of the interactions that occur between who you and your partner are as persons. In addition, unlike Jill, Frances is not making evaluations about possible futures with Ian, but evaluations about what her experience is with him *now*. This evaluation of the present is important for bringing about future possibilities. If a person reveals personality traits in the present which are in conflict with your own, there is no reason to expect that your future experiences with them will be good.

The strengths of Frances's approach are twofold. First, she attends to and values those qualities upon which a relationship's success ultimately depends—the meshing of *personalities*. Second, she seeks those individuals who already have those personality qualities she admires, since it is with those people that a gratifying future (in terms of a relationship) is most likely.

Appreciation

Soon Jill and Sam became magnets for one another. They could hardly wait until evening came when they could once again be together. At home they consoled one another over past hardships and delighted in revealing past tomfoolery. Sam sometimes felt that Jill was often too critical of how he acted and dressed, but he reasoned that he probably *could* use some personal revision. And besides, he thought Jill always looked so fiery and pretty when she would start correcting him. Jill was not crazy about the extensive list of casual lovers that Sam seemed to have, but that was the past. She loved him, he loved her, and from now on it would just be him and her. Of course, Sam was also chronically late, fairly demanding, and somewhat secretive, but Jill looked into the future and knew that all that would be different once they settled down with one another.

Once mutual attraction has been achieved (that is, the criteria for what makes someone attractive have been fulfilled), the lovely, loving and magical stage of appreciation begins.[1] During this time, every little behavior is perceived as just another example of your lover's charm, wit, intelligence, thoughtfulness, and so on. The rose colored glasses firmly in place, your ongoing experience becomes something special and cherished. It is as though you have just returned from a week of backpacking, hopped into a warm shower and then into the crisp, clean sheets of your own bed. You probably appreciated that shower and that bed in a way that you did not before your backpack trip.

In the early stages of a relationship, little is taken for granted. Because nothing is for sure, people tend to remain for the most part in the *present*, attending to what is good. The fact that there is mutual attraction is often all it takes to convince a person that a relationship is worth pursuing. In pursuing a relationship, they will continually be looking for examples of how their criteria are fulfilled by the other, and how they are fulfilling the other person's needs and desires. As did both Sam and Jill in the example above, dissimilarities between criteria and criterial equivalences tend to be either overlooked or in some way justified. Thus, criticalness becomes cute and useful, and that rakishness, tardiness and secretiveness belong to the past (or soon will). The emphasis is on maintaining the perspective that the other person is wonderful.

The appreciation stage is also a time when you do your best, give your best, and be your best. Feeling valued and appreciated, and being generous, thoughtful and respectful seem to come easily and naturally.

Jill's mistake is to appreciate Sam in the same way she was originally attracted to him: through the gauze of evaluations about the future, rather than present. What Jill is appreciating in Sam is not who and what he is now, but what she thinks he and they will be sometime in the future. She is responding to Sam in relation to a future she has *imagined*, rather than in relation to her ongoing experience of him.

Although Sam is also transforming Jill's disquieting behaviors into examples of just how precious she is to him, he is doing it in relation to his *present* experience, rather than some future considerations. The importance of the difference between these two ways of thinking is in the likelihood that Jill will ignore ongoing problems and differences in their relationship to a much greater extent and for a much greater time. Though both are distorting their experience, at least Sam is doing it in the present, providing him with more opportunities for feedback as to what *is* going on.

The moment-to-moment quality of appreciation may last for an hour, a week, several years, or even a lifetime.[2] And perhaps it should last a lifetime, provided that in appreciating your partner you are attending to the present; and you have a clear notion of what you value and want for yourself so that you can assess whether or not what you are appreciating makes it appropriate to move to the next stages of the relationship.

Security and Expectation

It wasn't hard for Jill to decide she wanted to marry Sam. They loved one another, they loved being together, and she wanted to have forever what they had had together for the past few months. Sam's walk down the aisle was not so easily made. The first time that Sam really worried about his relationship with Jill was when she raised the possibility of marriage. He was happy with the way things were, but after talking with Jill it began to dawn on him that if he didn't make a commitment to her, he would lose her. Lose that beautiful woman? Be alone again? Sam decided he couldn't stand either, so he bought the ring and asked that very special question. Jill's answer was yes.

When the present becomes good enough, people start going into the future, wondering what could be there and wanting what they imagine. It does not at all have to be a deliberate, conscious decision process. Instead, it may simply begin with the subtleties of knowing that you will be together on Saturday night even though you don't yet know what you will do together. The experience of belonging *with* one another takes root and begins to grow.[3] Soon, you find yourself projecting into the future and anticipating what life is going to be like together. It is usually at this point that people either make an overt or covert commitment, separate, or somehow define the limits and boundaries of their relationship. That is, they decide on what basis their relationship is going to proceed through time.

It is at this point in the relationship that short-term considerations and long-term considerations interact. In terms of the relationship, it is now time to apply your long-term criteria (what you want to be there in the future) and your short-term criteria (what has been there for you in your present interactions). Also, it is time to consider what is *not* there and what is *not likely* to be there. In our example above, Jill's mistake is in leaping into a committed relationship without attending both to what has been and is there now in their relationship. Though a commitment can certainly be based upon an evaluation about the future, in order for it to be an informed evaluation it must be made with respect to and in light of cause-effect relationships between the present and future. The fundamental question to ask is, "From what I know now about myself and this person, can I predict. . . ?" Jill has not been attending very much to what *is* and, so, has little basis upon which to make present-to-future cause-effect judgements if, indeed, she makes them at all.

Sam makes a similar mistake, the difference being that instead of ignoring short-term criteria, he ignores his long-term criteria in making a decision. She continues to be attractive to him, and he doesn't want to have the experience of losing her. What he does not consider, however, is whether or not she will continue to be the person he wants to be with ten, twenty and forty years down the road.

Again, this is a time during which we seek security through the fulfillment of expectations. This makes it important that those expectations be appropriately derived (through a consideration of the past, present and future) in order to prevent disappointment.

Of course, this is also the stage at which relationships frequently break down. Those individuals who invariably choose to dissolve the relationship rather than make a commitment at this point are often thinking about their experience in ways which do not include the possibility of change further down the road. The global interpretations that characterize such internal representations can turn even a small commitment into forever, leaving them feeling overwhelmed and trapped. In addition, such responses may be based upon criterial equivalences which identify *commitment* with being imprisoned, or *belonging* with a loss of self or the subordination of personal desires, or that *relationships* are opportunities to be hurt or disappointed. Rather than drawing upon the memories of the relationship going well and taking those into the future, these individuals will draw upon memories from unhappy relationships, put those into their evaluations of the future, and thus, feel compelled to run away. They will say to themselves, "I failed at relationships before, so I'll fail again." "I was left and hurt before, the same thing will just happen again."

It wasn't too very long before Frances and Ian were seeing each other often. They were in love, knew it, and were glad of it. It had seemed so very natural and matter-of-fact when the phone calls to arrange their dates gave way to the unspoken assumption that they would be together whenever they could. It started Frances thinking about a more permanent arrangement. Ian had been wonderful as a lover and friend. What about as a housemate and husband? In that department she wanted someone who was stable, not stodgy, and reliable and responsible. Well, Ian certainly fit that. Frances also wanted children, and Ian genuinely seemed to love children. Frances already had many memories of Ian going out of his way to play with kids. Frances was physically very active and wanted to stay that way. Ian certainly did not fit in there. Frances was under no illusions—the few times she had got Ian to join her in a sport it had only been after weeks of cajoling and nagging. Other than that, however, Frances decided that she wanted to be with Ian through time, to make a home and a life with him. And as far as the sports? Well maybe she would eventually be able to instill in Ian a fondness for sneakers, but whether she succeeded at that or not, she would make sure that she had friends with whom she could be active when she wanted to.

Fulfilled in her relationship with Ian, Frances begins to consider the long-term possibilities. Her short-term criteria have been satisfied, but that is not enough to reassure her that a long-term (lifetime) relationship with Ian will be satisfying. Accordingly, Frances sorts through her long-term criteria, trying to determine on the basis of her experiences with Ian (memories and present experiences) whether or not they would have a satisfying life together. That is, she makes future evaluations based upon present-to-future cause-effect.

As far as Frances can determine, she and Ian are compatible with one important exception: She values physical activity and he does not. Had Frances not had the ability to generate options and choices, this glaring difference between them could easily result in her regretfully deciding that they were incompatible and would have to go their separate ways. Instead, Frances was able to come up with a satisfactory way of fulfilling her need for physical activity (sports with friends). We want to stress that she is not entering this long-term relationship *ignoring* the significant differences between herself and Ian (as did Sam and Jill). Rather, in Frances's estimation, there is a great deal of congruence between what she and Ian value, *and* she has ways of satisfying for herself those criteria which she recognizes are *not* shared by them both.

Stacking

So, now you have made either an explicit or implicit commitment to be together. As a result, perhaps you are now living together, marrying, planning a Pacific sailing adventure, buying a house, or (the biggest of them all) having a child together. The commitment made, you settle into the pleasant and fulfilling experience of security. But secure about what? It is in this stage of the relationship that expectations about the future are generated: that you will be sleeping together tonight, tomorrow night, and every night for years; that disagreements won't be the end of the relationship; that every moment doesn't have to be ecstasy for it to still be a good relationship. Over the weeks, months and years that now follow, you attend to whether or not your expectations are being fulfilled. As long as they are, you can feel fulfilled as well as secure. But if they are not. . .

> Now married, Sam and Jill settled into the comfort and security of knowing just when, where and what they would be doing in relation to each other, every day. Sam's afternoon phone calls to Jill to see how she was doing no longer delighted her, but became part of their routine. And the praise that he used to lavish upon her for her lasagne and red hair dwindled, then disappeared. He still liked her hair and her lasagne, and she still liked his afternoon calls, but they were, well, *used* to all that now, so it was easy to forget about how nice they really were. In time, Sam started to forget to call. Jill did notice that, and each time he forgot she would feel a little more uneasy about his caring for her. Jill started wondering if maybe he were no longer as interested in her, or perhaps, even interested in someone else. What Sam noticed was that Jill wasn't dressing up like she used to, nor was she doing her hair the way she *knew* he liked it. Sam began to wonder if her recent neglect was a preview of the future. He had married a beautiful woman, and the idea of coming home to an unkempt, aging housewife in a housecoat filled him with anger and wariness. Now there was something else, too. Sam was finding that Jill's seeming passion for the future was starting to get on his nerves. He liked to reminisce, to kick around old times. But Jill hated that, and would actually leave the room when he would get to talking over old times with friends. He couldn't help but notice (and be offended by) the fact that she never forgot to renew their subscription to *OMNI*, but that she would invariably let lapse his subscription to *The Smithsonian*.

One of the hazards of the security phase that people often run afoul of is that of habituation. In the same way that you can become accustomed to a particular smell (even an offensive one) to the point of not noticing it, people can become habituated to experiences that at one time thrilled or pleased them. The meal prepared just the way you like it, the afternoon telephone call to find out how you are doing, the gentle kidding, the effort to dress-up—in short, all of those things that you found so gratifying and special during the appreciation phase—can become so expected that they come to be taken for granted. And so, even though you might still notice them, you now respond matter-of-factly or even indifferently to the special meals, the phone calls, the kidding, the new clothes, and so on.

This happened with Jill and Sam. Secure in their relationship, those things about each other that they used to delight in and appreciate came to be expected, and, soon were taken for granted. Not receiving the same kind of appreciative responses that they did when courting, it is easy to understand how Sam will start to forget to make his afternoon call, and for Jill to lose the desire and motivation to appear attractive for Sam. Through habituation, the phone calls and the cosmetics became *expected*, and so Jill and Sam start noticing when those things are *not* there. Sam and Jill start to wonder if their expectations are justified, which leads them into speculating about the possible significance of their mate not being the way they had expected. Accordingly, they start to accumulate and *stack* examples of those discrepancies with the result that they innocently (and, for the most part, unconsciously) begin building a new belief or understanding about the other person.

The other thing that often happens as people settle into the lull of expectations in their relationships is that other criteria, and things of importance that have previously been relegated to the shadows by the bright light of appreciation, begin to come to the fore. In the example above, once Sam is no longer in the thrall of Jill's beauty and the intoxication of a new relationship, he once again notices the pleasure and importance he places upon the experience of walking down memory lane. Unfortunately for Sam and Jill, it is only then that he discovers that the pleasure he takes in his strolls through the past is not shared by Jill. In addition to his fear and anger over Jill's apparent declining interest in her appearance, Sam must now also deal with the fact that there is something that he wants in a relationship that is not, has never been, and (as far as he can see) will never be there with Jill.

Sam and Jill make evaluations about the past, present and future based upon expectations they have had, their own emerging needs, and their fantasies about where this could all lead (these are imagined future possibilities that are treated as real information). By doing this they begin to accumulate example upon example of discrepancies between what they want and expect in the relationship, and what they actually have gotten, are getting, and can expect to get. Also significant here is that any considerations of how to positively influence the course of events through their own behavior are absent from their internal processes. The result is that the discrepant behaviors are not viewed as the product of their (the couple's) interactions, but as a problem that belongs to the *other* person.

As the examples mount, so does the pressure to change beliefs with respect to those examples.

Threshold

For Sam and Jill there followed a period of arguments about his waning interest in her (which he denied) and her no longer wanting to be attractive for him (which she denied). After each argument they would manage to make up—but they never forgot. One night, Sam and Jill reached flash point. He was arriving home late from work with two things on his mind. One was that it had been a long time since he and Jill had had a romantic evening, and that is what he wanted to have tonight. The other was that he had forgotten to call and tell her that he would be late, and so he had to think of a way to explain it away. When he arrived home he found her staring at the TV, dressed in a housecoat, no makeup, her hair unkempt, no dinner on the stove, and fairly oblivious to him. For Sam this was the last straw. He exploded and began loudly castigating her for her frumpiness and her disregard for herself and their marriage. Now he could see her shallowness for what it really was, just a cosmetic mask she had used to snare him. "You're not the woman I married!" he finally realized. Jill was upset, but she had no more tears to shed—she had shed them all earlier when she realized that Sam was not going to call today. Today was her birthday, and Sam had forgotten. The enormity of his neglect suddenly hit her and she realized that all she had ever been to him was a good lay. She should have known, she told herself ruefully, when she saw the way he was putting the moves on all the women at the party where they first met.

Often the result of stacking example after example of your mate's failings is that some level of tolerance is exceeded and you go over a threshold of tolerance. Once over threshold, the old positive beliefs become impossible to hold onto. Suddenly you start generating new, usually derogatory criterial equivalences (that is, applying new meanings) to your lover's behaviors. What was once perceived as outgoing is now seen as *exhibitionism*; his appreciation of women becomes *lechery* or *lasciviousness*; her close social circle becomes evidence of her *insecurity*; his wanting her becomes *demanding*; her playfulness turns into *irresponsibility*.

This change in perspective is not limited to the present, however, but extends into the *past* as well. Looking back from the present over-threshold vantage point, the past appears different. In her mind it is not that the husband who appreciates women is now a lecher, but that he *always has been*, and suddenly there are all of those examples from personal history which support that new perspective. Similarly, it is not that the wife with the tight circle of friends is now insecure, but that she has always been that way, and there are all of those examples which support this realization. The rose-colored glasses are now definitely off, replaced by lenses of less pleasing shades.

Once over threshold, it seems that there is little possibility of going back to the way things once were. Not only is the past and present view of your lover's behavior now *consistently* viewed as unsatisfactory, but the future is also perceived in the same way. When you now look at a past and present that unequivocally (in your perception, anyway) demonstrate the inherent shortcomings of your mate, the overwhelming tendency is to assume that the future will be no different. Some people even get to the point of perceiving their mate as an inherently bad or flawed person. At the very least, with no hope for change but full expectation of more of the same dissatisfaction, the future becomes bleak. Some accept the bleakness, and some separate and look for someone else who can fulfill their needs.

Going over threshold can be precipitated by the frequency or the magnitude of the examples of discrepant behavior. In the above example, Sam had come home and been disappointed many, many times by Jill's disheveled state. Finally, some *frequency threshold* for these experiences was reached and he went over threshold. Jill's beauty became, to him, an example of her shallowness and a ploy to ensnare him. What pushed Jill over threshold was not that Sam had failed to call (which he had done many times), but the enormous *magnitude* of disinterest he displayed by forgetting that it was her birthday. Suddenly, Jill knew that all Sam wanted—or had *ever* wanted—her for was as a sexual object. It needn't go this way, however:

> Frances was feeling uneasy quite a lot these days. For a year now, she had been trying to get Ian interested in starting a family, but every time she brought the subject up he would find cause to shrug it off, put her off, or simply, almost rudely, change the subject. Frances kept pondering his responses and trying new approaches, but the result was always the same. Finally, Frances started to worry that perhaps she had been wrong about Ian's love for children. She was afraid to ask directly, but realized that she had to. The answer was not what she had expected. Ian did not want children—he never had. He liked *other* people's children, but the thought of having his own filled him with fears of responsibilities that he simply wasn't willing to risk. Frances was disappointed, but she wasn't going to give up on her intention of having children. During the months that followed, she tried to change Ian's mind about kids, once even going so far as threatening to have someone else's child. At that threat, Ian had walked out and was gone all night. Their lovemaking became less pleasant, they started

avoiding meaningful conversations, and when they did talk they often ended up fighting over something trivial. One morning, Frances thought to herself, "Is this what we have to look forward to for the rest of our lives together?" And the answer, for her, was no. For Frances, having children was not the same as engaging in sports. She was not willing to give up having children and (for her) there was no way of getting that experience other than having her own. She realized that her differences with Ian were irreconcilable and that they needed to find other mates. She didn't want to hurt Ian—she loved him—but they would have to separate. Later, after they were divorced, they remained friends. Frances was unwilling to give up everything they had together, and she kept in touch with Ian, that wonderful man who didn't happen to want children.

Obviously, the difference between Frances's experience and that of Sam and Jill is that Frances did not go over threshold. In fact, she did not even go through stacking. Her usual response to Ian's reluctance or refusal to talk with her about children was taken by her as a situation in need of a perspective and approach that she had not yet tried. That is, her internal processes included varying the amount and kind of detail she was attending to, as well as an appreciation of past-to-present-to-future cause-effect. This provided a basis for generating new ways of responding. In this way she was oriented toward figuring out how to most appropriately approach Ian regarding starting a family. Eventually, however, her attempts were completely frustrated and she went for gathering more information from Ian. She discovered that she had misjudged the situation and that they were irreconcilably opposed on the question of children. They eventually separated over their differences, but on very different terms than did Sam and Jill. Frances was sad and disappointed, but she was not bitter. And, since she never stacked her experience into going over threshold, she left Ian with her fond memories and feelings for him intact. And, hopefully, she also left with a lesson learned about the importance of checking out explicitly, ahead of time, such important things as the bearing of children with her next prospective mate.

Fortunately, there is another alternative to going over threshold, one that involves using your sensory experience and flexibility of behavior to adjust your interactions with your mate in accordance with the needs of the relationship. The very essence of love and marital relationships is *accommodation*. Of course, as Frances found out, you may have certain wants, needs and expectations that cannot be accommodated to those of your mate, or by your mate to yours. But the fact is that the overwhelming majority of differences over which couples make each other miserable, fight and even separate are *not* irreconcilable. Rather, they are more often than not based upon misinformation and misconceptions about their respective wants and needs. For example:

It was important to Steve to have something new to look forward to. He hated going to the same old restaurants, taking the same old vacations, making love in the same old ways. His wife, Michele, valuing tradition, sought out the old haunts, decorated the Christmas tree just the same each year, and enjoyed making love the way they had always made love. When Steve suggested something new, Michele grew fearful of losing something of their past. And when Michele suggested something traditional, Steve felt disappointed and bored. Eventually they had fought over these responses in one another enough to find out what was going on. Once they knew, they cared enough about each other (and about the relationship) to accommodate to each other's needs. Steve began offering new restaurants or vacation spots to Michele as opportunities to start some *new traditions*. He also started admiring her ability to preserve traditions. For her part, Michele started willingly going along with some of Steve's new ideas, or at least acknowledged those ideas as being good ideas, even when she *also* felt that it was important to her to follow one of her traditions.

When Fred joined Sylvia in the kitchen that morning, all he got in return from her for his "Good morning!" was a sullen grunt and the cold shoulder. They had been married thirty-five years, but it was only in the last few months that he had been getting this kind of treatment from her. Fred decided to find out what it was all about. Sylvia answered angrily, "I didn't think you'd care—after all, you don't care enough about me to even say 'good night'!" It came out that Fred had recently fallen into the habit of simply going off to bed when he got tired in the evenings. Sylvia would go looking for him, wanting to share something with him or just be with him, and find him sawing logs in bed. She was hurt, she felt that he no longer cared about *them*. This was not the case, however, and Fred not only reassured her of that fact, but from then on he made sure to let Sylvia know when he was going to bed.

Laurie felt awful. Her head and shoulders ached, her sinuses throbbed, and her stomach wasn't doing too well either. When Greg got home he found her lying on the couch, trying not to move too much or too fast. He asked what was wrong, and Laurie replied, "I guess I'm coming down with another damn cold." Greg gave her a peck on the cheek and said, "Oh, I'm sorry to hear it. I'll be outside in the garden." When Greg came back in an hour later, Laurie was not only ill, but angry and in tears as well. She told him that she thought that he didn't care that she was ill because he never wanted to know anything about it, or take care of her—he just ignored it! In fact, ignoring her illness was *Greg's* way of showing that he *does* care, since when he is sick he prefers that he and his illness be left alone. He now realized that that was not *Laurie's* idea of caring and, since he does care, thereafter Greg was happy to give his love the attention and care that she wanted, needed, and deserved.

The point of these three examples is that instances of an unpleasant, disappointing or hurtful difference between you and your mate need not stack themselves to the point of threshold. The vast majority of such differences can be accommodated, provided you care enough about your own experience, your mate's experience, and the quality of your relationship to adjust your own behavior. If you have this commitment to the quality of your relationship, all that is needed in addition is an awareness of both your own responses and those of your mate, and the flexibility to adjust

your behavior when the quality of your responses or those of
your mate is other than what you would like it to be.

With Love in Mind

In this section we present the EMPRINT format for each of the
stages discussed in the previous section: attraction, appreciation, security-expectation, stacking, and threshold. You
will benefit from the insights and learnings provided by each
format whether what you want is to find the right mate, maintain a state of fulfillment and appreciation with your existing
mate, or bring love back into a failing relationship.

Attraction

In speaking about what it was like playing a woman in the
movie *Tootsie*, Dustin Hoffman described how rejected and
discarded it felt to be responded to as an unattractive woman.
Typically, men did not choose to pursue getting to know
Tootsie, and Hoffman felt that they were missing out on knowing a wonderful person. Hoffman's experience with crossing
the gender line exemplifies the problem that we described in
the previous section on attraction: being attracted on the basis
of external visual appearance, money, social standing, educational degrees, political power, or future possibilities for
romance. Selecting who you want to be with based on such
superficial criteria is devaluing and demeaning to others,
ensures that you will miss getting to know many fine people,
and is very likely to lead to disappointment sooner or later.

Whether your attraction strategy is based upon matching a
person's appearance with some set of external, visual standards (like Sam's), or is based upon imagining future possibilities with that person (like Jill's), in either case you are not
attending to and basing your judgements upon *who* that person *is*. What is needed is a strategy that is based upon more

elaborate *present-experiential standards* which are to be fulfilled *before* you reach the state of attraction.

Of course, to do that you need to know your criteria. In
sorting out your criteria you need to make a distinction between the short-term and long-term. Very often, people do not
realize that their short-term criteria can be significantly different from their long-term criteria. They then make the mistake of either testing for long-term criteria in the short-term
context of attraction (as did Jill), or testing for short-term
criteria in the long-term context of security (as did Sam).
Either way, disappointment is almost assured.

The most favorable situation in terms of finding satisfying
and lasting relationships is one in which you make sure that
your long-term criteria in some way *include or accommodate*
your short-term criteria. This will not happen if your long-
term and short-term criteria conflict. For instance, if you have
as short-term criteria *spontaneous, wild, reckless, challenging,
ornery,* and *indulgent,* and as long-term criteria *stability, security, companionship, gentleness, caring, concern,* and *sensitivity,* then your short-term criteria do not match your long-
term criteria. Anyone who satisfies your short-term criteria is
certain to disappoint you if and when your relationship enters
into the security and commitment phase. On the other hand,
you are likely to enjoy satisfying and lasting relationships if
your short-term and long-term criteria are a better match. For
instance, if you had as short-term criteria *fun, considerate,
intelligent, friendly, passionate* and *sensual,* and as long-term
criteria *family oriented, responsible emotionally, supportive,
nurturing,* and *responsive to other's needs and concerns,* then
the chances of the short leading to the fulfillment of the
long-term are much better. Moreover, your short-term criteria
are likely to continue to be satisfied when long-term criteria
become preeminent, as happens in a committed relationship.

We want to repeat that while long-term criteria are *not*
appropriate to test for when you are deciding who to be attracted to for casual dating, long-term criteria *are* appropriate to
test for when considering making a commitment. The significance of making the distinction between short-term and long-
term criteria, and of trying to adjust your criteria so that the
short-term lead to the long-term, is to help insure that when

you *do* make a commitment to a long-term relationship it will be able to continue to satisfy your wants and needs.

1 You should, then, make a list for yourself of your short-term and long-term criteria. Consider which of your short-term criteria naturally lead to, or are included by, your long-term criteria. Would you be content, once you were in a long-term relationship, with no longer having satisfied those short-term criteria that are incompatible with the long-term ones? If not, how can you adjust those short-term criteria so that they lead to, or are included in, your long-term criteria? Or, how can you adjust your long-term criteria to take into account the incompatible short-term ones? (Examples of accommodating long-term and short-term criteria were given at the end of the "Threshold" section.) To the extent that you can, make your short-term and long-term criteria compatible. Make your list and consider possible adjustments before going any further.

Criteria for Relationships

Short-Term   **Long-Term**

_____   _____

_____   _____

_____   _____

_____   _____

_____   _____

So now you have a list of short-term and long-term criteria that are important to you with respect to love relationships. In addition to knowing what those criteria are, however, you must have ways of knowing if and when the qualities that those criteria represent are present or absent in your prospective lovers and mates. Suppose that one of your criteria is *considerate responsiveness to others*. What behavior would be evidence that this quality was there? Perhaps as you and your date are passing an elderly lady who struggles upstairs with a bag of groceries, your date greets her and offers to help her with the bag in a way that says, "I know you can do it, but let me help your day go a little easier." Evidence of the *lack* of the quality of considerate responsiveness to others might be cutting in front of people in traffic or in waiting lines, or pushing past others to beat them into elevators. (Of course, these same behaviors could be taken as evidence of ability to survive if you are in New York City.) If you do volunteer work at the local SPCA and Audubon Society, a woman who wants a sealskin coat, thinks big game hunting is sexy and buys black market ivory is not evidencing behavior which is likely to represent the kind of criteria that you value.

2 Go through your list of criteria and consider what kinds of behaviors and responses would constitute evidence of those criteria being shared by another person, and what kinds of behaviors and responses would constitute evidence that your criteria are *not* shared by another person. This will give you the basis for informed responses to others, thus making your selection of mates and the fulfillment of your wants and needs much less haphazard. Give yourself this gift right now by identifying those behaviors and responses.

Another important consideration is that of past mistakes. Any mistakes that you have made in being attracted to and forming relationships with others should be used as information about what to do and not do in the future, rather than as examples of your stupidity, unworthiness, unattractiveness, and so on. If, for instance, the past mistake involved a mate who was a heavy drinker and his drinking spoiled your relationship, then it is probably wise not to fall for the champion tequila boilermaker drinker at the end of the bar, even if he *does* have soulful blue eyes.

3 Accordingly, at the end of this paragraph, take an inventory of your past mistakes in relationships and identify what specifically was the cause of those experiences being mistakes. You are looking for what it is that made those mistakes possible so that in the future you will know what to look for and what not to look for in a lover and a mate (as opposed to using those mistakes as evidence of your failings as a person). Take this inventory now; you are developing a useful set of guidelines for future success.

You now have an appropriate and promising basis from which to become attracted to others. You have made the distinction in your criteria between the short-term and long-term; have brought the short-term and long-term into accord with one another as much as possible; and have some idea of what behaviors are evidence of the qualities you are valuing in others.

In becoming attracted to others, the next step is to change your visual criteria from matching culturally-determined (usually media-determined) criteria of pretty, ugly, desirable, undesirable, and so on, to a *qualitative* judgment of the person's character. Appropriate here are questions such as these: How does this person look? Friendly? Caring? Intelligent? Hostile? Arrogant? Lonely? Bored? Does it feel good to look at them?

4 Take a moment when you reach the end of this paragraph to list seven or eight qualities or characteristics that you value in *anybody*. After making your list, identify someone of the desirable sex whom you were around recently (possibly at a social gathering) to whom you were not attracted, someone you could have met but declined to. Then identify someone recently to whom you were attracted but did not meet. Making as clear an internal image as you can of the first person, look at him or her and ask yourself the kinds of questions we described above, using your list of valued character traits as the content for those questions (e.g. "Does he look caring about others?").

Qualities Valued in Others

_____

_____

_____

_____

_____

_____

_____

5 After going through your list, ask yourself, "What kind of person does he or she look like beyond those traits that I value?" When you identify two or three of those, consider whether they are character traits that you also might value or at least find interesting, or are traits that you specifically do not appreciate. Do this now.

6 Next, consider how you feel as you look at that person. Do you feel good, bad, sad, curious, bored, careful, hopeful? Having done that, switch to the image of the person to whom you were attracted but did not meet, and take him or her through the same sequence of evaluation with respect to your list of valued character traits, the traits that are there that you have not considered, and how you feel looking at that person. Make these evaluations before proceeding to the next step.

7 The next quality to consider is the sound of that person's voice. Voice tones—shrill, resonant, nasal, soft, loud, flat, breathy—very much influence people's emotional states but, unfortunately, discriminations of voice tonality are usually out of consciousness for most people in our culture. Taking voice tonality for granted, you can spend a lifetime around someone who generates an unpleasant emotional state in you without your connecting that emotional state to the tonality of that person's voice. So, the next question to ask is, "How does that person's voice sound to you?" This will, of course, require much closer proximity (perhaps even engaging that person in conversation). Going back to the two people you had selected above (the unattractive person and the attractive person you did not meet), recall now the sound of each of their voices and attend to how your emotional state changes as you listen to their tonalities.

8 Now reconsider how you feel when you are with this person. Is your experience enriched? Are you happy to see this person? Do you feel valued and appreciated when with this person? Do you feel comfortable with this person? Sensually stimulated? Intellectually stimulated? If you now take a moment to search through your acquaintances for a person to whom you are not visually attracted but with whom you feel valued, and a person to whom you are visually attracted but with whom you do *not* feel valued, you will recognize immediately that an attraction strategy that is based upon matching external, visual criteria in no way guarantees that the person will be a satisfying and gratifying partner. Try this now.

If you review the steps that we have just taken you through you will notice that they all orient you toward your *present experience*. You will also notice that they require you to establish criteria that can be satisfied in each of the three primary sensory systems: visual, kinesthetic (feelings) and auditory. As we described previously, attraction is most appropriately done in the present and with a present evaluation, since it is only in that way that you give yourself the opportunity to discover what *is* there to appreciate, respond to, and possibly love. Such a present-oriented strategy (which includes a broad range of criteria and flexibility in ways to satisfy those criteria) produces behaviors and responses of getting to *know* people, of being curious and interested in them, before being attracted. In this way, a relationship between you and this other person is actually formed before the state of attraction can even be present.

Appreciation

As we noted before, the appreciation phase is that wonderful, rose-colored-glasses phase. If you have passed through the attraction phase you are almost certain to enter into the world of appreciation. Now your new lover shines in your eyes. Some people during this stage, however, will be appreciating the other person more for what they *could be*, rather than who they *are*. Though usually not a problem then, this does become a problem and the source of much disappointment later on when the relationship turns toward commitment, longer-term ongoing fulfillment and security. It is only then (and subsequently) that a person discovers that the things they had assumed would be there are not and probably never were. However, if your attraction was based upon, and grew out of, the kind of present reference and present testing described in the previous section on attraction, you will obviously be appreciating what *is*, rather than what *could be*.

1 Begin making present tests by taking an inventory of your mate's behaviors that are worth appreciating. Identify at least five things that he or she does on a regular basis that you really appreciate. They could be that your mate tells you the truth, keeps commitments, keeps the car's gas tank more than half full, lets you crawl into bed at night while he or she locks up and turns out the lights, throws his or her dirty clothes in the hamper, remembers to buy you a present on your birthday, picks up the dry cleaning, or treats your parents well. They can vary in importance, but they all should be behaviors that warrant appreciation. Use the following space to list five things your mate does that you appreciate.

What My Mate Does That I Appreciate

_____

_____

_____

_____

_____

2 Next, list five things your mate does *not* do for which you are appreciative. For instance, perhaps your mate does not lie, does not yell, does not squander money, does not drink to excess, and is not rude to your friends.

What My Mate Does *Not* Do That I Appreciate

_____

_____

_____

_____

_____

3 Now that you have thought about your mate's behavior, consider your mate's positive *qualities*. By qualities we mean traits or attributes such as being curious, ambitious, responsible, honest, loving, sexy, and so on. Pick five of your mate's qualities that you value, and then think about recent incidents that are exemplary of your mate demonstrating those qualities. Once you have identified five of your mate's qualities that you appreciate, and have recalled recent incidents that are demonstrations of those qualities, list the qualities in the following space.

My Mate's Qualities That I Appreciate

_____

_____

_____

_____

_____

This inventory of behaviors and qualities assures that your appreciation is justified, and not just a byproduct of rose-colored lenses. Going through this process also *enriches* your appreciation for your mate. Knowing that, anytime you want to *be* appreciated you might want to persuade your mate to make this same inventory of your behaviors and qualities.

In addition to the significance of placing your attention on the present and making your evaluations about present con- well means appreciating in a way that he or she can *perceive*. By letting your mate know what you appreciate about him or her you make it possible for him or her to know what to do in the future to be appreciated by you. Similarly, by discovering the behaviors that let your mate know he or she is appreciated, you know what to do in the future to give him or her that experience.

4 All you have to do to gather this information from your mate is ask. Questions like, "How do you know when I appreciate you?" and "What do I say or do that lets you know I appreciate you?" and "What is proof to you that you are appreciated by me?" will elicit the information about how your mate wants and needs to be appreciated. You will then know what you need to do in order to fulfill your mate's criterial equivalence for being appreciated. Go through this information gathering process for several different important criteria. It is important that you know about, and be able to match, how your mate knows they are loved, trusted, respected, and so on. After you have gathered this information, you need to let your mate know how *you* need and want to be appreciated, loved, trusted, respected, and so on. In this way you will give them the opportunity to appreciate you (and love you, trust you, respect you, etc.) in ways that are meaningful to you.

The magical experience of mutual appreciation needn't be only a phase, eventually fading from lack of information and neglect. Being appreciated by those we care about is an experience we all value and are likely to seek out, provided we know what to do to earn that appreciation.

Security-Expectation

The security phase is the time during which you start considering the possibility of making a formal or informal commitment with your lover to make the relationship in some way permanent. The pitfalls most commonly associated with this stage have to do with either a person's fear of making a commitment, or deciding to make a commitment based upon inappropriate, unrealistic evaluations. The security phase is also the time that expectations begin to develop, setting you up for the pain of disappointment.

The following EMPRINT format first addresses typical underlying causes of fears and concerns with regard to making a commitment to a long-term relationship. It then provides you with useful know-how for making lasting and satisfying commitments, as well as strategies for knowing how to get what you want from your mate in ways that are enriching to both of you.

The pattern which underlies a fear of committing to a relationship is usually similar to that involved in abusing the past. That is, on the basis of past unpleasant experiences you form criterial equivalences about relationships, commitments, marriage and yourself that are of the following kind, and which you express in the following ways: Relationships are really only for the satisfaction of one's own needs; commitments mean the subordination of oneself; marriage is just another opportunity to be hurt; I am not a lovable or dependable person.

1 In changing such criterial equivalences, the first thing to do is to identify *counterexamples*. That is, search through your personal history (or even the world itself) for examples which are inconsistent with your unwanted criterial equivalence. The importance of finding and recognizing the counterexamples is that it turns the default response of a criterial equivalence ("that's the way it is") into something about which there is at least the possibility of a choice response. For example, if you believe that commitments mean the subordination of oneself, search through your memories and find at least one example of a time when your character and needs were allowed complete expression and satisfaction within a committed relationship. If you are unable to find even one counterexample in your own experiences, you can search through the experiences of friends and acquaintances for such examples so that you can know that at least it is *possible* to be in a committed relationship without sacrificing one's self. If you have a fear of committing to a relationship, spend a minute or two right now to identify your undesirable criterial equivalences. Once identified, find counterexamples to each one.

2 Having stepped away from the default response of the criterial equivalence, you are now in a position to consider what made those failures from your personal history the mistakes that they were. Ask yourself, "How is this example of a positive experience [the counterexample] *different* than the bad experience I had?" Answering this question will assist you in ferreting out just what were the causes of that bad experience. Once known, you can then use that information to set criteria and standards of behavior for the future which will insure that you do not repeat the same mistake. The questions then become, "How am I different now?" and "What am I doing or *what will I do* so that the remembered unpleasant outcome won't happen again?" Answer these questions before going on.

3 The other common problem at this stage is making commitments based upon inappropriate evaluations. Relationship commitments are about going through a certain amount of time into the future together, so it is at this point that your long-term criteria become significant. It is now appropriate to apply your long-term criteria (as well as your short-term criteria) to the experiences that you have accumulated with your lover in order to determine whether or not it is likely that you will be able to satisfy those criteria with this particular person. In other words, you need to realistically determine what is there and what is not, and what is likely to be there and what is not likely to be there. Before proceeding to the next step, take the time to make this realistic evaluation.

4 In making your evaluation you probably discovered that there are both matches and mismatches between what is important to you and what is important to your lover. People are far too diverse for it to be otherwise. Too often people attend only to the matches and ignore the mismatches, but the mismatches will almost always catch up with them eventually. With any mismatches, then, it is important that they be addressed in at least one of the three ways listed at the end of this paragraph. Moreover, if you are currently considering making a commitment to a relationship, or if you are presently in a relationship, it would be useful first to identify for yourself one or more discrepancies and then apply the following ways of addressing such mismatches:

■ Suppose that the discrepancy could *never* be resolved, that is, that you could never get a particular desire or need met in your relationship. Would you still be content and fulfilled? (As in Frances's situation, the relationship is still fulfilling even though it will not be possible to share athletics with her mate.)

■ Can you adjust your desire/need so that it is in accord with what is and would be available in the relationship, and at the same time *satisfactorily fulfills at least some of your original intent?* (The desire to have children can become the desire to care for others.)

■ Are there ways to fulfill your desire/need outside of the relationship without jeopardizing the integrity of relationship?

(Frances engages in sports with people outside of her relationship with Ian.)

Any discrepancy that cannot be resolved in at least one of these three ways will stand as an irreconcilable difference. That desire/need will not be met in any way within the relationship, nor will it be met satisfactorily outside of the relationship.

The fact that there is an irreconcilable difference between two people does not necessarily mean that the relationship is doomed. That depends upon the relative importance of the matter about which the couple disagree. Recalling Frances and Ian, the discrepancy that she faced was not resolvable for her in any of the ways we have listed: (1) she would not be happy without a child, (2) caring for Ian in the same way that she would care for a child was not acceptable, and (3) working in a day-care center was not acceptable. The fact that having a child was of tremendous relative importance to Frances made it a situation that she simply could not shrug off and ignore. Had their differences centered around something that was (for Frances) considerably more trivial, such as Ian's insistence on elaborate security systems for the house, the fact that Frances hated those systems and could find no way to reconcile that hate, is not likely to bring about the end of the relationship. It may bring tension, it may bring humor, but it is something that Frances can accept as beyond her influence and worth enduring for the pleasures of being with Ian.

It is also important to consider the flexibility of your criterial equivalences when making a commitment. It is especially significant to consider after a commitment has been made and you are living together in the security phase. For Jill, the way that she knew that Sam cared was that he called her during the day to see how she was doing. Accordingly, when he didn't call, she felt uncared for. Having only one way of satisfying a criterion means that you will be able to experience fulfillment with respect to that criterion *only* if the necessary circumstantial requirements are met. The world is complex and capricious enough to guarantee, however, that there will be times when those circumstantial requirements will *not* be met. What then?

It is far more useful (as well as gratifying) to have many ways of satisfying your criteria. Obviously, the more ways there are for you to feel loved, the more often you will get to have that experience. For example, if you are a woman you could feel loved when he calls if he's going to be late; when he locks the house up and turns the lights off at night; when he asks what movie you would like to see; when he makes fine love to you; when he says no if he really doesn't want to make love; when he turns down business opportunities that would take him away from you for long stretches; when he doesn't flirt with other women; when he challenges you if you need it; when he tells you the truth even if it is not what you want to hear. All of these (and much more) could serve as indicators that you are loved. (It is particularly helpful if they are all behaviors your mate can't not do—that is, if they are behaviors which naturally occur as byproducts of his or her own personality.)

In this regard it is important to note and realize that it is very likely that your lover is letting you know that he or she loves (respects, cares for, enjoys, appreciates) you in many ways that *you* do not recognize as examples of that love. Asking you what you want to see at the movies may be just common courtesy to you, but to your lover it may be an expression of love for you.

5 At the end of this paragraph, identify some experience (like having fun, or feeling believed in or trusted) you very much like to have within your current intimate relationship, but that you don't have *as often as you would like.* Then sort through your interactions with the other person and try to identify ways in which that person is actually trying to give you that experience, ways that you have, until now, not recognized. Once you have identified those ways you can, if you wish, ask that person directly what their intention is in doing whatever it is that they do in that situation. (Several good examples of this were given at the end of the "Threshold" section.) Complete this step before moving to the next.

6 Having done that, consider the criteria (standards, matters of importance) that you want to be sure are satisfied within your relationship. Pick three or four of these criteria and, for each of them, think of at least four ways (other than those you are accustomed to) that would serve as examples to you of this person fulfilling your criteria. Do your very best to make your choices with regard for your partner's *existing* behaviors. Remember, the more ways that your criteria can be fulfilled, the better your ongoing experience, and the richer and more secure your relationship will be. Before you go on, make this important evaluation.

What Is Important To Me   **How I Can Know I Am Receiving It**

_____	_____
	_____
	_____
	_____
_____	_____
	_____
	_____
	_____
_____	_____
	_____
	_____
	_____
_____	_____
	_____
	_____

One of the potential dangers of the security phase is the tendency to become habituated to those things that you used to appreciate about one another. In coming simply to expect those once special behaviors and responses, they are taken for granted. As we described, this is often the beginning of the end for the relationship. Once taken for granted, what becomes noticeable is the *absence* of the behavior or response, rather than their presence. This leads to the stacking of examples of when you don't get what you expected and wanted, and, if that stack reaches critical proportions, to threshold. Both in terms of preserving your relationship and maintaining that special quality of appreciation, it is important to avoid being lulled into expectation and habituation.

Probably the best way to avoid expectation and habituation in your relationship is to be aware of the cause-effect connections which make possible your and your lover's moods, behaviors and the satisfaction of your and your lover's criteria. For example, suppose you appreciate and value the fact that your husband helps out with the housework. You might determine that the cause of his helping is his experience of doing something *together* with you. As soon as you recognize this cause-effect relationship, two things happen. The first is that his helping becomes much less possible to expect and, so, ultimately less possible to take for granted. His helping with housework, as you now recognize it, is not an inherent response of his, but one that is caused by certain conditions, namely, the perception that it is a joint endeavor.

The second thing that happens as a result of recognizing the cause-effect relationship is a shift from stacking to what might be termed interaction. Instead of the passive noticing when things are there or (more commonly) are not there that characterizes stacking, you become an *active* member of an interaction, determining how to bring into experience those moods or behaviors that you and your partner want and value. For instance, if you are not considering cause-effect, and you ask your husband to take down the drapes to be washed and *he balks*, the common response is to notice that he doesn't seem to want to help with the housework the way he used to; and the incident gets stacked upon previous, similar examples that you are storing up. Perceived as cause-effect, however, your response becomes one of wondering what about your request and this particular situation led to his demurring, rather than eagerly jumping in. If you know that the sense of teamwork makes the difference in his response, you can then approach the situation accordingly. You could suggest taking the drapes down together, ask him to take down the drapes as part of a general house cleaning that you are also involved in, or indicate it would help you get to other things that *both* of you recognize need to be done.

7 Now it is time to apply what you have learned about cause-effect to your situation. Identify several areas within your present relationship that are sources of disappointment to you in that they are examples of behaviors and responses that were once characteristic of your partner and that you appreciated, but which your partner no longer seems to be willing or able to do. For example, when you were courting, your lover may have been prompt, or generous, or helpful, or concerned, but now, months or years later, he or she no longer evidences those qualities and responses, and you miss them. You will use this information in the next step, so identify these sources of disappointment before proceeding.

8 Next, for the response you want to have, determine what caused it when it was there, and what caused it not to be there when it wasn't. If you have difficulty in finding the cause-effect relationship, try the following: Take the first one of those situations, recall an example of when your partner *did* have the response you cherish, and an example of when your partner *did not* have that response. Comparing the two incidents, ask yourself the question, "What is the same and what is *different* about these two examples?" In order to check out and refine the cause-effect relationship you have discovered, check the differences you find against a couple of other examples of the response being there and not being there. You can then use this information to create an atmosphere which is appropriate for the natural elicitation of the kinds of interactions that you and your mate want and appreciate (as in the drapery example). Taking one of your examples, discover the causes involved and then create ideas for how to interact in the future to elicit the responses you appreciate.

There is one additional and important (though often overlooked) way of finding the cause-effect relationship underlying the kinds of interaction you cherish: Ask. If a relationship has not yet gone over threshold, it is usually the case that all those concerned have the best intentions for each other.

These good intentions are not always fulfilled in behavior, however, and when they are not, most people will be glad for the opportunity to correct the situation. Therefore, simply tell your partner that you have always appreciated a particular response of theirs or a certain kind of interaction that you have with each other, and then ask them what used to make that response or interaction something that they wanted to do. This will often directly get you the information you need to help make those responses and interactions a part of your ongoing experiences.

By being aware of the cause-effect relationship between circumstances (which very much includes your behavior) and the quality of the interactions you have with your mate and lover, you will never take it for granted that those interactions will just be there. And, when they are not there, you will have a way of reestablishing those interactions by becoming involved in creating and recreating the kind of environment within which those interactions can flourish. And there is one additional consequence of this perspective and approach to nurturing and maintaining relationships—you will never get into the stacking of disappointments that eventually leads to threshold.

Threshold

When your disappointments with another person stack up beyond a certain critical level, or when you are plunged into a disappointment that is sufficiently appalling, you go over threshold. As we have already described, going over threshold leads to the formulation of a new belief about the inherent unsuitability of the other person, and a resorting of the past and future in relation to that new belief. Although going over threshold may have a useful outcome, such as getting a woman to leave her wife-beating husband, in general, going over threshold is not useful. All it does is cast another person in a villainous light, *usually ignoring the cause-effect relationships* which made the rounds of mutual miscommunications and disappointments possible in the first place. Without that information, there is little to insure that you won't repeat the same mistakes in your next relationship.

It is not difficult to persuade someone to go through the motions of giving their relationship another chance, but it is something else entirely to intervene such that they can see their partner through unprejudiced eyes. LCB and ML have developed two procedures that address the phenomenon of going over threshold. The *threshold neutralizer* is appropriate if your present response to your mate (or whoever you are over threshold with) is one of overwhelming disappointment, anger, hate, dissatisfaction, and so on. The intention of the threshold neutralizer is to make it possible for you to remain separated in a healthy way (if you are already separated), or to make it possible for you to *begin* to realistically reevaluate your relationship, if that is what you want to do. A thorough reevaluation is the purpose of the *relationship evaluator*, the outcome of which is either to motivate you to fully reengage in making your relationship work (though on a more appropriate footing), or to assure you that your decision to separate is appropriate. The balance of this section is devoted to a presentation of the steps for both procedures. For a more detailed presentation of these procedures, together with examples of them being used with clients, read Leslie Cameron-Bandler's book, *Solutions: Practical and Effective Antidotes for Sexual and Relationship Problems.*[5]

When you are over threshold you are associated into the past painful memories concerning your partner, and dissociated from the past pleasures. You can remember both, but the painful ones are much more real and compelling. In addition, your pain and dissatisfaction is attached to, and associated with, your partner. The purpose of the threshold neutralizer is twofold: first, to separate the pain and dissatisfaction from the partner (without dismissing that it has occurred); and second, to regain access to pleasant memories. The steps for using the threshold neutralizer are as follows (take your time with each step, proceeding to the next one only after you have completed the one you are on):

1 Establish a baseline for your experience by imagining unexpectedly meeting the person with whom you are over threshold. Pay close attention to your response since you will use this same imagined meeting as a test later. The degree to

which there will be a more positive response will be the degree of success.

2 Think about the qualities and characteristics, large and small, that make *you* uniquely yourself. Look at yourself through the eyes of someone you know loves you (whether or not you love them is not important right now), and enjoy the positive attributes that can be appreciated in a fresh and new way through the eyes and perception of someone who loves you. Use this fresh perspective on your wonderful qualities to help you get in touch with strong feelings of self-appreciation. *Hold on to those feelings throughout the entire process that follows.* (Being able to feel good about yourself while seeing the other person separates the bad feelings from being attached to all aspects of the other person, as well as giving yourself more of the experience of choice concerning your responses when around that person.)

3 Picture the other person in a still shot (that is, as if in a photograph) as he or she looked when you first met. While you are looking at that picture, be sure to maintain your feelings of self-appreciation. When you can look at the remembered image of that person *and* maintain your feelings of self-worth, view that person as being separate from you, an individual in his or her own right, who lived a life that did not include you up until that point in time. Recognize that he or she is a complete person, separate and distinct from you, with his or her own unique set of qualities and characteristics. Picture him or her in the future, living in a different place, with friends and loved ones that are strangers to you. Then, recall the qualities or attributes that drew you to him or her in the first place.

4 Having done that, recall a past pleasant memory you share with that person. Recover this memory in as full a representation as you can, seeing what you saw, hearing what you heard, smelling what you smelled, and feeling what you felt at that time, *recognizing as you do, that this is your memory, and that nothing should be allowed to take it away.*

5 Come back to the present, bringing your feelings of self-appreciation with you.

6 Again imagine a chance encounter with the other person. (If you are still living with that person, make it a surprise meeting, so that your response is in a situation other than your usual meeting times. You could imagine one of you coming home early, running into each other at the store, or any other unexpected, nonritualized encounter.) How is your response this time different than the first time you imagined running into him or her (in step 1)? Are you still appalled, or delighted, or somewhere in between? (If you are still appalled, then go back to step 2 and go through the process once again, this time making sure to maintain the state of self-appreciation, and increasing your sense of separation between yourself and the other person (step 3).

The *relationship evaluator* is a process that assists one or both members of a couple in identifying and evaluating their criteria and behavior in connection with relationships. This process includes an evaluation of whether or not each can get his or her wants and needs fulfilled by the other. Depending on the outcome of the evaluation, you and your mate will either come to the conclusion that you are no longer appropriate for each other (allowing you to be assured that a decision to separate is an appropriate one), or you will both be motivated to positively reengage in satisfying, and receiving satisfaction from, each other.

This is a long and varied sequence of experiences designed to assist you in evaluating needs and wants, and in establishing specific guidelines concerning how to reach and maintain fulfillment in personal relationships. You will recognize that it is lengthy and brings much material up for further exploration at each step. Accordingly, it is appropriate for you to spread the process out over a period of several days, allowing yourself the opportunity to explore you and your relationship thoroughly.

The relationship evaluator is presented as a sequence of questions/directions, and can be done together by you and your mate. (If you do not do it together, you should first gather information from your mate regarding the first three questions in the sequence.) Be thorough in answering those questions and in following those directions; each is important in assisting you and your mate in usefully evaluating your wants, needs, and expectations with regard to relationships in general, and to your present relationship in particular. Following the first six questions are sample responses to assist you in orienting to each question.

1 What do you really want from a relationship now? That is, what do you want now, not necessarily from your existing relationship, but from an ideal relationship? (e.g. Companionship, a partner and a friend, someone I can trust to stand by me, not someone I always have to entertain or please, but someone who will "go for it" with me.)

2 How does this differ from what you wanted in your past? Go back to several years ago and, looking through younger eyes, see what it was you wanted then. What attracted you, what filled the needs that you had back then? (e.g. Then I really wanted to be taken care of—I didn't believe in myself enough to think it could be otherwise. Also, I wanted to be entertained, stimulated.)

3 Moving from the past to the present and now into your future, go forward in time to discover what you will be wanting and needing in the future that differs even from now. (e.g. Well, it's more difficult to know for sure, but it feels a lot like what I want now, only deeper. I'm more aware of wanting affection. I want to be sure that there would be lots of affection. Funny, it seems even more important then—in my future—than now.)

4 Which of your wants and needs has your mate satisfied in the past and the present (e.g. He was entertaining and he tried to take care of me.)

5 What does your mate do now that would satisfy you in the future? (e.g. I'm not sure. Maybe, well certainly he loves the children.)

6 What has your mate given you in the past that you didn't even know to ask for? (e.g. He challenged me; made me believe in myself more. I guess when he left me alone a lot I also had to learn more about myself, about how to take care of myself.)

7 Do a thorough evaluation of how being with your mate has made you more than you would have been without him or her.

Regardless of whether all of your experiences felt good or comfortable, how have you been compelled to be more of who you want to be (or appreciate being) because of the experiences you have had together? How will you be more of who you want to be in your future as a result of your past together, regardless of whether you stay together now?

8 Now that you have made one brief journey into the future, generate several different possible future scenarios in the following way: Using examples of your mate's *existing* qualities and behaviors—not his or her past or future possibilities—evaluate whether he or she can give you what you want. Generate one possible scenario in the future, checking for what you *are* getting for yourself from him or her. Compare this to a future scenario based on your spouse's *possible future qualities and behaviors*. Are you getting more from the future that is based on your mate's existing qualities and behaviors, or the ones you project as future possibilities?

9 Describe some of the behaviors that your mate does to which you strongly object. Going through them one at a time, determine what would have to be going on inside of *you* so that you would generate the same behavior. (So, if you really hate his walking out of the room while you are arguing, imagine *yourself* doing just that, walking out in the middle of an argument. What's going on with you that you would be compelled to do that? Is it the intensity of how angry, frustrated, or threatened you feel? What are the possibilities of what lies behind that objectionable behavior which make it understandable—not necessarily likeable or even acceptable—but at least understandable?)

10 While reviewing each of several situations where your mate has expressed such behavior, attend to the possibilities which compel him or her to be expressive in that way, and imagine how it would have been different if you had responded or behaved differently. Try a few different forms of behavior for yourself in each of those past situations and recognize how it could have been different if you had responded to how your mate was feeling on the inside, instead of what he or she was doing.

11 Looking at those examples of objectionable behavior from still another perspective, determine how each is a manifestation of an attribute that you enjoy or benefit from in some other situation. For instance, with one couple he was incensed when she was late, which was often. However, once he recognized that her being late was a byproduct of how fully she attended to the needs of whoever she was with, he could recall how often she had postponed, cancelled, or been late for appointments with others in order to attend to *him*. Explore how these instances of your mate's objectionable behavior could be byproducts of some appreciated and valued attribute.

12 As you consider your own qualities that you most value, and the ways in which you manifest those qualities through your behavior, go back to some awful past interaction involving your mate. Pay attention to yourself and to what your mate's feelings were behind his or her behavior. Identify how you also were not being all of who you want to or could be. See yourself there in that situation. Choose one of your highly valued attributes that would be useful in that situation and see yourself generate different forms of behavior that are reflective of those attributes. Notice how the entire interaction is transformed by your living out your own attributes. Repeat this process with at least two other awful past interactions.

13 Now, having accumulated several examples of new, more useful behavior to influence your interactions, take them into one of those possible futures you created in step 8 and play them out. How differently do events transpire? How much more of what you want do you get?

14 Knowing that you could have made the past different, and that you can make the present and future different, do you want to? Are you willing to make the necessary changes to make those interactions come out differently? Is it worth it to you?

15 *If the answer is yes*, then see yourself behaving in those new ways and influencing the course of events of your relationship. As you do, feel how it feels knowing you have made a crucial difference in bringing your relationship from bad to better, perhaps even to good or wonderful. Then, see your mate, recognizing his or her positive attributes that are worth appreciating, and feel that appreciation. When is the next opportunity for you to test your different forms of behavior to discover how much you can influence the direction of your relationship?

If the answer is no, then ask yourself what you have to lose—what of your wants and needs may go unsatisfied—if you are without that person in your life. What might you miss that you are getting now? How will you fulfill those needs without that person?

The relationship evaluator resolves problems in two ways when either you or your mate have gone over threshold. One possibility is that the process of thoroughly evaluating your criteria concerning primary relationships will bring you both to the conclusion that you are not appropriate for one another (that is, there is no possibility of satisfying each other's wants and needs any longer because you and/or your mate are unable or unwilling to meet those wants and needs). In this case, both of you end up with objective understandings that are the basis for appreciating what of value you have received from one another, as well as the basis for assuredness in your decision to separate, and confidence in moving into the future.

The second possibility is that the process will serve to reengage your flexibility of behavior and your attention to the emotional states of your mate. In addition, all this now occurs in light of a more explicit understanding of what each of you wants and needs, both now and for the future. In this case, each of you takes responsibility for making your life together all that it can be, by actively manifesting your own best attributes, while equally actively recognizing and responding to the other's valued qualities. Thus, a mutual knowledge of and concern for fulfilling each other's wants and needs becomes a meaningful commitment to yourselves and to your futures.

Deciding whether or not to continue a relationship is an important consideration. By including the above steps in such an evaluation, you will be insuring that you consider the criteria and criterial equivalences that are inherently appropriate for making this kind of decision.

Whatever you decide, your decision will be in the form of an opinion, judgement, goal, outcome, desire, etc. You can now take this new wish or want through the format for going from wishing to having that is presented in the section "Making It Come True For You" in Chapter 4. By doing so, you will be able to assess, from another perspective, whether or not this new goal or desire is really worth pursuing. If it is, you will develop the plans, perceptions, and flexibility of behavior that will allow you to move confidently into the future, knowing that you have the know-how for converting that future possibility into a present reality.

10 Parenting

There is probably no more important job, nor greater privilege, than to be a parent. And all you have to do to qualify is have a child. Suddenly, placed within your hands and arms is the awesome responsibility of raising a human being. The manner in which you fulfill that responsibility over the next eighteen years will determine to some extent (and, perhaps, to a very great extent) the character, cognitive and perceptual skills, and values that your child will enjoy (or not) throughout his or her life. And, of course, as our children grow, so grows our society and our culture. Despite the importance of the evolving relationship between parent and child during childhood, few people are taught how to create the kinds of nurturing and mutually enjoyable relationships that they would like to have with their children. We now turn to a few of the ways in which such relationships can be fostered, making this, perhaps, the most important chapter of this book.

Growing with Your Child

Certainly one of the most distinctive characteristics of childhood is *change*. Children grow larger, their proportions change, facial and body characteristics change, their abilities to comprehend and reason develop, their command of the language and of countless skills increases, and on and on. For some people, this development comes to a halt somewhere in their twenties, but at least up until that time that person is changing daily. As a child moves from infancy to being a toddler, to being a mobile youngster, to puberty, to adolescence, and then to young adulthood, his or her wants, needs, and abilities also continue to evolve. Though the fact of these changes is known by everyone as a piece of information, there are still many of us who neglect to respond accordingly. Growing with your child means adjusting your own expectations of, and interactions with, your child in accordance with *his or her* still-evolving world rather than according to other inappropriate standards.

> Douglas's tenth birthday was coming up. He looked forward to it with a confusing mixture of hope and hopelessness. For the fifth year in a row he was going to ask his mother, Tess, for a bicycle. That evening he found her sitting on the sofa in the living room, reading. Douglas sat down on the chair opposite her. "Mom?" She looked up from her book, smiled warmly, and held out her arms to him. "Come here, baby. I've hardly seen you all day." Douglas shuffled over and sank down beside her. Tess enfolded him with an affectionate hug. "Mom, you know what I want for my birthday?" "What?" she asked. "A bicycle." She tugged him back close to her. "Oh honey, but they're so dangerous. I can't have my baby out in the streets." Douglas expected this, but his heart grew leaden and sank anyway. "But mom, I'll be careful." "Careful? Why you're practically a *baby*!" The next day, after his mother had dropped him off at school and had driven out of sight, Douglas, shamefaced, once again borrowed his friend's bicycle to ride around the school for awhile.

Whether or not it is safe for Douglas to ride a bicycle, at ten years old he is certainly *not* "practically a *baby*." What *is* still true is that Tess persists in responding to him as he once was (as a baby, fairly helpless, vulnerable and incompetent), rather than as he *is* (a ten-year-old, keen eyed and eared, in enviable command of his body and senses, and utterly intent upon finding out what that body and those senses can do). In this case, Tess is not attending to the present experience of her son as a ten-year-old, but is using her memories of him as a toddler as a basis upon which to evaluate his having a bicycle. In addition, she is using criteria, and evidence of what fulfills that criteria, that belong to Douglas's toddler years instead of today's reality.

Responding out of memories and criteria from the past (with their out-of-date associations), Tess continues to not observe the facts of his present stage of development, competency and needs. This is demeaning to Douglas, robbing him of the recognition of his developing competencies. It is also possibly injurious to his further development, since as a baby he is denied opportunities to have experiences necessary or useful in his evolution as a full-fledged human being.[1] Her criterion of safety is one that any responsible parent would hold dear no matter what age his or her child was. But what constitutes safety (that is, the criterial equivalence for safety) necessarily changes as the child changes. For an infant, safety with respect to knives means not handling them in any way. But later on, this criterial equivalence must be amended to include using knives in a safe way. Like it or not—recognize it or not—your child will inevitably handle knives. In the interests of safety, therefore, it is best if the child has learned to handle them properly when that time comes. This is not, however, the only way that such inappropriate responding can be generated.

Harold took great pleasure in opera, a refinement that he wanted his seven-year-old son, Joseph, to share. Harold poked his head into Joseph's room and said, "Joseph, get your shoes and coat on. We're going to see *The Magic Flute*!" Lost in the strange form emerging from his pile of Legos, Joseph did not register his father's presence and continued clicking the little plastic pieces into place. Irritated, Harold's tone grew stern, "Joseph!" The boy looked up at his father. "You know better than to ignore someone speaking to you. Now get your shoes and coat on." The Legos would have to wait.

At the opera house, the seat kept folding up and trying to swallow Joseph. He couldn't see without getting on his knees, then his legs would cramp. Whenever he tried to straighten them out, his dad would hiss at him, "Be still and enjoy the performance!" Joseph tried. The sets were pretty, but it was hard to figure out what was going on since the people up there weren't talking English. He wanted to go to the bathroom, but Dad said, "Wait." He was hungry, Dad said, "Hush!" He was thirsty, and Dad threatened Joseph in a raspy whisper, "If you don't settle down, we're leaving!" Joseph thought about that for a moment, then asked if he could run down the aisles.

Just as a seven-year-old is no longer an infant, neither is he or she an adult. Accordingly, it is inappropriate to respond to a child as though he or she has the sophistication, biology and values of an adult. It is wonderful that Harold wants to expose his son to the beauty and passions of the opera, but it is disrespectful of Harold to do it in a way which ignores *Joseph's* ability to appreciate beauty and passion, as well as the needs and predilections that he has as a seven-year-old boy. This does not mean that Harold should not have taken his son to the opera. What it *does* mean is that Harold should expect Joseph to act like a seven-year-old boy, which does not usually include sitting quietly for three hours, being interested in an art form that he does not understand, going long stretches without food, drink and pit stops, and so on. Instead of responding to Joseph as he is, Harold responds to him as he will be someday (that is, an adult).

There is nothing inherently wrong with Harold's criteria. Harold's mistake is in applying them according to criterial equivalences that are appropriate for adults, rather than for seven-year-old children. For seven-year-olds, attentiveness is expressed in much shorter intervals than it is for adults. For a seven-year-old to sit attentively for half an hour without the relief of some distraction is a major accomplishment. (Similarly, we know of a mother who, when her six-year-old daughter asked for a dress that she had fallen in love with, told the little girl that she would buy it for her, but that she first had to be good for the whole year!) You can certainly expect a seven-year-old to find the opera set pretty and the music nice, but it is unreasonable to expect him to care about the plot unfolding onstage, find the Queen of the Night's aria particularly stirring and well done, and so on. In short, while Tess is not responding to Douglas in the present but to what Douglas had been, Harold is not responding to Joseph, but to what Joseph *will be* (at least in Harold's mind). In their interactions with their children, both Tess and Harold lack accurate feedback in the present regarding their children, as well as criteria that are current, practical and fair.

Another way to express Tess's and Harold's misalignment with their children is to say that they were expecting their children to meet certain standards that are normally characteristic of people either younger or older than their children actually are. However, just because young Joseph does not share his father's same notion for what it means to be appreciative, it is not necessarily the case that Joseph does not have a concept of what behaviors or experiences constitute appreciation. Like any adult human being, children have their own *personally characteristic* criterial equivalences through which they evaluate and respond to the world.

An example comes from one of LCB's experiences in raising her child, Mark. When Mark was about eight years old, LCB could not help but notice that he was frequently reluctant (sometimes downright afraid) to tackle new situations involving physical skills, despite LCB's vigorous and consistent encouragement. For instance, martial arts classes were consistently avoided, and learning to swim was a terrifying prospect, despite LCB's assurance that "I've seen you do great things with your body before. I know you can do it and will do well at it!" In one of these situations LCB asked Mark what, in his view, was a success and what was a failure. Mark's responses were that a success was "doing something that you or someone else thought you couldn't do," and that a failure was "not doing what you or someone else thought you could do." LCB realized that, *given Mark's criterial equivalences* for success and failure, her way of encouraging him was inadvertently setting him up to fail. Telling Mark that she knew he could do it immediately created (in his mind) the looming possibility of *failure* if for any reason he was unable to do it. That is, he would not have done what his mother thought he could do and, so, he would have failed.

Accordingly, LCB adjusted her behavior and communications in such a way as to better fit Mark's idea of success. Instead of reassuring him that she was confident that he could swim the length of the pool, she would tell him, "I don't know how far you can swim." Or, "Of course, you can't expect yourself to do it just as good as before, after all, it's been awhile since you last did it." Or, "Let's try it and find out how much you remember." The significance of these encouragements was that they did not convey to Mark the idea that his mother had certain expectations about his performance (as well as suggesting to him that he not have any either). Therefore, he was no longer in danger of inviting the horrible experience of failure by going ahead and trying, while any improvement was unexpected and so a success. Once LCB had readjusted her communications to Mark to take his associations into account, the situation changed dramatically, and he soon found himself diving into the very situations that he had previously found so intimidating. LCB also interacted with Mark to generate increasingly flexible means of fulfilling his criterion of success (i.e., learning, doing his best, having fun, and so on). Similarly, consider:

Maribeth was visiting at the home of friends one evening when their three-year-old daughter, Kim, emerged from her bedroom, clutching her blanket. When her parents asked her why she had gotten out of bed, she confessed that she was frightened of the monsters in her room. Her parents insisted that there was no such thing and ordered her back to bed. Kim reemerged five minutes later, still genuinely worried about the monsters. Her parents told her that she was being silly and ordered her back to bed, whereupon Kim started to cry. There was a brief, loud battle of wills, which ended when Kim's father picked her up, stuck her back in bed and made it clear that she better stay there.

The next morning, Kim and Maribeth found themselves alone with each other. Kim meekly asked Maribeth if she ever had monsters in *her* room. Maribeth answered that she *used* to, but that she had found out how to get rid of them. Instantly interested, Kim asked how she did it. Maribeth told her that she had discovered that monsters are afraid of milk and covers. So, as long as she drank her milk they stayed away, and if any came near, all she had to do was pull the covers over her head and they would go away. Kim was delighted with this information and specifically asked for milk before bed that night. Subsequently, Maribeth found out from Kim that she had had no more trouble from monsters in her room.

Although their efforts at disabusing Kim of her belief in monsters was well intentioned, her parents were nonetheless responding to her as though she were older than she was. For many (perhaps most) three-year-old children, nighttime monsters are a reality. Even if it was not generally characteristic of children of her age, the present reality is that *Kim* believes in these monsters. Rather than respond to Kim as she *is*, her parents responded to her as though she were five years old (or, perhaps, even older). To our minds, it would have been equally inappropriate for her parents to have responded to her monster fears as though she were still an infant, cradling and rocking her, cooing and telling her that everything will be alright. Kim needed more than that, and was certainly capable of responding on a higher level.

Maribeth, on the other hand, responded to Kim with respect to the fact that she was three years old and facing monsters in her room at night. To begin with, Maribeth accepted Kim's experiences as being valid. (Her parents' "there's no such thing" is, even if unintended, tantamount to saying, "you're crazy.") In doing this she is recognizing that Kim is three, not five, ten or twenty. Maribeth then provides Kim with a way to banish the monsters, which recognizes that Kim is three, and not two or one and, as such, is capable of appreciating cause-effect relationships.

The most significant feature of Maribeth's computations is that she is making evaluations in the present with respect to Kim's present experiences and capabilities (perhaps including experiences generated from a vicarious projection of what Kim's experience must be like). The significance of these evaluations and experiences, used as a data base, is that they orient Maribeth to Kim as she is in the present. Obviously, Maribeth may choose to ignore Kim's present and respond with regard to the past or future, but at least that decision will be made with knowledge of, and (hopefully) respect to, that present.

By responding to your children as they *are*, you help ensure that your interactions and responses to them are in accord with their needs and capabilities. As we will point out in the section "Enjoying Your Child," an ongoing awareness of your children's needs, capabilities and personal attributes will also provide you with a basis upon which to appreciate and enjoy them.

Nurturing Your Child

Lucille steered her shopping cart down the aisle while her five-year-old daughter, Vivian, skipped along behind her. Because Vivian was feeling older today, she wanted to take a more active part in the day's shopping. She tugged at her mother and said, "Can I get the things down for you, Momma?" Lucille was busy scanning the shelves. "Can I?" came the plaintive question once again. It got through enough this time that Lucille grunted in response. Vivian took this as a yes, so she started looking for what they needed. She glided over to the fruit section and stopped in front of a glistening pile of apples stacked cannonball fashion. "We need apples," she decided, and reached out for the one closest to her. It was one near the bottom of the stack, and when she tugged it out, a rumbling shower of apples poured down upon her and onto the floor. This *did* get Lucille's attention. Looking back, Lucille was filled with disgust and embarrassment as she saw the other shoppers tittering or glaring at Vivian, or trying to pretend she wasn't actually standing there surrounded by apples. Lucille came unglued. She stalked over to Vivian and yanked her out of the fallen apples. "Now look what you've done!" she scolded. "I can't take you anywhere! You obviously can't be trusted!" As Lucille started to pick up the fruit, Vivian reached down to help her. "Don't you move! You've done enough damage for one day!" As Vivian started to cry, she was thinking to herself how really sorry she was that she was a troublemaker.

This scene is one we have all seen in one form or another in the supermarket. (Shopping seems to be one of those situations in which parents do not experience their children as being an integral part of the task at hand.) There is no question that Vivian made a mess. There is also no question that Lucille has reason to be peeved about that mess; after all, she will probably have to clean up much of it. So, was Lucille's response to the spilled apples appropriate?

The answer to that depends in large part upon what you perceive the role of a parent to be. If you think of it as being that of simply controlling children, then perhaps Lucille's response is fine. If, however, you consider the role of a parent to be to *nurture* children, then Lucille's response was inappropriate. (In using the term "nurture" we are referring to *the support, training and education given a child during his or her stages of growth.*) A woman recently mentioned to us that her grown children were a big letdown to her. She complained that their homes and lives were completely chaotic. Then she wistfully recalled what perfectly behaved children they were. "Whenever we went to visit friends, they would sit and not say a word or move until I told them to," she sighed over this fond memory. (After her kids left home she took up dog training.) While you might argue that this woman was educating her kids to sit quietly, the fact is that there is just not much call for that particular skill out in the world. That niche is already well filled by furniture and rocks.

It is our opinion that the role of a parent is not to keep children from doing things, but to teach them *how to do things well*. This is not to say that there are not things that children should not do. Below a certain age, children need to be kept out of the street, off high places, away from sharp knives and poisons, and so on. The physical well-being of your child must be protected. But too often, parents fail to realize that protecting even their child's physical well-being involves teaching him or her how to behave in those dangerous situations safely. Instead, many parents simply forbid the child from being in those situations. It is inevitable, however, that your child will be engaged in all of those dangerous behaviors and situations, and how he or she handles them will depend in large part on the information and training you have offered. Telling your child not to stick anything in outlets, and not to touch them or electrical cords does *not* tell that child how to safely plug or unplug an electrical appliance. And like it or not, they will do it. And because they are inherently curious and know you don't want them to, they will probably do it when you are not around to instruct (or call the doctor).

Of course, this does not mean that you teach a one-year-old how to safely cross the street or handle electrical plugs. The child has to be developmentally ready (both physically and mentally) to be able to appreciate and follow your instructions. The problem comes when the child *is* developmentally ready and yet you still do not provide the opportunity to learn. This includes not only dangerous situations, but almost all situations. In the example of Lucille and Vivian, for instance, Vivian had reached a stage in her development at which she wanted to start helping with the shopping and was tall enough to actually do some of it. What was the upshot of her learnings for that shopping trip? The fact that the apples collapsed does not necessarily mean that she learned about the necessity of taking them from the top of the pile. Adults often take their own sophistication and logic for granted, failing to realize that their children may not make the same sense out of an experience that an adult would. Perhaps all Vivian learned was not to touch the apples. That is about as useless a learning as one could have. What she needed to find out from her mother was how it happened that the apples fell, and how to pick apples properly. The other thing that Vivian may have learned was that she was a troublemaker. That required almost no figuring at all—her mother simply told her so.

If Lucille was not attending to how to educate her daughter at the supermarket, then what was she attending to? Lucille (as we discovered when we interviewed her) was responding to the situation in the *present* with respect to criteria such as decorum, efficiency, and control. Whether such criteria are appropriate or not, they are certainly destined to be violated in an outing involving a five-year-old child. With such criteria and an overwhelming emphasis on the present, Lucille looks around her and sees that her daughter (an extension of herself) is making a scene, is costing her time and trouble, and is not under her control; and so finds the situation an utter violation of her present criteria. If her criteria had been having fun and making waves, obviously she would have had a very different response to the incident.

In addition to her inappropriate evaluation and criteria (in terms of an educational opportunity for the child), Lucille also shows a lack of choice in responding (default response) and imagines how she looks to other people because of her daughter's lack of decorum, efficiency, and control. This immediate vicarious projection of other people's opinions and responses forms the basis of Lucille's embarrassment over her *daughter's* mess. Her subsequent response of yelling at and castigating Vivian amounts to inflicting punishment (that is, a penalty of physical or emotional pain, loss or confinement) for wrongdoing.

Responding with punishment may come from other than the present, however. For instance, upon seeing her child dump a load of apples on the grocery floor, a mother might associate the mistake with other, previously committed transgressions made by the child. She then might respond as though the present incident were yet another example of the child's disobedience, thoughtlessness, or whatever.

The compelling aspect of this kind of experience is from the *past*. Obviously, upsetting the applecart, leaving pajamas on the floor, and getting into mommy's makeup are all different transgressions. If, however, you group all such behaviors into one set or type, then these misbehaviors will all be perceived and responded to as examples of the *same thing:* disobedience or thoughtlessness. Operating out of internal processes based upon such an emphasis on past transgressions all grouped together makes it very easy to reach the limits of patience quickly, since any and all misbehaviors and mishaps get lumped into the same experiential bag. And once that bag is full, the slightest misstep on the part of the child will elicit sudden storms of punishing anger and frustration.

Another common response is, upon seeing the spilled apples, to imagine the child in the future being, for example, an out-of-control delinquent as a consequence of not having learned discipline now. Often the response to this future possibility is to punish the child in order to teach him or her to mind and thus forestall that dire future.

Here the evaluations that compel behavior are of the future, but they are of a particular nature: They are a large-scaled generalized description (out-of-control delinquent). Evaluations are then made as to what is believed will happen if this behavior continues. The effect of such evaluations of the future (which make that undesirable future completely real) is to create in the parent the emotional state that they would have if the future had actually come to pass, which in turn creates a compelling need to respond right away and decisively. Again, the result is usually some form of punishment intended to stop the child from ever repeating his or her transgression.

Although all three computations described above rely on different time frames for their evaluations (past, present and future), all three have the same result as far as the child is concerned. That is, he or she is (perhaps) informed about what *not* to do, but not informed of, or guided to, the behavior that they *are* to do. In other words, these computations result in punishment, rather than education. In speaking of education here we are referring to *an interaction which assists a child to gain competence within a particular area*, whether that area be social, personal, academic, physical, or behavioral. Consider, then, an example of education:

Alex and his father, Paul, left the store. Halfway across the parking lot, Paul noticed something clutched in Alex's four-year-old paw. When asked about it, Alex proudly revealed the colored pencil he was holding. Paul squatted down beside Alex and asked where he got it. "From the store," Alex admitted. Paul explained to Alex that the pencil belonged to the people who owned the store and that taking it without permission or paying for it was stealing. Paul asked him what he thought they should do. Alex didn't know, so Paul suggested they go back to the store and return the pencil. Paul explained the situation as Alex handed the pencil back to the cashier. A week later, Paul and Alex were again walking out of a store when Alex pulled his dad to a stop and sheepishly held out his hand. In it was a sticker shaped like a heart. When Paul asked where it came from, Alex replied, "From the store." "Remember what that is called?" Paul asked. Alex nodded, "Stealing. I better take it back." Paul waited outside the door while Alex went back in and returned the heart to the place he had found it.

What is striking about this example is that, faced with the fact that his son has stolen something, rather than becoming angry or worried, yelling, berating, spanking and otherwise punishing Alex for an obviously bad behavior, Paul responded by giving Alex the information and experience he needed in order to make more appropriate choices in the future. That this worked was evidenced by Alex's subsequent testing of his recently acquired knowledge. When we asked Paul about what went on inside of him when he saw what Alex had done, he replied, "Well, I knew that I didn't want him to steal, so I started thinking about what I could do that would teach him not to steal. Having him take it back seemed like a good idea." Evident both in what Paul did, and in his description of what his thinking was at the time, is that he was making computations based upon evaluations of compellingly real futures about helping Alex to learn. In other words, instead of trying to get Alex to avoid doing the wrong thing, Paul taught Alex how to do the right thing.

Like the parent we described who envisions a horrendous future and so punishes the child to avert it, Paul makes meaningful evaluations of the future based upon cause-effect relationships between the present and that future. The difference is that Paul uses his evaluations about the future to determine how to create an experience for Alex which will lead toward the outcome he (and perhaps they) are after. This difference in orientation and flexibility comes from perceiving the future he is considering through the presupposition of choice, an ability to vary the size and scope of what is being considered, and the criterion of *learning*, which sets the tone for the kinds of possibilities he will consider.

We do not mean to convey from this one example that we are equating education with painless interactions, or punishment with painful interactions. What is of significance, in our view, is not whether the child goes through pain and tribulation, but whether that pain and tribulation is intended to provide the child with an experience for what *not* to do (punishment), or what *to do* (education). Consider the following example, which comes from the child-rearing experiences of Milton H. Erickson, M.D., perhaps the most consistently effective psychotherapist that the profession has ever known:

My son, Robert, one evening announced that he was big enough, old enough, and strong enough to take out the garbage. I expressed my doubts, but he assured me he was big enough and strong enough. I said he might forget, he assured me he wouldn't. I said, "All right, beginning Monday you can do it." So Monday night he took it out, Tuesday night he took it out, and Wednesday night he forgot. So I reminded him on Thursday. He apologized for forgetting on Wednesday; he took it out Thursday night but forgot it Friday and Saturday. It just happened that early on Sunday morning at 3 a.m. I awakened. I had been very good to Robert—I had let him stay up till past one o'clock. But I had awakened at three o'clock. I awakened Robert, apologized very profusely for not having reminded him to take out the garbage, and asked him if he would please dress and take out the garbage. So Robert, with many unknown thoughts, sighed deeply, dressed, and took out the garbage. When he came back in, he got out of his clothes, into his pajamas, and into bed. I waited til he was very sound asleep and then I awakened him again. I apologized very sincerely, very profusely, explaining that I didn't know how that one piece of garbage got overlooked. Robert made a more extensive, minute search of the kitchen, took that piece of garbage out to the garbage pail, and then walked back to the house slowly. I was watching through the curtained window. He reached the back porch, turned and ran out to the alley and checked around the cover of the garbage can. He came in and thoughtfully undressed into his pajamas. I never again had to remind him.[2]

In contrast to the example with Paul and Alex, Erickson provided his son with an undeniably unpleasant experience. The examples are the same, however, in that both provided guidance about what *to do*, rather than simply punishing them for what was done. In another example, Liz, a colleague of ours, was having trouble with her two-and-a-half-year-old daughter heedlessly pinching, biting and banging into her ten-month-old brother. Explanations were repeatedly made to the little girl, but had no effect. One morning Liz was sitting nearby the two children when she observed the little girl bend over and bite her brother. Before the boy had even registered the bite enough to begin crying, Liz bent forward and bit her daughter. The girl was surprised at first, then got down to the business of joining her brother in a good cry. The effect of what Liz did was to provide her daughter with a compelling and almost simultaneous experience for her brother's experience in being bitten. The result was that the sister stopped her indiscriminate hurting of her brother.

Now, you may or may not agree with some or all of the lessons that were taught, or the way in which the parents went for those outcomes in each of the three examples described above. What to teach your children and how to teach them is a personal matter, to be decided by you and your mate. The point to note about each of these examples, however, is that in each case the parent responded by providing the child with a learning experience that would give him or her the opportunity to learn what *to do*, rather than simply punishing them for doing what they ought *not* to do. Liz's biting of her daughter was not done out of rancor or in retribution. It was, instead, timed to occur almost simultaneously with the girl's biting of her brother, providing her with an immediate representation of, and feedback for, her actions from the boy's point of view—something she had not been able to grasp before. In this particular case, the timing was crucial. If Liz had waited until the boy had already reacted by bursting into tears, it would have raised the likelihood that her daughter would have associated being bitten as *punishment* for somehow having created her brother's now obvious distress.

We noted above that Liz's intervening was done without rancor, which is also true of the other two examples given. In this regard, we must mention that the form that punishment often takes (or at least includes) is some kind of attack on the child's personhood and self-worth. Lucille's angry characterization of Vivian as untrustworthy and a trouble-maker was an example of this kind of identifying self-worth by behavior. There is a world of difference between telling a child that she made a mistake, or even that she did something bad, and telling her that she *is* untrustworthy, or that she *is* bad. The former approach recognizes that she has things to learn and perhaps change about herself but leaves her self-concept and integrity intact. The latter approach, on the other hand, turns her behavioral lapses or ignorance into comments upon, and demonstrations of, her as a failure and an inadequate person.

The difference between the two forms of communication may strike you as subtle, but their differing effects can be profound. As an example, take a moment to recall among your past child-rearing experiences some incident in which you responded to your child in a way that you are ashamed of or regretful of. Perhaps you spanked or yelled at your child when they did not really deserve such harsh treatment. Or perhaps you treated them in a way that hurt them deeply, and may even have threatened your relationship with them. Whatever it is, find that moment when your parenting was not what it should have been.

Recalling that incident now, consider:

> How could you have been so inconsiderate? So unfeeling? So unaware? What kind of person are you? That was certainly *not* the kind of thing that a good parent does, and if you know what's good for you and your child, you'd better not ever do that again.

These kinds of remarks are similar to the rancorous, punishing remarks that are often used in responding to children's misbehaviors and mistakes. Contrast the assaulted feelings you had in response to those remarks with your feelings as you now consider:

> Your response to your child in that incident was probably not what you would have wanted it to be. What would you rather your response to have been? How can you change your perspective on what your child was doing and the situation so that the next time you are in a similar situation you can respond the way you *want* to respond (and be the person you want to be)?

You probably experience this second response to your parenting misbehavior or mistake as being much more respectful of your feelings of self-worth and self-concept, and helpful in terms of orienting you *toward useful learnings*. Similarly, keeping behavior separate from self-worth fosters a child who, as he or she grows, responds to mistakes as something that must be addressed and responded to in order to prevent future recurrences. They are *not*, however, crushed or cowed by their failure, nor are they fearful of their eventual ability to be competent within that particular situation. Making behavior contingent upon self-worth, on the other hand, engenders pervasive and lasting feelings of inadequacy, as well as fearfulness of engaging in those situations for which they have ample demonstration of their inherent inadequacies.

We want to reiterate that the thrust of what we are describing here as a computation underlying appropriate nurturing of the development of a child neither precludes nor vilifies such unpleasant responses as being angry, hurt, and disappointed, or such behaviors as spanking and deprivations. In our experience, such responses fall within the bounds of nurturing, *provided* that such responses are expressed and such behaviors are employed in ways which provide your child with information and experiences that are intended to help them move *toward* some competency within a particular situation; *and*, that this be done in a way which is respectful, if not supportive, of the child's personhood ("I am a trustworthy person," as opposed to "I am not a trustworthy person") and self-worth ("I am good," as opposed to "I am bad").

The internal processing which we have discussed above as being appropriate naturally leads to both of the outcomes that we have just described. In the first place you are led naturally to consider what is necessary to enable your child to have the results you and he or she wants. This is based on internal processes most concerned with future well-being, the criterion *learning*, choice of response, flexibility in considering a wide range of goals (goals of different levels of specificity), and present-to-future cause-effect relationships (that is, the present behaviors that produce the all important future results). Secondly, these internal processes are about what to *do*, rather than detecting what is wrong (as was the case with the three inappropriate responses we described). This places the situation into the appropriate world of behavior, and takes it out of the realm of inherent weakness or failings. In other words, it is no longer a matter of being a good or bad boy, or a trustworthy or untrustworthy girl, but of determining what kinds of experiences are likely to lead this child to acquire appropriate social, personal, academic, and physical skills.[3]

Enjoying Your Child

As we noted at the very beginning of this chapter, change and growth are two of the most distinguishing characteristics of children. Between protecting them from danger, nurturing their constantly evolving emotions, bodies and intellects, and supplying their seemingly constant need for food, clothing, coloring books and uniforms, keeping up with those changes is pretty much a full-time job for most parents. The reward for our twenty-one years (minimum) of effort? Well, there are many. Though some parents treat the raising of their children as the mere performance of a duty, for others there is the satisfaction of seeing their children safely off to the pursuit of their independent lives. For others, children provide their lives with feelings of significance, or with a sense of immortality. For many parents, how their children distinguish themselves in school, dating, marriage, and the workplace, reflects directly upon the parent's feelings of accomplishment and self-worth. Unfortunately, most of the kinds of child-rearing rewards that we have just listed come and are enjoyed only after milestones and long periods of time have passed (graduations, marriage, first job, turning twenty-one, and so on). Pete Seeger, the folk singer, has a different view, saying that parents "do it for the high wages—kisses!" The virtue in doing it for the kisses is that it is something you can enjoy every day of those twenty-one (and more) years.

> "Look, dad! I wrote my name!" Susan proudly held the piece of paper aloft. Mel, her father, was eager that Susan learn to write. He had expected her to be much further along by now than she seemed to be, so it was with the anticipation of great things that he took the sheet from the five-year-old and examined what his daughter had done: ZUZAN. Mel couldn't help it—he was disappointed. Surely she could have done better than that. "When are you going to learn to write letters properly?" he wanted to know. He handed the paper back to Susan and walked off.

Mel *wanted* to enjoy his daughter's triumph. Instead of responding to the progress she had made, however, he responded to the progress he wants her to make. That is, the comparisons he is making are between her present writing ability and his notions of what her present writing ability could and should be. The evaluations that he is making, then, are about the present, but they are in relation to future possibilities/probabilities which Susan has not yet matched. He is applying these future possibilities to the present and cannot be other than disappointed. The result of his expectation that the future occur in the present is for Susan a devaluation of her accomplishment, and for Mel a missed opportunity to join her in taking pleasure in that accomplishment.

As indicated above, in addition to his evaluations based upon future possibilities that he expects to be occurring in the present, Mel's kind of response also usually involves evaluations based on a relatively detailed level of specificity. This is the difference, for example, between thinking about progress as *correctly* writing letters, or *getting better* at writing letters. Both can be perceived as indicators of progress, but correctly writing letters is very much more specified than is getting better at writing letters and, so, *is not so easily satisfied*. The range of Susan's behavior that will satisfy such a detailed and specific representation of progress (i.e., correct) is very narrow, while the much broader range offered by the more general *getting better* provides the opportunity for many more ways to demonstrate progressing competency and thus, many more opportunities to revel in a child's accomplishments.

Mel's exchange with his daughter would have been one of those moments of satisfaction and pleasure if he had evaluated her present accomplishment in light of her *past* rather than her future. Writing her own name was something that Susan had never done before. Comparing what she can do now to what she was able to do yesterday reveals progress that Mel can enjoy. Compared to last year's scribbles, today's backward letters are as thrilling as they are amazing.

By way of contrast, consider the response of a teacher who told us about a parent that came in to consult with her about the woman's five-year-old daughter. After listening to the woman complain—in the presence of the little girl—for ten minutes because her daughter was not achieving at the level which Mom thought she should, the teacher got fed up. She interrupted the tirade and said, "In the last five years, your daughter has learned to walk, run, jump, tie her shoes, draw, paint, color, build things, get along with others, fight and make up with others, feed and dress herself, use a toilet, ride a bicycle, count, think in abstractions, learn rudimentary logic, recognize numbers and the letters of the alphabet, read many words *and* learn to speak a language fluently. Now, what have *you* learned in the last five years?"

The obvious contrast between this teacher and Mel is that while both are making present evaluations regarding progress (evaluations about what a child *is* able to do), the teacher makes these evaluations with reference to the *past* whereas Mel's evaluations are made with reference to the future. The only other significant difference is that the teacher is able to vary the range and degree of specificity of experiences which she uses to fulfill her criteria (e.g. think in abstractions, recognize numbers), which makes it possible to respond to all of her student's varying accomplishments as examples of progress, which is a source of enjoyment for them both.

Noticing how your children have progressed is not the only way to enjoy them, however.

At seventeen, David felt self-reliant and self-responsible. Actually, he had felt that way for a couple of years, but with high school graduation and his departure for college nearing, the feelings were particularly strong now. David was just on his way upstairs to his room when his father, Ned, stopped him. Inwardly, David groaned; he had been through this before and already knew what was coming. His father started right in about how David was making a mistake about the college he had selected. David temporized for a few minutes. Then, suddenly, he had enough. He angrily shouted at his father, "It's none of your damn business!" and stomped upstairs. Before he had even reached his bedroom, the enormity of what he had just done was already sinking into his stomach like a swallowed cannonball. He had never talked to his father like that before. David waited for the knock at the door, but it never came. The next day Ned greeted him cheerily. David warily waited for the ax to fall, but it never did, and neither did his father ever again bring up the matter of his college choice.

Years later, David recalled the incident and asked his father if he had been mad at him for that curse. "Mad?" he answered. "No, I was proud of you." David cocked his head to one side and asked, "Did you say 'proud'?" "Sure," Ned continued. "I was wondering when you were going to finally stand up to me. Once you did, I knew that you would be taking care of your own decisions from then on."

Ned was probably no more eager than anyone else is to be told, "It's none of your damn business!" Accordingly, had he responded to being cursed with concern for the present only, he might very likely have taken offense and retaliated in some way. Instead, Ned took the present into the *future*, where he was able to see his son's present defiance as harbinger of the boy's growing independence—a quality which Ned thinks his son will need. On this account, instead of feeling hurt, Ned feels proud and hopeful of his son's future ability to stand on his own two feet.

Ned's response includes a demonstration of the point we made previously: The effects of how a criterion can be fulfilled differ when specified with more or less detail. In specifying in rigid detail how his criteria would be fulfilled, Mel had severely narrowed the range of behaviors that would match his criterial equivalences. For instance, specifying in rigid detail, Mel's criterial equivalence for *independence* might be owning car and house, married and supporting family, and has a well-paying, secure job. (In fact, we have met individuals who have even narrower, more rigidly detailed representations in which the kind of car, type of house, wife or husband and job are also specified.) Based upon such highly detailed specifications, Mel would have to await the satisfaction of each of those particular conditions before he could enjoy his son or daughter's independence.

The more general, flexible level at which Ned operates in this situation, on the other hand, involve searching for evidence that is more on the order of *being responsible for yourself.* The range of situations and behaviors which might stand as examples of such independence is tremendous, even including such otherwise unpleasant experiences as being cursed at and ignored by your own son or daughter.

There is another kiss that is available to every parent every
day, and yet it is usually overlooked. It is the enjoyment that
is to be had by sharing your child's reality. Obviously, your
child's world is different than yours, and it changes and
evolves with every stage of development that he or she goes
through. Those realities used to be your own many years ago
when you were growing up. Perhaps they are now inappropriate for functioning as an adult in an adult world, but the
respite and the possibility of new perspectives that those
younger, now somewhat alien, realities offer are well worth
exploring and enjoying. Inherent in that doll house, the
Legos, the climbing tree, the baseball glove, the dressing up,
the rock and roll, the dates, and the noisy cars are ways of
perceiving the world that may be enjoyable in and of themselves, and that may, in the contrast with your own world,
reveal to you new, interesting and refreshing perspectives.

How To Bring It All Home

In this section we will be guiding you through the EMPRINT
format for each of the three areas of parenting previously
discussed: growing with your child, nurturing your child, and
enjoying your child. These EMPRINT formats are designed to
teach you how to be a more effective, fulfilled and satisfied
parent. You may discover that the skills and abilities you will
learn as you participate in each exploration or exercise are the
ones you wish your parents would have had while raising you.
Read through each step, and then be sure to carry out the
instructions for each step. In this way you will be learning to
perceive and respond in ways that will benefit both you and
your child.

Growing with Your Child

If you look back over the three sections on parenting that we
have just completed you will notice that all of the useful
internal processes we have described depend upon some

knowledge of your child's present stage of development. Growing with your child depends upon being able to recognize the nature of the world that he or she lives in and, at this time, is capable of appreciating. It is this recognition that allows you to interact with your child in a way that is in accord with who he or she presently is. In addition, having a present understanding of your child's model of the world and capabilities makes it possible to *enjoy* their progressive mastery of various skills and qualities. And, those present understandings keep you apprised of aspects of your child's development that perhaps need some of your *nurturing* attention.

As a parent, therefore, you need to make an effort to recognize the physiological, social, cognitive and behavioral needs and abilities that your child presently has. To illustrate, recall a recent incident in which you interacted with someone who was giving you instructions/directions that presupposed a greater sophistication on your part than you actually possessed, and which were given in such a way as to leave no room for you to ask questions. Examples of such experiences may be found in having your car's problems and repairs described to you by a condescending repairman, or in taking a question about your computer to an unsympathetic computer dealer, or in trying to fill out long forms for the IRS. Also, recall a recent incident in which someone was talking down to you, presupposing much less sophistication than you actually possess. Perhaps at twenty-eight you are still getting calls from your mother reminding you to wear something on your feet in the morning. Or perhaps there is a librarian who, when you ask for a certain book, insists upon taking you through the procedure for using the card catalog and then shows you how to look through the shelves for the book. Both kinds of examples can serve as reference experiences for what it is like to be responded to at a level of competency other than your own. The feelings of inadequacy and resentment that you probably felt in those experiences are the same kinds of feelings that children have when they are responded to at a level of understanding and development that is either beyond or behind where they actually are.

If you want to grow along with your child, in the sense of being able to interact with him or her appropriately and with mutual satisfaction, then it is imperative to know your child in a way that is congruent and representative of *who* your child actually *is*. As we illustrated above, two mistakes that parents sometimes make in this regard is either to perceive their children as being younger than they actually are, or older than they actually are.

1 In order to orient yourself to a present assessment of your child which is congruent with your child, the first thing to do is to identify at least two other children who are two or three years younger than your child. In your mind's eye, imagine those two younger children standing beside your child. As you look at them, compare their bodies; compare height; torso, limb and head proportions; weight; musculature; development of facial features. Make this simple comparison before going on.

2 Next, when you reach the end of this paragraph compare those children with your own as to how they move, play, and interact with others. Compare their voice tonalities. Compare their interests, and their physical and mental abilities. Compare the kinds of things they are learning in school. Compare the differences in their responses to situations such as being punished, rewarded, asked to do things, and so on. The goal here is to differentiate your child's physiology, behavior, intellect and emotions from those of younger children. (If your imagined comparisons seem unconvincing to you, get your child together with a couple of these younger children and actually watch and listen to the differences between them as they interact.) Take the time now to make these comparisons.

3 The next step is to see in your mind's eye your child as he or she was a *year ago*, and your child as he or she appears now. Compare those two images in the same way that you did with the younger children. (If in looking at the two images, your child appears the same in both, get a photograph of your child taken about a year ago and use it to refresh your memory of how your child looked then.) As before, notice how your child's body, face, voice, movements, physical and academic interests, school subjects, reasoning, and responses to various situations have changed.

4 The next step in appropriately orienting yourself to who your child *is* is to make the same kinds of comparisons described above between your child and children who are *older*. To begin with, select two or three *adults* you know. Picture those adults and your own child side-by-side, and compare them in terms of physical development. Then compare them in terms of behaviors, intellectual abilities and interests, kinds of emotional responses, and so on.

5 Having done that and noticed some of the gulfs that still separate your child from the adult world, select a couple of children that you know who are about two years older than your own child. Again, make comparisons between those two children and your own child with respect to physical, physiological, behavioral, intellectual, and emotional differences. As before, the only goal here is to make you aware of some of the ways in which your child is different from individuals who are older. If you do not find the comparisons compelling, then we suggest that you actually get your child together with two or three adults, and then a few somewhat older children, and make your comparisons by actually watching and listening to their interactions.

In making the comparisons that we have described above, you have begun to locate your child appropriately in his or her developmental sequence. However, although this is an improvement over responding to your child as though he or she is younger or older than he or she actually is, it is not enough. Like any adult, a child has his or her own characteristic physical, emotional, and cognitive qualities, abilities, and interests. It is surprisingly easy to forget this, and so inadvertently end up treating your child as a certain-age-kid. It is therefore important to maintain some awareness about *who* your child is, so that you can interact in an appropriate and mutually satisfying way.

6 To begin, take an inventory of each of the following categories for your son or daughter (the parenthetical examples are for the five-year-old boy of one of the authors). Use the space that is provided to list the information for your child.

■ **Physiology** What is his/her body like in terms of size, strength, agility, musculature, body hair, hip size, breasts, shoulder breadth, voice tonality, skin texture, smells, and so on? (e.g. slight; not particularly strong; tall for his age; tires easily)

My child's physiology ⸻⸻⸻⸻

⸻⸻⸻⸻⸻⸻⸻⸻

■ **Physical Abilities**   What gross and fine motor activities does he/she do well, and what does he/she not do well? (e.g. uses tools well; great fine motor skills; good at climbing)

My child's physical abilities ⸻⸻⸻⸻

⸻⸻⸻⸻⸻⸻⸻⸻

■ **Physical Interests**   What does he/she like or not like to do with his/her body? (e.g. wants to know what his body will do; likes running and gymnastics)

My child's physical interests ⸻⸻⸻⸻

⸻⸻⸻⸻⸻⸻⸻⸻

■ **Cognitive Abilities**   At what kinds of mental computations and reasoning is he/she competent? (e.g. uses vocabulary and reasons beyond his years; counts and adds; writes; great memory)

My child's cognitive abilities ⸻⸻⸻⸻

⸻⸻⸻⸻⸻⸻⸻⸻

■ **Personal Qualities**   What are his/her values, personality traits, emotional wants and needs? (e.g. concerned about the welfare of others; strong sense of family; easily embarrassed; artistic; tends to quit things not quickly mastered; considerate; protective of his sister; comfortable playing with much older children)

My child's personal qualities ⸻⸻⸻⸻

⸻⸻⸻⸻⸻⸻⸻⸻

■ **Interests**   What does he/she like, seek out, or appreciate, and what does he/she dislike, avoid, or ignore? (e.g.

likes art, books, and cartoons; hates medicine; likes planning projects)

My child's interests _____

_____

Once you have gone through these six categories of experience and behavior with regard to your child, you will have specified for yourself much of what characterizes your son or daughter at this time in his or her life. If you want to grow along with your child (in the sense of interacting with him or her in a way that the child can appreciate), then you need to do so with regard for the characteristics that you have just identified.

For example, Mark, a friend of ours, has an eleven-year-old son, Jordon, who has excellent fine motor coordination—a skill which has translated itself into record video game scores in arcades throughout the city. For whatever reasons, however, the coordination between eye and hand that Jordon enjoys does not extend to the rest of his body. He is an artist in the arcade; on the basketball court, he is a klutz. Aware of these qualitative differences in Jordan's physical skills, Mark adjusts the nature of his interactions with his son with regard to the situation. For example, when they are playing video games (a situation involving fine motor coordination), Mark challenges Jordan to do better, is suitably impressed by his son's triumphs, and commiserates with Jordan over his failures. When they go out to play basketball, however, Mark readjusts his interactions with his son, building them around having a good time (rather than doing well).

Similarly, a distinctive personality attribute of Paul's five-year-old son Alex is his ongoing sensitivity to the responses of others. Always very attentive to voice tonality, facial and body expressions of others, Alex is very quick to recognize a change in the emotional state of anyone around him, and responds accordingly. For instance, he tries to cheer up his little sister when she is unhappy, and puts on his mother's favorite music when he notices that she is irritable. As mature as his responses often are, Alex is still a five-year-old and does not yet understand certain nuances of communication, such as sarcasm, kidding, spirited disagreement, and so on. Consequently, it often happens that Alex misconstrues the significance of a communication (particularly those directed toward him) and winds up hurt and in tears. Paul is, therefore, respectful of his son's feelings by either not using such (to Alex) ambiguous forms of communication, or by making sure to establish ahead of time that the nature of the interaction is going to be kidding around, arguing for the fun of it, and so on.

From the comparisons that you made above it should be evident that your child changes from year to year (in fact, at least month to month, as you will see if you make those same kinds of comparisons for those shorter time periods). Thus, it is not enough to take the above inventory once. Rather, as long as it is important to you to interact with your child in a mutually satisfying way, it is incumbent upon you to maintain an ongoing awareness of your child's characteristics and development. No matter how informal, such an inventory needs to be taken constantly, in the sense of being a part of your ongoing consciousness about your child.

7 In this regard, we know of no better way of keeping in touch with your child's world (and, thus, the various distinctions we have been describing) than occasionally to interact with him or her in *his or her* environments and on *his or her* terms. Match your tempo to that of your child by talking, moving, and reacting at the same rate as he or she does. Attend to the words and concepts he or she uses. Talk about and do the things that he or she wants to do, and in the way that he or she wants to talk about and do those things. Just being with your children in their room or on a walk with no intention other than gathering information about what is important, meaningful, attractive, and enjoyable to them will reward you with the most compelling personal and vicarious experiences that you can obtain for who your children *are*.

8 Included in this information gathering should be some knowledge of the meanings (criterial equivalences) through which your child is perceiving the world. As LCB's experience with her son illustrated, children, like any adult, have criterial equivalences which they use to assess their experiences and guide their responses. As we illustrated, making sense out of your child's behaviors and being able to interact in an appropriate and useful way with your child may hinge upon your knowing just what those criterial equivalences are. (In LCB and Mark's case, knowing that *failure* = not doing what you or others thought you could do made it possible for LCB to present challenges to Mark in such a way that he was willing to tackle them.) Even though criterial equivalences can be one of the most profoundly affecting aspects of your child's experience and behavior, it is nevertheless one of the easiest pieces of information to gather. Simply ask. You will almost always net a statement of your child's criterial equivalence within a situation when you ask questions like, "How do you know when you have succeeded . . . have failed . . . are interested . . . are loved . . . are listened to . . . ?"

9 Points of misunderstanding and conflict between parents and their children (between any two people, actually) often arise as a result of the two people unknowingly operating out of different criterial equivalences within the same situation. Go through your own recent interactions with your children and identify two of those frustrating, disappointing and/or upsetting incidents or moments in which your child failed to respond in a way that you expected or would have liked. (For example, your eight-year-old son continually interrupts your conversations with your spouse.) For each of those incidents note the criteria that were important to you at that time and were not being met by your child (perhaps considerate or respectful in our example). You will use this information in the next step, so be sure to identify these criteria before proceeding.

Times When My Child Failed To Act or Respond as I Wanted

The Standards My Child Failed To Meet at That Time

#1 _____   a. _____

b. _____

#2 _____   c. _____

d. _____

10 Next, specify *your* criterial equivalence for each of those criteria or standards (e.g. considerate = responding to other people's wants and needs). Having specified these criterial equivalences for yourself, now go to your child and ask for *his or her* criterial equivalences for those same criteria. (For example, you could ask, "How do you know when you are or someone else is being considerate?" or "What does it mean to be 'considerate'?") You will find your *child's* understanding of that criterion, or you might discover that your child does not have a criterial equivalence for that criterion. (In which case you have the opportunity to introduce one.) Gather this information now and write it in the following spaces.

My Criterial Equivalences for the Standards Not Met at Those Times	**My Child's Criterial Equivalences for the Same Standards**
a. _____	_____
_____	_____
b. _____	_____
_____	_____
c. _____	_____
_____	_____
d. _____	_____
_____	_____

11 Once you have this information, compare your child's criterial equivalences to your own. How are they similar and dissimilar? How do those differences make your child's responses sensible in those situations which you found so trying? And how could you use your understanding of your child's criterial equivalences to assist him or her in growing and learning? Using our example, your child might respond that being considerate means not hurting people. When you compare his criterial equivalence with yours (responding to other people's wants and needs) you discover that they are similar in that both are about others, but that they differ in their scope (hurting compared to the much broader needs and wants). Given his criterial equivalence, it is obvious that your son will not recognize his interruptions as being inconsiderate. Understanding this, you can either change his criterial equivalence to include a broader scope, or you can use his present criterial equivalence to assist him in changing his behavior by explaining that *people often feel hurt when they are interrupted.*

Having an understanding of who your child *is*, however, does not itself necessarily prevent you from wanting and expecting more from your son or daughter than his or her present capabilities. Nor should it, since it is part of your role as a parent to provide your child with challenges and opportunities to go beyond their present boundaries. Sometimes, however, parents' eagerness to have a child evolve eclipses their recognition of the child's present ability to meet those expectations. What was intended to be encouragement on the part of the parents, then, becomes *impatience.* And impatience almost always conveys to the child a sense that he or she is *inadequate.* If you do become impatient with your child's development, take yourself through the following sequence (steps 12 through 17):

12 First, identify some important skill (e.g. count to one hundred, go without diapers, make friends) or attribute (e.g. concern for others, shares, tries new things) that your child has recently mastered. Go back to that incident or moment when you realized that this skill or attribute was now in your child's repertoire, recapturing the feelings of pride and relief (and perhaps surprise and satisfaction) you had when you realized this. Relive that incident or moment; it is important that you get in touch with and reexperience these feelings before proceeding.

13 Next, travel back through time until you reach that era in which your child had not yet mastered that skill or attribute, but a time that you nevertheless *expected or wanted* that skill or attribute from your child. (For instance, you notice that your son, Bobby, is now able to share his things with others. Moving back through time you come to an incident six months ago in which, despite your suggestions, encouragement and admonishments, Bobby's friends had to be sent home because he would not let them touch his toys.) Locate that time now.

14   Reliving that moment, step into the frustration, disappointment or anxiety of that past, *but this time* do it knowing (now) what you did not know then: *that your child will eventually acquire that skill or attribute, but that it is not YET a feature of his or her development.* Notice how your response changes (probably becoming more patient, perhaps even curious about the future) in relation to and within that situation. Go back through this same sequence with several other skills or attributes that you once expected and fretted over, and that your child has now mastered.

15   You can now use the change in emotional response that comes from going through this sequence for your benefit in the actual present. Select some skill or attribute which you *currently* expect your child to demonstrate in his or her behavior, but which (to your frustration, disappointment, and/or anxiety) they do not. Remembering and keeping in touch with the state of patience you got from the previous sequence, now recall a recent example of your child behaving in a way that demonstrates that they do not yet have that skill or attribute that you want them to have, realizing that they *will* have and manifest that skill or attribute in the future. How does your response to their present deficiency change?

16   Now take other examples of skills and attributes your child does not evidence but that you are anxious for them to have and run those expectations through the same steps.

17   Having done that, it is important to take the time to insure that your new responses will occur in the future. Identify two or three upcoming situations in which you want to respond to your child with these new, more patient and assured responses. Taking them one at a time, fully imagine being in these futures; seeing everything around you, hearing other's voices, feeling the sensations that are present in that future. Mentally rehearse responding to your child as you intend to, making any adjustments necessary for your response to be aligned with your new perceptions and emotional state. Be sure to notice and appreciate how you have learned to convert problem situations into opportunities for loving and supportive expressions. Take the time now to complete this final and important step.

The purpose of this sequence is not for you to become complacent or satisfied with the way your children are, but to reassure you (based upon your own experiences) that your child can and is eventually likely to acquire the skills and attributes that you, as an adult, know to be important. The patience that comes with this reassurance will convey to your child a sense of your confidence in their ability ultimately to master these important skills and attributes. It will also provide you with a perspective that is more conducive to your being able to enjoy your children as they are, and for who and what they are.

Nurturing Your Child

As we have just noted, the goal is not to become complacent about your child's evolution. Indeed, it is your responsibility as a parent to help guide your sons and daughters toward the attainment of those skills and personal attributes that you think or know will make it possible for them to enjoy gratifying lives. In fact, the attainment of those skills and attributes leading to a gratifying life *must* be your goal as a parent, otherwise your role is reduced to little more than that of temporary warden.

The following EMPRINT format teaches you how to apply your special concerns and personal values to the creation of learning experiences that will influence your child's future well-being. All parents influence their children, and therefore their children's future well-being. This EMPRINT format is designed to give you the know-how that you need to do so knowledgeably and effectively. In orienting yourself with respect to the evolution of your son or daughter from childhood into fulfilled adulthood, we are talking about an emphasis on the criterion of *learning*, and about setting those learnings within the frame of a long-term future.

1 Take a moment to consider what you want your child to learn in the long run: *What do you want your child to learn as a*

youngster, a teenager, a young adult, and an adult? Several times later in this section you will be directed to consider these learning goals, so write them in the following spaces.

What I Want My Child to Learn

As a youngster _____

_____

As a teenager _____

_____

As a young adult _____

_____

As an adult _____

_____

There are two reasons why it is important to specify to some extent the kinds of goals that you have for your children. The first is that by making those goals explicit you provide yourself with the opportunity to evaluate whether or not those goals that *you* want for your child are congruent (or potentially congruent) with *who your child is as a person* (recalling the previous section on "Growing With Your Child").

2 Accordingly, at the end of this paragraph take a moment to evaluate this list of goals you intend for your child with respect to what you know about him or her as an individual. Are the goals congruent with your son or daughter? If not necessarily congruent now, could they become congruent at some later point in his or her life? How can you readjust basically incongruent goals to fit the personality and the physical, emotional, and cognitive skills of your child? Evaluate your list of goals now, using these questions as a guide.

The second reason it is important to be aware of your intended goals for your children is this: You will have explicit outcomes to relate to and move toward in your interactions with your children. A goal becomes an outcome in a *plan*. In order to be useful in planning, however, the criterial equivalence for the goal needs to be appropriately specified in relatively small behaviorally-based details. For example, if you want your child to be considerate, then you need to know that for you (perhaps) considerate means not interrupting others, doing things for others without having to be asked, and being prompt. If you want your child to be self-reliant, then you need to know if that means (for you) doing things without asking for assistance, being able to safely go places alone, and correcting correctable mistakes without help from others.

The difference that having an explicit representation of the goal can make is often tremendous. Merely *telling* your children to be considerate fails to provide them with any specifics about *what to do* in order to be considered considerate, no matter how many times or how loud you tell them. Similarly, thinking *only* in terms of the overall desired goal/response also leaves *you* in the dark about *what you can do* to help your child become a considerate person. As soon as you start specifying your criterial equivalence at the level of behavior, however, you immediately provide yourself and your child a knowledge of what will constitute being considerate. Now you can explain, demonstrate, or provide experiences to your child exemplifying just what to *do*.

3 For each of the goals that you listed for your child, specify for yourself just what kinds of behaviors and responses are, to you, indicative of that goal.

Goal   **Specific Behaviors and
                                Responses**

_____   _____

                                _____

_____   _____

                                _____

_____   _____

                                _____

_____   _____

Now that you have the goal specified, what do you do next? The general answer is that you provide your child with experiences that, hopefully, will assist him or her in learning what you think he or she needs to learn. We can further specify this answer by dividing such learning experiences into three types that we have found useful.

First, if your child is a youngster (younger than six or seven), very often all that is needed in terms of providing guidance is an explanation and/or demonstration of the kinds of behaviors and responses that you want and expect from them. Young children often have not, as yet, formulated criterial equivalences for many of life's skills and attributes. That lack of preconception together with the child's insatiable appetite for learning creates a tremendous readiness to absorb and emulate those explanations and demonstrations. This was exemplified in the way in which Paul explained to Alex the significance of stealing the pencil, then walked him through the behavior of returning what was taken and making amends. This provided Alex with a set of learning experiences that he could then use later when in similar situations.

A second strategy for providing learning experiences is to create an experience for the negative (unpleasant, dangerous, scorned) consequences of not emulating certain skills or attributes. We saw an example of this when Milton Erickson apologetically and repeatedly awakened his son to remind him to take out the garbage. Similarly, we know of a father whose teenaged son incessantly teased the members of the rest of the family. Determined to do something about it, the father went up to his son and started firmly poking him in the arm. At first the boy took it as a joke, but when his father continued to poke him the boy became irritated and wanted his father to stop. Dad wouldn't, and the boy's irritation spilled over into anger and resentment. Once the boy had become thoroughly indignant and exasperated, his father stopped and simply said, "That's what it's like for us with your teasing." The teasing stopped. Again, what this man provided was an experience for the negative consequences (to the family) of his son's behavior, a learning experience that the son could then use to readjust his own thinking and behavior. The previous example of Liz providing her daughter with an experience of what it was like to be bitten is another example of providing an experience of negative consequences.

A third strategy involves providing your child with a learning experience for the positive (pleasant, rewarding, endearing) consequences of operating in the world in certain ways. For example, an acquaintance of ours who wanted to teach his son perseverance obtained a very simple airplane model and guided his son in the construction of it. Whenever the boy got stuck while building it, his dad would ask those leading questions that would make it possible for the boy to continue, then praise his son for being able to do it. After repeating the same interaction several times with additional and progressively more difficult airplane models, the boy started emulating perseverance in his own behavior. That is, whenever he got stuck after that, he naturally assumed that there was something he could do to keep going, and would diligently search for that way.

4 Underlying all of the examples given above is an emphasis on *learning* as perceived within the realm of the future, and the cause-effect relationships that will (or are likely to) lead to that future. Taking one of the skill or attribute goals that you previously listed as an example (e.g. sharing), make an image of your child sometime in the future being able to behaviorally express that goal (e.g. see and hear little Cathy sharing). Do this before moving to the next step.

5 Next imagine what kinds of learning experiences you could help create that would make that future a reality (that is, the cause-effect steps linking the present to that future). In order to assist you in this, we suggest that you apply as a guide each of the three learning experience strategies that we described above. For example:

■ Describe the criterial equivalence you want your child to operate under; demonstrate it in your own behavior, and/or guide the child through the behavior. (Using sharing as an example, the result of your planning might be to explain the significance of sharing to Cathy; make a point of sharing with her and/or in front of her; and then pointing it out to her.)

■ Provide the opportunity to experience the negative consequences of not emulating the skill or attribute. (Engage Cathy in mutually enjoyable play. Then when she inappropriately refuses to share something, describe your disappointment and leave; find something that you have that Cathy wants and, when she asks for it, refuse to share; point out the unpleasantness of the internal state to her, then share with her to provide contrast.)

■ Provide the opportunity to experience the positive consequences of emulating the skill or attribute. (Set up a situation in which Cathy is given something to give to one of her peers, then interpret to her the giving of it as sharing, and praise her for it.)

Use the following space to note the ideas you develop from using each of these three strategies for one of your goals.

Goal   **Learning Experience**

_____   #1 _____

                                           _____

                                           _____

                                           #2 _____

                                           _____

                                           _____

                                           #3 _____

                                           _____

                                           _____

Once you have taken the goal through each of these strategies you will probably have at least three possible ways of interacting with your child that could assist him or her in moving toward the goal. The salient point here is that of generating a _learning_ experience for your child which provides a reference experience that will be useful. The usefulness of the three strategies is in guiding your thinking along those lines.

6 We therefore suggest that you take the other skills and attributes on your list and process them through these strategies. Also, continue to use the strategies in your daily interactions with your children until you discover (in those moments when there is a discontinuity between what you want *for* and expect *of* your child, and what he or she does) that you naturally turn to responses which involve creating useful learning experiences for the child.

Two points still need to be made. First, guiding your children toward new skills and attributes usually requires consistency on *your* part. Although sometimes change may result from a single, compelling experience, more often your child will be oriented as a result of repeated exposure to a particular experiential or behavioral skill or attribute. As a parent, then, you need to remember and be guided by significant interactions you have had with your child (threats, promises, praise, lessons, agreements, and so on). This will enable you to respond consistently over time. For instance, it is inconsistent to make your child return something that he has taken from a store, but then ignore the next time he takes something that does not belong to him. Such inconsistency is not likely to provide your child with a set of learning experiences that will be useful when finding himself in a situation in which he is thinking about taking something that belongs to someone else.

7 *Future-pacing* is useful in keeping yourself consistent in dealing with your child. By imagining yourself responding appropriately and consistently in possible upcoming situations that are similar to the one in which you have just interacted with your child, you can help insure that you will respond appropriately and consistently over time with your child. Take a few moments when you finish this paragraph to identify an upcoming situation in which you will have the opportunity to respond consistently with a previously made threat, promise, agreement, or action. Imagine being in that situation. As fully as possible experience actually being in that future time and place, then respond consistently in that situation, realizing and appreciating that you are acting in the best interests of your child's future well-being. Before proceeding, use this method to future-pace your new, more consistent responses.

The second point is this: By our emphasis on computations based on future learnings we do not mean to imply that you should always respond in this way to deficiencies in your child's behavior. Obviously, it is often the case that responses based upon present or short-term future considerations are called for. Anyone who has just spent a rainy weekend in the house taking care of the kids, finally gotten them to bed, then gratefully collapsed upon the sofa, only to be aroused minutes later by little voices arguing about who had the biggest cookie, knows what we are talking about. You certainly could consider some interesting response which would give them a useful learning experience regarding what is really worth arguing about. But at half past nine at night after two days of indoor coping, who cares? If it works, why not simply yell down the hall from your slumped place on the sofa, "Hey you kids! Knock it off and go to sleep!"? There are times, then, when it is your intention and desire to nurture your child, and other times when nurturing is simply not appropriate or not of interest to you. We think it important, however, that you consider whether or not the attention that you devote to nurturing your child is adequate, and whether or not the nurturing you do is appropriate and useful in helping your child evolve. In that regard, the computations that we have introduced here can make the difference between your being a warden and a guide.

Enjoying Your Child

What is there to enjoy about children? Certainly one of the most enjoyable aspects of having children is witnessing their evolution from infants to (hopefully) happy, fulfilled adults. As parental guide and teacher (rather than a keeper), a precious reward is the pleasure that derives from seeing your child master and enjoy new skills, from knowing that each of these changes can help make your child's future a little better, and from the personal pride you may feel in having done well on your child's behalf. You *want* your children to prosper emotionally, intellectually and socially. And one of the most deeply pleasurable moments in parenting is when we recognize that our children are prospering in one or some of those ways.

Enjoying your children in this way means being able to *recognize* that they *have* made progress, that they *are* prospering. If you recall, Mel missed an opportunity to enjoy his daughter's progress because he was not able to recognize it as such. Instead, he attended to what she had not yet achieved, and so was unable to share in Susan's accomplishment. What he was lacking was a reference to his memories regarding what his daughter had previously been able to do with her writing. Such a reference would have provided him with the basis for a comparison that would have made his daughter's progress palpable to him.

This is easily done if the orientations and internal processes we have described in the previous sections on growing with and nurturing your child have begun to become familiar to you. Two of the important things we had you do in those sections were (1) take the opportunity to orient yourself to your child as he or she is, and (2) evaluate the skills and attributes you want for and from your child in light of who he or she is. With some ongoing appreciation for your child's qualities and yet-to-develop skills and attributes, all that is left to do in order to be able to delight in your child's progress is a *memory* to which you can compare their present skills and attributes. The ongoing yardstick used in measuring your child's progress, then, becomes that of improvement (rather than mastery).

1 If you have any recent examples of your child not mastering some skill or attribute that you want him or her to have, take a moment to move back through time to examples of when your child was even *further* from mastery of that skill or attribute.

2 Now compare those examples with what they are able to do now. Notice the improvement and progress that is evident by this comparison. (Obviously, another possible outcome from making this comparison is that you discover that your child is now *further* from mastery than he or she was before. Though probably not a source of enjoyment, such information is nonetheless important to have, and may indicate that it is time to make plans to intervene in some useful way. See the previous section on "Nurturing.")

Another way to enjoy the satisfaction that comes with recognizing your child's progress is to notice how his or her present skills and attributes will serve the child well in the *future*. If you recall, this was exemplified by Ned's response to his son telling him to mind his own business. The boy's response may have been rude and impertinent, but Ned also perceived it as indicative of his son's growing independence—something which Ned wanted him to learn.

3 Recall a recent incident in which your child surprised you with a somewhat new and (to you) either unpleasant or pleasant behavior. (As an example: Your five-year-old son is sitting too close to the TV. As he stands up to comply when you tell him to move back, you slide his chair back for him. He becomes angry and socks you in the leg because, "I wanted to do it myself!")

4 Next, with regard to the behavior, you need to change what first captures your attention in the present into an example of a more significant and positive attribute in the future. The intent here is to go from the behavior itself to what it indicates in terms of a *useful* attribute. (So, your son's behavior is indicative of a growing self-reliance, which is on a more generalized level than his being angry, hitting, and wanting to do it himself.) At this point it is important to keep the attribute separate from the behaviors that are its manifestation. This separation makes it possible to respond to your child's behavior in relation to the larger picture of his or her developing personality, rather than just to the immediate offensiveness of the behavior. As it was for Ned and his son, this recognition and separation of behavior and attribute can be reassuring and pleasing. Using the incident you recalled in the previous step, change the offending behavior into an example of a positive future attribute.

If the behavior your child has used in expressing that attribute is appropriate, then the matter can be left as it is. If, on the other hand, his or her behavior was somehow inappropriate (dangerous, unpleasant, self-defeating), then more needs to be considered.

5 Now that you have an idea of where the behavior is leading in terms of an attribute, you next need to make sure that your child has appropriate behaviors to express and fulfill the developing attribute. After all, the *attribute* is something worth preserving. Your task, then, becomes one of helping your child find more appropriate ways of expressing this attribute. Move from the attribute itself to the kinds of behaviors that would be more appropriate in expressing that attribute. Those behaviors, then, are what you want and need to convey to your son or daughter. (Your interaction now becomes one of nurturing.) In our example, your son's angry, hitting response is certainly inappropriate and ultimately not useful, so you praise him for wanting to do it himself, but explain that you had no way to know that before, that people can't read his mind, and that from now on he needs to let others know what his intentions are so that they can cooperate with him. Given the attribute you have identified, what are appropriate behaviors for your son or daughter? How will you convey this message to your child? Spend some time now answering these questions.

And finally, in addition to taking pleasure in your child's evolution, another source of enjoyment that is *often* overlooked by parents is the *child's* world. Although part of your role as parent is to bring your child to adulthood, the fact is that they do not yet share with you all of the perceptions, distinctions and beliefs that make up the adult world. If you are willing, your children can take you back to a way of perceiving the world that is perhaps more characterized by awe, wonder, curiosity, possibilities, perceptual flexibility, acceptance, and freedom than is your adult world. And, every stage of their growth and development brings with it changes in those perceptions.

We have already described how to step into your child's reality when we talked about entering into your child's world as a way of finding out who they are. The only addition we are suggesting here is one of expanding the emphasis of the experience to include *your* enjoyment of this younger world, as well as gathering information about it. The most effective way to enter your child's world is to match your own movements, tempo patterns, speech patterns, intonation patterns, and activities to those of your child. Many adults find this difficult to do either because they feel that there are other things that they should be doing besides simply hanging out with their kid, or because they worry about appearing foolish. If you find it difficult to step into your child's world for either of these reasons, we suggest that you plan ahead and set aside a certain private time with your child for the express purpose of stepping into his or her reality. Once you discover the freshness of perspective and warmth of interaction to be had by stepping, for awhile, into their reality, you will probably seize every opportunity that comes your way to once again share their world.

Children grow up and opportunities that are missed are often lost. This is a precious time of your life. Don't waste it. Put the learnings from this section into play.

11 Envoy

The descriptions and EMPRINT formats we have presented in this book are for the purpose of acquiring talents, abilities, and experiences, not for the diagnosis of problems. Despite the fact that throughout we have described various problems that people commonly face, and the ways that some people successfully respond within those same problem situations, in none of these cases do we say *why* some people have a certain problem and *why* others do not. Instead, our purpose has been to describe the internal processes that individuals use to generate their overall experience—their understandings, insights and emotional states—and their behavior. And we have described those internal processes in such a way that they can be made available to any other person needing or wanting to have access to similar experiences and behaviors. This orientation harkens back, of course, to Edward Hall's desideratum in which he calls for "the equivalent of musical scores that can be learned, each for a different type of man or woman in different types of jobs and relationships, for time, space, work, and play," the purpose being to "have a means for making life a little less haphazard and more enjoyable."

Furthermore, candidates for this acquisition include not only those so-called good experiences and behaviors that some people manifest, but the problem ones as well. As we have tried to indicate throughout, all experiences and behaviors are useful and appropriate, depending only upon the situation in which they are manifested. Thus, every human being—including you—is a resource, harboring a wealth of experiences and behaviors that are the very things another person needs to turn his or her failures, disappointments and frustrations into enriching experiences and gratifying successes.

Therefore, what we have presented in these pages is only a sampling, a taste of what is available and what is possible. The internal processing distinctions that we have described can be found in *every* thought, interaction, deed, skill and response that human beings have. The method that organizes those distinctions is *not a map* of human beings, but a *way of mapping* them as they move through the many situations that make up their lives. Life does not have to be a series of default responses, determined by worldly happenstance. In providing you access to the otherwise hidden realms of internal processing that underlie every person's experiences and behaviors, the understandings and formats presented here can become for you a means of personal evolution. Applied to large groups of people who could benefit from having new choices about their experiences and behaviors, these understandings and formats (and the EMPRINT method itself) can become a means of social and cultural evolution as well.

We hope that as you live each of your days, there will be incidents, comments, or stray notions that raise questions in your mind that will bring you back to this book, searching for information and understanding. We did not write this to be read and then put in a bookcase, to help keep dust off the shelf. We intend it to be used to provide practical and accessible ways of achieving goals in general, as well as the specific goals described in each chapter. We intend it to be an experiential presentation of a method capable of generating those learnable human musical scores Hall describes. And we intend it to raise questions—questions whose merits lie not in the answers, but in the quest for those answers.

Notes

Notes for Chapter One

1 Perhaps the first published attempt at describing the behaviors which characterize human beings cross-culturally was Charles Darwin's *The Expression of the Emotions in Man and Animals*. Of course, cross-cultural comparison of experiences, behaviors, and social structures has long been one of the endeavors of anthropologists; a recent example is Colin Turnbull's, *The Human Cycle*, in which he explores those patterns which seem to be characteristic of all cultures.

Notes for Chapter Two

1 The formats presented in this book were generated by using the EMPRINT method, an accelerated skill acquisition process developed by the authors. The EMPRINT method, together with its uses and applications, is presented in *The EMPRINT Method: A Guide to Reproducing Competence*, another FuturePace book written by the authors.

2 In *The Structure of Scientific Revolutions*, Kuhn provides further evidence of this pervasive influence of individual models in his description of a series of experiments conducted by Bruner and Postman. They asked their subjects to identify playing cards, one at a time. The subjects were unaware, however, that in the pack were anomalous cards, such as a red six of spades, black four of hearts, and so on. At short exposure times, subjects identified the bogus cards as being normal (thus a black six of hearts was identified as a "six of spades" or a "six of hearts"). When exposure times were increased, subjects became confused and hesitant to answer. Further increases of exposure time made it possible for some subjects to identify the anomalous cards, and from that point on they had no trouble picking them out:

A few subjects, however, were never able to make the requisite adjustments of their categories. Even at forty times the average exposure required to recognize normal cards for what they were, more than 10 percent of the anomalous cards were not correctly identified. And the subjects who then failed often experienced acute personal distress. One of them exclaimed: "I can't make the suit out, whatever it is. It didn't even look like a card that time. I don't know what color it is now or whether it's a spade or a heart. I'm not even sure now what a spade looks like. My God!" (p. 63)

Kuhn goes on to note that one of the experimenters (Postman) confided that even he found it uncomfortable to look at the incongruous cards:

Surveying the rich experimental literature from which these examples are drawn makes one suspect that something like a paradigm is prerequisite to perception itself. What a man sees depends both upon what he looks at and also upon what his previous visual-conceptual experience has taught him to see. In the absence of such training there can only be, in William James's phrase, "a bloomin buzzin' confusion." (p. 113)

Notes for Chapter Four

1 It may occur to you that the computation that one uses in *doing* will determine whether or not you *procrastinate* (that is, procrastination is chronically putting off doing). We have found, however, that procrastination is much more a function of whether or not you have generated rich and compelling future representations capable of motivating you either toward or away from something. Pro-

crastination, then, will be determined by the nature of the computations made during *wishing* or *wanting*.

Notes for Chapter Five

1 Everything we have modeled and will be presenting in this chapter is aimed toward healthful eating patterns—*not* toward dieting and losing weight. You need to eat appropriately and get some exercise in order to be healthy, to feel and be fit. Often people eat and exercise in certain ways in order to match criteria generated in the media regarding appearance, beauty, attractiveness, control, and so on. We are more interested, however, in people operating out of their own *internally generated* criteria. Your weight is going to be the simultaneous consequence of your eating and exercise habits, and your genetic make up. If you eat and exercise appropriately, then your genetics will take care of establishing your normal weight. If you want to reduce your weight below that point, you should recognize that you may be bucking a genetic predisposition, which may be difficult and involve a life-long commitment to certain deprivations. Before embarking on such an endeavor, you should consider whether you are doing it to satisfy internally or externally generated criteria, and whether or not the effort will be worth the satisfaction of those criteria. (The "From Knowledge To Experience" section of this chapter will assist you in determining the answers to these questions.)

Notes for Chapter Seven

1 The nicotine in cigarettes takes the place of certain neuro-transmitters that are involved with generating states of euphoria and well-being. If nicotine is used over a prolonged period of time, the chemical processes which are responsible for making those neuro-transmitters "realize" they are not needed, and shut down. The result is a physiological dependence upon cigarettes and their nicotine in order to maintain feelings of well-being. When you quit smoking, suddenly there is an absence of both the neuro-transmitters and the nicotine, resulting in the depression, nervousness and anxiety many people experience when trying to give up the habit. This physiological dependence gradually eases, however, as your neuro-physiology registers the need for the missing neuro-transmitter and eventually resumes producing it.

2 We want to make it clear that we are not talking about alcoholism here. Alcoholism is a very much more complex situation (both experientially and socially) than the problem of occasionally drinking inappropriately.

Notes for Chapter Nine

1 All things considered, mutual attraction happens with surprising frequency. We suspect that this frequency is largely due to the fact that being found attractive fulfills for many people many of the criteria regarding someone else being considered attractive. That is, "That he/she wants me demonstrates what a smart, sensitive, wonderful person he/she is."

2 Appreciation based upon evaluations about the future (as in Jill's case) may also last a very long time. In fact, appreciation based upon what will be in the future may last longer than appreciation based upon evaluations about the present. Future-based appreciation will fade only when enough compelling experiences are acquired to convince the person that the future they have been expecting is no longer possible. Reaching this conclusion can take a very long time, however, keeping the person in a relationship that they would have ended long before had they been according more significance to their *present* experiences.

3 Belonging *with someone* should be differentiated from belonging *to someone*. The two are often confused. Unlike a relationship, once you buy (say) a sofa, it *belongs to you* and you no longer have to do anything to keep it. Relationships, on the other hand, are never done, requiring ongoing efforts ("doing") to keep them.

4 This is often the situation of the married person who has affairs. With separate, non-inclusive criteria for the short and long-term, affairs become the only way they know of to have all that they want and need in relationships.

5 Leslie Cameron-Bandler's, *SOLUTIONS: Practical and Effective Antidotes for Sexual and Relationship Problems*, contains not only a more in-depth discussion of the threshold pattern, but also discusses many other aspects of relationships. It includes many approaches (not covered in this book) that are useful in making those relationships enjoyable and fulfilling.

Notes for Chapter Ten

1 Though the emphasis in this section is on parents and their pre-adult children, we wish to note that some parents continue to respond as if the past is the present even when that child becomes an adult, married and with children of his or her own (a situation for which you can probably find examples from your own acquaintances).

2 This particular example is adapted from *PHOENIX: Therapeutic Patterns of Milton H. Erickson*, (Gordon and Meyers-Anderson). Erickson's approaches to handling family matters were unique and always instructive, and are best presented in Jay Haley's, *Uncommon Therapy: The Psychiatric Techniques of Milton H. Erickson, M.D.* Reading and re-reading this book will reward you with perspectives on family interactions that are as intriguing as they are useful.

3 We certainly feel that both familiarity and flexibility with all of the experiential distinctions and useful computations described in this book should be two of your goals in nurturing your child from infancy to adulthood. We do not, however, presume to tell you what your goals for them should be in terms of their self-concept and self-esteem (other than making the general observation and recommendation that those areas of your child's experience be nurtured and supported). More specific information regarding the beliefs and values which contribute to an appropriate self-concept and gratifying self-esteem can be found in many books on the subject. Two which we would recommend are *Self-Esteem: The Key To Your Child's Well-Being* (Clemes and Bean), and *Uncommon Therapy* (Haley).

For those interested in many more examples of nurturing approaches that are both respectful of the child and strategic, we very much recommend the delightful *Mrs. Piggle-Wiggle* books, by Betty MacDonald. Each is filled with stories about exasperated parents discovering how to easily, naturally, and effectively affect their child's social and personal development. Required reading for all parents.

Glossary

Cause-Effect   those experiences, occurrences, situations or behaviors which are, or are perceived to be, contingently related to one another, such that the expression or occurrence of one leads to the expression or occurrence of the other.

Choice Response   the ability to generate more than one emotion or behavior as a response to a specific situation.

Compelling Future   an imagined future that is capable of influencing a person's present experience and behavior.

Criteria   the standards on which an evaluation is based.

Criterial Equivalence   the behaviors, perceptions, qualities, circumstances, etc. which constitute fulfillment of a criterion.

Counterexample   an experience, memory or piece of information which is inconsistent with a generalization or belief.

Default Response   the fact of having only one emotion or behavior as a response to a specific situation.

Emotional State   an individual's overall feelings at a moment in time (such as happy, curious, confident, etc.).

Evaluation   the process of applying your criteria to a specific context in order to determine whether or not, or to what extent, your criteria were, are being, or could be fulfilled (also referred to as a Test).

Feedback   all of the responses (both your own and those of others) that occur in a situation that could be used to inform and guide a person's thinking and actions.

Future-Pacing   a technique for helping to insure that new responses will occur when needed by stepping into the future and imagining as fully as possible the experience of using those new responses in the needed situation.

Internal Processes   ways of thinking; the interaction of criteria, criterial equivalences, presuppositions of cause-effects, references, representations, and evaluations resulting in an individual's experience and behavior within a specific situation.

Present-to-Future Cause-Effect   the fact or belief that an action, event, evaluation, experience or situation occurring in the present will determine to some extent what occurs in the future.

Presupposition   an assumption or belief that, knowingly or unknowingly, influences your experience and behavior.

Reference Experience   what an individual is using as his or her source of information within a specific situation.

Representation   the internal pictures, sounds and feelings that a person is using when making an evaluation.

Subordination   ignoring or overriding evaluations about one time frame in favor of evaluations about another time frame (e.g., ignoring the future in favor of the present).

Vicarious   gaining experiential information by imagining what someone else's experience is.

References

Aaronson, Bernard S. "Behavior and the Place Names of Time." in Waker, Henri, Ed. *The Future of Time*. New York, NY.: Doubleday, 1971.

Ashby, W. Ross. *Design for a Brain: The Origin of Adaptive Behavior*. New York, NY.: John Wiley & Sons, 1960.

Bandler, Richard and Grinder, John. *The Structure of Magic*. Cupertino, CA.: Science and Behavior Books, Inc., 1975.

Bleibtreu, John N. *The Parable of the Beast*. New York, NY.: Collier Books, 1968.

Cameron-Bandler, Leslie. *Solutions: Practical and Effective Antidotes for Sexual and Relationship Problems*. San Rafael, CA.: FuturePace, 1985.

Cameron-Bandler, Leslie and Gordon, David and Lebeau, Michael. *The EMPRINT Method: A Guide to Reproducing Competence*. San Rafael, CA.: FuturePace, 1985.

Clemes, Harris and Bean, Reynold. *Self-Esteem: The Key To Your Child's Well-Being*. New York, NY.: Zebra Books, 1981.

Darwin, Charles. *The Expression of the Emotions in Man and Animals*. Chicago, Ill.: The University of Chicago Press, 1965.

Dossey, Larry. *Space, Time & Medicine*. Boulder, CO.: Shambhala Publications, Inc., 1982.

Erickson, Milton H. "Pseudo-Orientation in Time as a Hypnotherapeutic Procedure," J. Clinical and Experimental Hypnosis, 1954, 2, 261–283.

Frankl, Viktor E. *Man's Search for Meaning*. New York, NY.: Washington Square Press, 1963.

Gordon, David. *Therapeutic Metaphors*. Cupertino, CA.: Meta Publications, 1978.

Gordon, David and Meyers-Anderson, Maribeth. *Phoenix: Therapeutic Patterns of Milton H. Erickson*. Cupertino, CA.: Meta Publications, 1981.

Haley, Jay. *Uncommon Therapy: The Psychiatric Techniques of Milton H. Erickson, M.D.* NY, NY.: W.W. Norton & Co., Inc., 1973.

Hall, Edward T. *The Silent Language*. Garden City, NY.: Doubleday & Company, 1959.

———. *The Hidden Dimension*. Garden City, NY.: Doubleday & Company, 1966.

———. *Beyond Culture*. Garden City, NY.: Anchor Press/Doubleday, 1976.

———. *The Dance of Life*. Garden City, NY.: Anchor Press/Doubleday, 1983.

Kuhn, Thomas S. *The Structure of Scientific Revolutions*. Chicago, Ill.: The University of Chicago Press, 1970.

MacDonald, Betty. *Mrs. Piggle-Wiggle*, and other titles. Philadelphia, PA.: J.B. Lippincott Co., 1975.

Mann, Harriet; Siegler, Miriam, and Osmond, Humphry. "The Psychotypology of Time." in Waker, Henri, Ed. *The Future of Time*. New York, NY.: Doubleday, 1971.

Miller, George A. and Galanter, Eugene and Pribram, Karl. *Plans and the Structure of Behavior*. New York, NY.: Holt, Rinehart and Winston, Inc., 1960.

Newell, Allen and Simon, Herbert A. *Human Problem Solving*. Englewood Cliffs, NJ.: Prentice-Hall, 1971

Pribram, Karl. *Languages of the Brain*. Englewood Cliffs, NJ.: Prentice-Hall, 1971.

Sheehy, Gail. *Passages*. NY, NY.: E.P. Dutton & Co., Inc., 1974.

Turnbull, Colin M. *The Human Cycle*. New York, NY.: Simon and Schuster, 1983.

Dear Reader,

We would like to send you a gift.

While doing the research for this book we developed many more techniques and formats than could be included here. They are similar to and certainly as effective as the formats presented here, but they fall outside the scope of the content we ultimately chose for this volume. They include formats for converting mistakes into learnings, effective negotiation skills, investing wisely, management skills, and learning how to learn.

If you would like to receive more of our work, please let us know and we will send you, at no charge, an unpublished format together with information on Mental Aptitude Patterning^{SM}. We will also keep you informed of our current work with the EMPRINT method.

LCB/DG/ML

To receive an additional format and more information on Mental Aptitude Patterning and The EMPRINT Method, please send your name and address to:

The Know How Authors
c/o FuturePace, Inc.
P.O. Box 1173
San Rafael, CA 94915